The TRANCE ZONE™

Unleashing
The POWER
Of Your
SUBCONSCIOUS
MIND

Written by:
Edward J Longo

(See "About the Cover" Page 211)

> Note: This hypnosis manual is intended for reference only. It is not to be used for medical advice, or as a guide for treatment of illness. If a medical problem is suspected, the reader is urged to seek competent medical help. The information herein is not to be used as a substitute for treatment ordinarily prescribed by your doctor.

The Copyright Law strictly prohibits any copying of material from this hypnosis manual, ***The Trance Zone***™, other than for personal use. Use of this manual, other than for the purpose of self-hypnosis, is strictly prohibited.

Only those receiving express written permission to practice hypnosis on others, or to teach ***The Trance Zone***™ hypnosis technique, are hypnotists, hypnotherapists, or other qualified professionals who receive legal certification signed by the author.

The Trance Zone™ **Hypnosis Power Course** is also available for those interested in becoming Certified Hypnotists, or Hypnotherapists. Only after receiving this valid Certification, will the Exclusive Rights to practice ***The Trance Zone*** technique be validated.

NOTE: Any form of lecture, presentation or seminar based on this hypnosis manual is strictly forbidden unless authorized by the author / founder, Edward J Longo

All inquiries about this manual, or Certification should be addressed to the publishers at EbookSites.Org 503 East 78th Street, New York, New York 10075

The Trance Zone Hypnosis Manual: ISBN 0-9713623-0-0
ISBN13 0-9713623-0-7

Copyright (C) Edward J Longo – Affinity Zone. All rights reserved.
Except for one-time personal use, no part of this manual may be reproduced by any mechanical, photographic or electronic process, or in the form of a phonographic recording. Nor may it be stored in a retrieval system, transmitted, or otherwise copied for public or private use without prior written permission of the author.

The Trance Zone ™

CONTENTS

Introduction 5

Forward 10

PART ONE

Chapter 1   **A Brief History of Hypnosis** 16
Within the pages of this chapter, you will be provided with historical facts, as well as being provided with a full understanding of hypnosis.

Chapter 2   **Functioning As A Hypnotist** 23
Through the hypnotist, WORDS will paint images on your mind. These images will aid you in mastering control over your life in an ideal, creative way. This chapter reveals the power of hypnosis, as well as the might of mental imagery.

PART TWO

Chapter 3   *The Trance Zone* – **The Concept Behind The Book** . . 31
In this chapter you will learn, in detail, all the tools necessary for entering the subconscious state of *The Trance Zone,* including the use of "The Hypnotic Eye."

Chapter 4   *The Trance Zone* - **Reaching The Initial State Of Hypnosis** . 42
This chapter provides full induction illustrations on hypnosis and self-hypnosis.

PART THREE

Chapter 5   **Unleashing The Power Of Your Subconscious Mind** . . 58
This chapter explains how the mind can alter the brain. It includes techniques that will aid in activating the endocrine glands that cause the body to become relaxed, receptive and supple.

Chapter 6   **Hypnosis Induction Techniques** . . . 67
This chapter goes into intricate detail explaining the **Techniques** used to "Go Into" *The Trance Zone*

PART FOUR

Chapter 7   **Hypnosis Induction Illustrations** . . . 81
This chapter goes into detail in explaining the **Illustrations** used to "Go Into" *The Trance Zone*

Chapter 8   **Hypnotist's Posthypnotic Suggestions Induced To Subject** . 96
This chapter demonstrates, in full depth, how the hypnotist successfully hypnotizes the subject through the use of suggestions, and Guided Imagery.

CONTENTS (continued)

PART FIVE

Chapter 9   **Trance Manifestation**   .   .   .   114

Through learning the <u>Secrets Of Attracting Luck</u>, you will finally come to understand hidden meanings. Here, through the use of the **Trance-formation Visualizer**, you will learn how to use luck to acquire manifestations of the highest kind.

Chapter 10   **Self-Hypnosis Induction Techniques**   .   .   .   125

This chapter demonstrates how the subject successfully induces the complete self-hypnotic **Techniques** used to "Go Into" *The Trance Zone.* These inductions have been translated into "the first person" for the convenience of those wishing to use self-hypnosis effectively.

PART SIX

Chapter 11   **Self-Hypnosis Induction Illustrations**   .   .   .   144

This chapter demonstrates how the subject successfully induces the complete self-hypnotic **Illustrations** used to "Go Into" *The Trance Zone.* These inductions have been translated into "the first person" to enable practicing self-hypnosis effectively.

PART SEVEN

Chapter 12   **Inducing Majestic Trance Spells**   .   .   .   155

This chapter illustrates, by a special positioning the hands and forming "The Observing Eye," how to induce the highly effective, self-hypnotic, **Majestic Trance Spells**.

Chapter 13   **Self-Hypnosis Behavior Modification**   .   .   .   169

Through a special reprogramming process this chapter illustrates, in full detail, specialized mind-altering inductions. For persons desiring to make permanent changes through self-hypnosis, these special inductions will prove highly beneficial.

PART EIGHT

Chapter 14   **Unified Physical Therapy Technique™**   .   .   .   187

Those committing to this **UPTT** technique will find this as the elixir to the mind and the spirit, as well as the physical body. In doing so, they will be surprised to find it strengthens the will, activates the organs and inspires the spirit.

Since exercise is definitely the staple of life, don't hesitate to become fully engaged in *The Trance Zone* technique. The benefits of this technique will not only prove to be rewarding; they will rekindle your natural desire to live a healthy life.

About the Author - Contact Information   207

INTRODUCTION

INTRODUCTION:

"Life does not consist mainly – or even largely – of facts and happenings. It consists mainly of the storm of thoughts that are forever blowing through one's mind."

------ Mark Twain – renowned poet

INTRODUCTION

Your decision to purchase this book is probably one of the best decisions you have ever made. What you are about to discover is that you have gained access to something more valuable than any possession you could ever hope to acquire. What you will uncover is so powerful a device that you will become enabled to take control of your mind's infinite potential.

By utilizing the principles and techniques of ***The Trance Zone***, you will not only gain the opportunity to improve your mind; you will be enabled with such power you will become alive, more so than you have ever dreamed. The secret to tapping the depths of the mind is to go into the subconscious, where the true source of power rules. Here, you can unleash the power of your subconscious mind, and change negative habits of thought and action into what you desire them to be.

This is where, and how, you can begin reprogramming your mind so that you can utilize your brain's unfathomable resources. This highly creative approach to hypnosis provides an intellectual powerhouse, regarding mastery of the mind. More importantly, it initiates the total performance of the capabilities of the brain.

The Trance Zone is an altered state of consciousness whereby, as if by some mystical power, the whole psyche shifts into an exaggerated state of positive exuberance. It is similar to that of "the Zone" that athletes talk about when an inner force takes over and places the participant into a state where every movement seems effortless. Tennis players and runners call it "the second wind" where every challenge seems a breeze; every, barrier becomes an invitation to a winning frame of mind. In other words, there is a surge of energy where everything, remarkably, falls into place. These remarkable states of euphoria could also be referred to as "Success Zones."

The Trance Zone hypnotic state provides that kind of dynamics. The theory behind this technique is one intended to stimulate that part of the psyche which brings the participant, or subject, to that very pinnacle. It is designed to enlist that pinnacle where, seemingly, nothing is impossible, nothing can go wrong, or interfere with achieving only the best results. The most important thing about hypnosis is that the nervous system cannot tell the difference between real and imagined experiences. By gaining access to the subconscious you can induce a trance and go anywhere, achieve anything, or be anyone you wish to become.

In utilizing ***The Trance Zone*** technique, the four D's: Diet, Discipline, Dexterity and Determination are synonymous, as far as achieving results. Through bypassing the conscious mind and going into the hypnotic state, you have the benefit of altering your mind to the degree you don't have to struggle with quitting smoking, addiction, or any other dysfunction. When you succeed at developing self-esteem and see yourself as that perfect and complete human being, all those bad, negative gremlins simply fade away. In this hypnotic state, everything becomes simple -- yet nothing is impossible.

As a simplistic illustration as to how being in ***The Trance Zone*** works, think of a large, empty soda bottle, with the cap representing the conscious mind. While the cap represents the limitations and restrictions of the conscious mind, the bottle represents the enormity of the subconscious mind.

Through bypassing the conscious state (the cap), you can easily access the unlimited attributes of the altered, subconscious state (the bottle). To further illustrate this point, if you are not satisfied with what is in the bottle, you can alter its contents to your satisfaction. Accessing the subconscious mind is that simple, using the principles demonstrated in ***The Trance Zone.***

(Also see The Ketchup Bottle Demonstration, Chapter 1, and also repeated in Chapter 10, Page 146 for self-hypnosis purposes.)

The Trance Zone manual is the ideal hypnosis, or self-hypnosis, program where you will become enabled to fulfill your innermost, precious ideals. Used efficiently, this hypnosis technique could become as your own omnipotent transformer, enabling you to energize your spirit, curing even the most complex of dysfunctions. In essence, achieving the power of hypnosis is tantamount to finding the "missing chord" of your being, thus completing a rich, harmonious cycle of happiness. In any case, the hypnotist must strive to maintain the highest degree of integrity, honesty, fairness and compassion, whenever dealing with a subject.

(Note: Please be advised that any attempt to use these hypnosis procedures in a harmful, or evil way will only backfire on the person violating the moral principles of hypnosis. Any attempt to harm anyone will be thwarted by the same person who is attempting to violate these principles.

Also Note: Generally, sentences appearing in ***italics*** throughout this manual represent the ***voice***, or WORDS, of the subject or hypnotist.

Both the WORDS of the SUBJECT and the WORDS of the HYPNOTIST are always shown in *italics*. The main difference between the dialog of the SUBJECT and the HYPNOTIST is that the subject's WORDS are always shown in the "first Person.")

OF SPECIAL NOTE

*The title **The Trance Zone** practically speaks for itself. It is that spiritual state of being, that **Trance** state of mind, that is reached upon being placed into the "**Zone**," under hypnosis.*

I came up with the name **The Trance Zone** because I thought it would make the ideal way for subjects to understand exactly how I approach the transformation of the mind, through hypnosis. If you have concluded that I mean to imply that I treat persons by placing them into a trance state in order to renew their spirits, you would be right. All people are spiritual beings, whether having religious beliefs, or not. And since the spirit is supernatural in essence, it would follow that the mind should be penetrated on a subconscious level, rather than trying to communicate with its earth-based, conscious counterpart.

Since the spirit is a supernatural state of mind, it is best reached by bypassing the conscious state and going directly to the subconscious, in order to enable reprogramming. This is because the conscious mind always tends to interfere due to its critical, skeptical, and other negative conditioning. But the subconscious is just part of what makes up our supernatural state.

Nearly all scientists, physicists, and psychologists (especially Carl Jung,) have come to agree that the mind is made up of genes handed down through time by our ancestors. This being the case, it would explain why going into the subconscious is so effective. It is because that's precisely where our minds first took root and became formulated. Tapping into that source is the challenge and the secret to unlocking the true power of our mind - our subconscious mind. And since the subconscious rules our thoughts, this is the place to begin the transformation process. This is for certain -- the reason it is difficult to reach the conscious mind is because of ***deception, distortion of truth, or faulty programming***.

If Acquiring The Hypnosis Power Doesn't Appeal To You, Remember This:

When you decide not to employ the power of your subconscious mind, someone else becomes its employer. In essence, you enable an outsider to empower your thoughts, most often without restitution.
Edward J. Longo - ABH, CCH, RBT
(Certified: American Board of Hypnotherapy - American College of Hypnotherapy.)

THREE PREREQUISITES IN USING *THE TRANCE ZONE* TECHNIQUE:

DESIRE – Without desire, going into the state of hypnosis, or transforming the mind will become difficult. Whatever it is you wish to accomplish or become it must be desired with a **healthy attitude and well-intended purpose**.

BELIEF – "*Whatever you can believe, you can conceive*," Robert Goddard once said. And he should know – he was one of the scientists who helped develop our first missile rockets. Not only should you believe in the process of self-hypnosis, but you must also have faith in the induction process when engaging the services of a hypnotist. Belief and trust go hand in hand when striving to accomplish anything meaningful, or purposeful. For hypnosis to work properly there must be a mutual feeling of trust between the subject and the hypnotist.

EXPECTATION – To **expect** is to anticipate the coming of something you desire. To anticipate it is wise to prepare, muster up hope, and believe that what you wish for will come to fruition. The preparation is **being willing, ready, and able to accept** what it is you desire to happen. Success can only be achieved through the expectation of positive results.

Finally, the **LUCK** you've been chasing and hunting down ceases to elude you. All at once, it comes to you just as if you found the *Horn-of-Plenty*.

FORWARD

FORWARD:

"Man finds himself isolated in the cosmos, because he is no longer involved in nature and has lost his emotional 'unconscious identity' with natural phenomena. These have lost their symbolic implications... His contact with nature has gone, and with it has gone the profound emotional energy that his symbolic connection supplied."

------ Carl Jung - noted psychoanalyst

FORWARD

For more than 15 years, I have been researching the relevance between psychology and the subconscious mind. Through my vast life experiences, including the study of acting, being a chauffeur for the rich and famous, and the observation of complex personalities, I became qualified and then certified as a hypnotherapist. The title, **<u>THE TRANCE ZONE</u>** became developed out of my experiences with physiology, human behavior, and the study of the correlation between the conscious and subconscious mind.

Through my understanding of the miracles Jesus performed through His remarkable spirit, it is of my opinion that He possessed, not only the powers of a healer and psychologist, but of hypnotist as well. What he did, primarily, was to heal and cast out demons, so no matter where Jesus went He performed a miracle. This was His supernatural gift from God. The fact that the term "Christ Consciousness" has evolved makes this even more convincing. Obviously, Jesus Christ possessed the highest knowledge of the subconscious mind, as well as possessing the utmost of supernatural powers.

I don't profess to have such powers, but through my discovery of this revelation, I became interested in the spiritual world, as well as implementing the powers that surround us in this physical realm. And, yes, I do believe in the devil and his workings. This is why I feel so strong about working with the subconscious mind, for I have come to believe that all disease and mental problems are caused by the influence of negative forces – some lesser, some increasingly pronounced by the dark and sinister, evil forces.

However, this is why I believe my work to be of a supernatural nature. Not unlike Jesus, in some regard, I always look to God to intercede, whether I am teaching, working, or performing my hypnotic trances.

(Note: All relative information regarding office hours and fees can be found in my Web site. Just type <u>AffinityZone.com</u> in the Http://address window.)

***THE TRANCE ZONE* BENEFITS**

WHAT YOU ARE CAPABLE OF ACCOMPLISHING:

While functioning within ***The Trance Zone*** you will gain the advantage of unlimited benefits. This is because you will learn to gain supernatural powers while inducing self-hypnotic trances in conjunction with the many following categories and inductions.

In refusing to succumb to subversive habits, such as smoking, alcoholism, drug addiction, overeating, and the like, you place your future on a straight path, healthy and dynamic, toward achieving your ultimate goals. The psychosomatic energy incurred by alleviating these degenerative habits will boost your confidence and energy levels to such a degree it will induce transformation, and in turn, manifest your ideals, wishes, desires, and innermost dreams.

Conversely, to succumb and administer to any form of life-sapping habit is tantamount to being unable to resist a dark glass of anti-matter presented by death's own hand. Degenerative habits are the devil's invented diversions to personal esteem, gain, needs, heart's desires, and all forms of positive energies associated with the progression of life-giving forces. Please, seek and develop constraint – better yet, cessation, of these vices.

***The Trance Zone* Categories:**

- Hypnotic Inductions
- Self-hypnosis
- Nutritional Rehabilitation
- Prayer and Affirmations
- Posthypnotic Suggestions
- Mind & Brain Replenishment
- Physical Therapy Exercise
- Altering Personality Traits

-- And more . . .

***The Trance Zone* Inductions:**

- Supernatural Spirit
- Mental Stability
- Manifest Dreams & Desires
- Instill Motivation
- Physical fitness
- Weight Control
- Good Fortune
- Overcome Insomnia
- Reciprocal Love
- Cerebral Perception
- Chronic Fatigue Syndrome
- Physical Rejuvenation
- Physiological Adjustment
- Relieve Stress
- Prosperity
- Personal Magnetism
- Overcome Disease
- Habit Modification
- Smoking Cessation
- Personality Development
- Keen Visualization
- Develop Self-esteem

-- And more . . .

THE SECRET 7 GOLDEN RULES

The Trance Zone hypnosis technique is extremely effective through its application of Hypnotic Inducements, Posthypnotic Suggestions, Self-hypnosis Affirmations, and Majestic Trance Spells. This is a highly spiritual technique influencing dramatic changes for the good and best in life, where ideals, dreams, and heart's desires actually manifest into reality – even miracles. The techniques used in this book can become extremely beneficial regarding the informative and creative utilization of exercise, nutritional rehabilitation, and prayer.   During your process of learning hypnotism, remember to keep in mind the Secret 7 Golden Rules as outlined below.

1. If you like the way your life is going, great – enjoy it.
2. If you don't like the way certain things in your life are going, avoid them.
3. If you are not happy with certain things and cannot avoid them, change them.
4. Provided you are not content with the way certain things are, and cannot avoid, change or detach from them - then accept them.
5. To accept certain things you can try changing your point of view about them – perhaps consider changing your mind.
6. Provided you cannot change your point of view about things, or change your mind about them, then draw upon the positive aspect of your subconscious mind to alter the situation according to your needs and desires.
7. Everything you are, or may become, is based on your **attitude**. Seek and incorporate the following **motivations** in order to change your **situation** and you will be able to look forward to a full and complete life:

    Purpose – With enough reasons to change your situation in life there must be something you wish to accomplish more than anything in the world – then go for it.

    Commitment – You must take a stand, whether it is something you believe in, or whether there is something you must do before you can move on – find out what that is, and stick to it, no matter what.

    Focus – The key to success of every form is concentration. No matter what it is you wish to accomplish, learn to develop a direct plan of attack, a laser-beam focus, and hone in on it like a falcon going after its prey.

(continue)

THE SECRET 7 GOLDEN RULES (continued)

Passion – Find out what it is that makes your blood boil every time you think about it, then make it happen using every fiber of your being.

Interest - Money invested wisely produces interest. Invest wisely in yourself and investigate every avenue of endeavor until you can become excited about living a fulfilling and gratifying life – know and feel that you are worth it.

Drive - If your body was a vehicle and you wanted to make it from the East Coast to the West Coast, you would need to plan every detail to make sure you could reach your destination safely. Your mind is also a vehicle. With the proper strategy and a purposeful path, you should be able to reach your destination blindfolded – living a gratifying, rewarding life takes that kind of **discipline** and **determination**.

Mental Balance – If you are not able to develop a sound mind through prayer, music appreciation, exercise, health and proper nutrition, then you must be lacking in some other physical or spiritual way. Another way to develop stability is change your pattern of sleep, environment, behavior, motivations, morals – even the way you dress and perceive yourself has an effect on your subconscious mind. Find every possible way to make every aspect of your life positive. "Love thyself" helps – "Know thyself" helps even more.

Prosperity – Seek this in every way, with one exception – do not focus on money as your idol, for you will only become subjected to the root of all evil – greed. Money is not the root of all evil – it is the unscrupulous extremes that people use to acquire it.

Finally, when you find out what it is that you love to do with a passion, practice transcending that love. And further, become open to receiving love. Then, live your life to the fullest, making the most out of every hour of every single day.

Not only can ***The Trance Zone*** hypnosis be used to advance your own growth, but after learning the techniques herein, you will have developed the potential to become a certified hypnotist, and thus be able to perform hypnotism on your own subjects. However, many states require licensing where many others do not.

(See Chapter 14 to find out more about how you can become a certified hypnotist, or to order my book or tapes on hypnosis.)

PART ONE

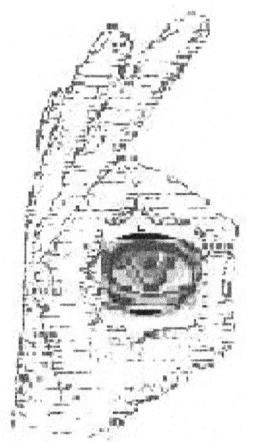

CHAPTER ONE
1

A BRIEF HISTORY OF HYPNOSIS

---

1   HYPNOSIS
HISTORICAL FACTS:

Autosuggestion became Emile Coue's doctrine during 1857-1926. He claimed that the hypnotist creates in the patient's subconscious an image of the desired effect, and that it is brought about primarily by the patient. He also claimed that each individual is a powerful hypnotist.

"Learn to cure yourself. You can do it. I have never cured anyone. This power is within you. Call on your mind for help. Make it the servant of your mental and physical well being. It will be present; it will heal you. You will be happy," he would say to his patients. He would also direct his patients to repeat the following affirmation twenty times, morning and evening: "<u>Every day, in every way, I get better and better.</u>"

CHAPTER ONE
1

A BRIEF HISTORY OF HYPNOSIS

Hypnosis sometimes occurs automatically, whether you are aware of it or not. This is the inherent state of mind where perception, ideas, and daydreams occur regularly. For example: You are cruising along in you car, lost in your worldly thoughts, when you suddenly arrive at your destination. You haven't the faintest idea of how you got there. The truth is that, since you've driven along this path so many times before, your subconscious mind had memorized the entire route. In effect, you were placed in the hypnotic state. How did you get into the hypnotic state? Were you asleep? Of course not! The fact of the matter is that you were a lot more alert than you realized -- that magnificent trance state of your mind shifted to automatic pilot, since your conscious mind became focused somewhere else.

That's the key: <u>focused</u> attention; that's when the subconscious mind comes into play. When the conscious mind becomes completely engrossed in something, the subconscious mind kicks in automatically and takes over. Why does this happen? The trance state becomes activated because the conscious mind can only concentrate on one thing at a time, so the subconscious has to intercede. That's what happens when you are under hypnosis. Since your conscious mind becomes easily distracted, your unconscious mind becomes activated by what's being said -- you begin to engage the most productive part of cerebellum. The juices begin to flow, creativity becomes predominant, and your mind becomes susceptible to all kinds of images and positive suggestions.

Hypnosis has been a part of every culture since the inception of the intellectual man. Four thousand years before Christ the Sumerians were already practicing it. In India's book of the Law of Manu an ancient Sanskrit refers to hypnotism as "the ecstatic sleep." Ancient Egypt used hypnosis as a therapeutic measure, exhibited on the Ebers Papyrus. In fact, Egyptian priests had their patients fixate on metal disks until so fatigued they went into hypnotic trance. In the eleventh century, monks of the Hesichastic Order, cloistered on Mount Athos and inaugurated the principle of self-hypnosis by contemplating their navels.

Hypnotism was refereed to as "Mesmerism" in the 1700's when Franz Anton Mesmer became known as the father of hypnotherapy. He believed that his "animal fluid," described as "Fluidum," could be stored up in magnets and transferred to patients to cure them of illness. He believed his "fluid" was transmitted by "passes" - making hand movements from top to bottom along the body. The Austrian doctor recognized this ancient healing phenomenon and incorporated it into his theory of "Animal Magnetism."

But Mesmer eventually discarded the magnets. He regarded himself as having the magnetic force. Thousands of sick but hopeful people flocked to his treatment center and he had a tremendous rate of success. However, his theory of Animal Fluid finally became discredited and ridiculed.

"Mesmerism" became the forerunner of hypnotic suggestion, although his cures were attributed only to the imagination. Magnets are still used to relieve pain and discomfort, facilitate healing of broken bones, and the health industry is using MRI's (magnetic resonance imaging) to replace x-rays because it is safer and more effective.

Hypnosis began receiving serious study during the 1800's and it was during this period that it received its name. An English ophthalmologist James Braid coined the word, "hypnosis", derived from the Greek word, Hypnos, which means sleep. Braid also showed that hypnotized subjects were very impressionable due to suggestions given verbally. Hypnosis was being used to perform more than 1800 surgical operations painlessly, in London. In India it was commonly used as the sole anesthesia for major operations, such as amputation of limbs.

Autosuggestion became Emile Coue's doctrine during 1857-1926. He claimed that the hypnotist creates an image of the desired effect in the patient's subconscious, and that primarily the patient brings it about. He also claimed that each individual is a powerful hypnotist. "Learn to cure yourself," he would say to his patients. "You can do it. I have never cured anyone. This power is within you. Call on your mind for help. Make it the servant of your mental and physical well being. It will be present; it will heal you. You will be happy." He would also direct his patients to repeat the following affirmation twenty times, morning and evening: "**Every day, in every way, I get better and better**." Accordingly, this generated a conditioned reflex, and therefore would become identified with the patient's personality.

In the early 1890's Sigmund Freud, the father of modern psychiatry, used hypnosis in his own practices and even delivered two papers on it. But by the late 1890's he began rejecting hypnosis in favor of his own theories, free association and dream interpretation. So with the rise of psychoanalysis in the first half of this century, hypnosis declined in popularity. But then a reversal occurred. Beginning in the 1950's hypnosis experienced a rebirth. In 1955 the British Medical Association approved the use of hypnotherapy as a valid medical treatment. And in 1958 the American Medical Association (AMA) followed suit. There are now more than 15,000 professionals who use hypnosis in their practices. Recent studies show that 94% of patients benefit from hypnosis, even if the only benefit is relaxation.

As of May 1998, three of New York City's most prestigious institutions – Beth Israel Medical Center, Columbia-Presbyterian Memorial Center, and Memorial Sloan-Kettering Cancer Center have announced ambitious plans for programs that promise to feature mind-body medicine. There are even plans to "hook up" the Dalai Lama to learn more about Tibetan meditation. *The Trance Zone* technique is clearly amidst the new wave toward the practice and understanding of hypnosis. Within a short period, you will come to find that the mystery surrounding hypnosis is no mystery at all – that it is merely a misconception.

So, what can hypnosis do for you? Not only can it be used to improve your physical and mental functioning, but it can also be used as a tool to have you achieve a great level of success and self-esteem. Although being under hypnosis is not in any way harmful, it is understandable that someone may be slightly apprehensive their first time. After one or two visits with a hypnotherapist, you will come to realize that hypnosis is a very healthy way to arm yourself for the 21st century.

UNDERSTANDING HYPNOSIS

The subconscious mind encompasses the entire mind, whether conscious, in the trance state, or completely asleep for the night.

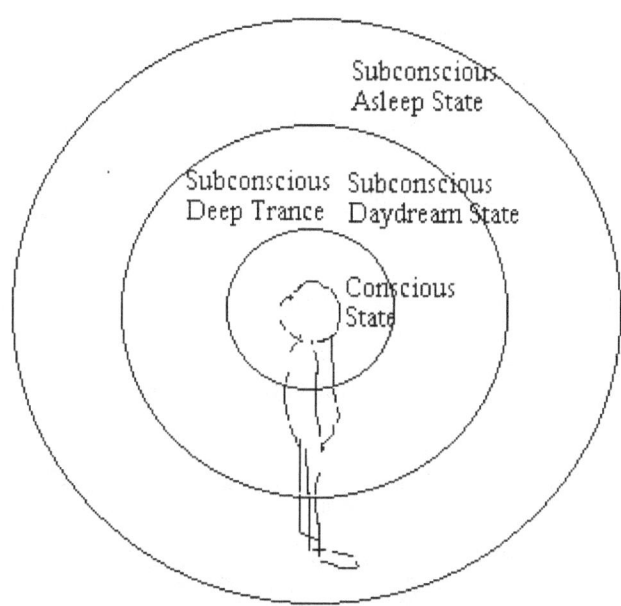

Although the subconscious mind can never stop processing and operating – terminating only in death -- it can shut down as it does when it goes into its deepest sleep mode. When the mind is fully awake, in the conscious state, it is still controlled by the subconscious mind; it is not even able to control how many times the eye blinks every minute. But it is a cinch for the subconscious; it performs billions of tasks without conscious awareness. It does all this automatically -- and this is how the conscious mind can be reprogrammed through hypnosis.

In the hypnotic state there are, primarily, two levels:
The **Subconscious Daydream State**, and the **Subconscious Deep Trance State.**

Although most people would disagree, more than 80% of subjects are able to become hypnotized into the **Subconscious Daydream State** needed for most hypnotherapy. Under hypnosis, the hypnotist may influence the subject with helpful suggestions providing soothing, rhythmical tones where the subject readily enters this state of subconscious.

As the subject relaxes, the breathing becomes calm, the temperature goes down, the pulse rate slows, and the blood pressure falls. There may be signs of rapid eye movements (REM's), and then the hypnotist attempts to discover the underlying causes of anxieties that have been suppressed.

Despite rumors to the contrary, it is virtually impossible to hypnotize anyone against their will. No person under hypnosis can be made to do anything against what they consider to be wrong, or against their principles – if there were a treat, they would simply snap out of the trance and return to the waking state.

Rest assured - there is no such thing as someone becoming transfixed into a trance state. Speaking of rest, the worst thing that could happen is that the subject would fall asleep naturally, which would only be for a short duration, inevitably to awaken completely out of the trance.

The best subjects are those who are imaginative enough to picture the ideas suggested by the hypnotist. Influenced greatly by the hypnotist's guided imagery, such susceptible subjects often drift off into a relaxed dream state, eventually reaching the **Subconscious Deep Trance State.**

Although going into a trance is thought of as being asleep, this is a misconception. The trance state is not much different than the normal daydream state, the only differences being that the eyes are closed, and that suggestions are being administered by a hypnotist.

Before anesthetics became widespread in the middle 19th century, hypnosis had been commonly used in surgery. However, the use of hypnosis in America today is becoming increasingly popular, especially in surgery as an alternative to anesthetics, which can have unpleasant and sometimes dangerous side effects. Because it is so effective, hypnosis is increasingly being used to treat many disorders such as anxiety, stress, addiction, insomnia, and other psychosomatic complexes.

As far as stage hypnotists go in America, law has restricted hypnotism used for entertainment purposes. The only hypnotist that I know of who is doing well today is Paul McKenna, and the reason is because he knows the true value, as well as the benefits of hypnosis, on, or off stage.

EVERYTHING WE ARE COMES FROM THE SUBCONSCIOUS

The subconscious mind is programmed like an endless tape, implanted within the complex synapses and cells of the brain. Actually, you <u>become</u> what your subconscious mind thinks. Then, thoughts transform us into our character.

You may think you can always consciously control your emotions, but after experiencing a crisis you may have wondered why you behaved so erratically, even sporadically. Actually, your subconscious mind is in control of every function necessary to keep you alive and well, functions that the conscious mind is not capable of performing. Try maintaining your heart rate, your blood count, your cell structure, or how many times you blink every minute of the day - (a little known fact is that the eyes even move and blink at night, during sleep.)

How about taking complete control of your memory? Properly accessed, it is possible to go into that subconscious tape and play back every word; every picture; every incident you've ever experienced even from the very day you were born. In fact, the trauma of birth has had, in some way, a lasting effect on each and every person.

Going beyond that, since the subconscious is Ancestral in development, you could feasibly tap into your past lives - this is because the subconscious is also supernatural in spirit. The good news is that, even after death, your spirit continues to live on, for the spirit is eternal. According to Einstein, energy never dies.

Since hypnosis works best in the state of relaxation, it is highly recommended that you predispose yourself to exercise, affirmations, and positive thinking, as well as listening to tranquil music and the many wondrous sounds nature has to offer.

More about this In PART TWO

The Ketchup Bottle Demonstration

To understand the basic concept of all hypnosis, consider the following example: Imagine that the ketchup bottle, below, (**Demonstration 1-1**) represents the physical and spiritual makeup of a human being. Imagine the **cap** as representing the conscious mind, and the contents of the bottle representing the subconscious. If this being was told that the contents inside was Green instead of Red, it would not readily accept it because the visual, critical, and conscious, mind has accepted Red as being a fact.

cap

Demonstration 1-1 Now, while undergoing hypnosis, and removing the **cap**, or the conscious mind, the being was told that the contents was Green, instead of Red, it would readily accept it. This is because the subconscious mind does not know the difference between fact and fiction. Relatively speaking, without going into the subconscious (the contents), this new belief would not be possible, since the conscious mind edits, criticizes, denies, and restricts information. The principle of **penetrating the subconscious mind** is as simple as offering a positive suggestion, a new thought, or a different truth. This is where the memory functions at its very best.

The Right Ear Demonstration

To further demonstrate the principle of **penetrating the subconscious mind**, try the following example: Form "**the hypnotic eye**" with the left hand and focus on it while cupping the fingers of the right hand just behind the right ear. Now, hold the palm close to the ear, serving as an amplifier while reciting the following words into the palm of the that hand placed at the right ear:

Every minute of every hour, I am feeling positive, uplifted, and fortunate because of receiving this remarkable power. This I have already accepted, in the name of Jesus Christ, Lord of every awakening hour.

Repeat the above phrase three times, not too loudly, focusing on the palm near the right ear. By doing this, the message is delivered directly to the subconscious because the right ear responds to it within the left hemisphere of the brain, where language is assimilated. In this instance, the words entering the right ear bypass the conscious mind, whereas words entering the left ear would only stifle the message. Many a New York City straphanger has, unwittingly, applied this practice when they would switch the phone to the right ear in an attempt to diminish the resounding noises of incoming trains.

CHAPTER TWO
2

FUNCTIONING AS A HYPNOTIST

2   HYPNOTIST
FUNCTION:

Through the hypnotist, words will paint images on your mind. These images will aid you in mastering control over your life in a creative and ideal way. During this process of <u>Guided Imagery</u> you will not become under any control; rather, through unleashing your own unconscious powers you will become enabled with the creative mind's most powerful tool - hypnotism.

In the state of hypnosis, the subconscious mind becomes fully accessible, processing two hundred million sensory messages every second. Conversely, in the conscious state, the mind is less than ten percent operational, processing only a handful of instructions at any given time.

CHAPTER TWO
2

FUNCTIONING AS A HYPNOTIST

The hypnotist's function is to see that the subject becomes relaxed and focused. The intention is that you become capable of receiving suggestions and directions that will motivate you into taking complete control of your destiny. Since this book is about hypnosis as well as self-hypnosis, I will also be addressing the subject. When you reach the trance state you will not do anything to violate your own values. Know that you always have the power to terminate the hypnotic state at any time. Hypnosis is not the sleep state, but an altered state of consciousness where our mental images, far deeper than our thoughts, aid in controlling our lives. This is the state of deep relaxation in mind and body commonly known as the trance state.

The objective of the hypnotist is to give helpful guidance along with positive images and have them take root in the subconscious mind. The end result of the learned experience is that you will become empowered to be master of your own fate. Hypnotism is effective in discovering the full potential, as well as the depth and nature of the person being hypnotized, so that growth, self-esteem, and success may be achieved. Through the hypnotist, words will paint images on your mind. These images will aid you in mastering control over your life in a creative and ideal way. During this process, you will not become powerless or out of control; rather, through unleashing your own unconscious powers you will become enabled with the creative mind's most powerful tool - hypnosis.

The wonderful thing about hypnosis is that the nervous system cannot tell the difference between real and imagined experiences; so by gaining access to the subconscious, you can into a trance and go anywhere, do anything, or become anyone you wish to. Just imagine - You can create an ideal reality in the privacy of your own mind, and actually feel, as well as experience all its benefits. Creating and developing mental images is certainly a great way to sense what it's like to be successful, or what it feels like to be loved and wanted. In this same manner, your mind's eye could allocate and then conceptualize the kind self-image you would be delighted to portray.

THE POWER OF HYPNOSIS

As you strive to fulfill your dreams, you will come to realize that you alone are in complete control of your destiny. In the state of hypnosis, the **subconscious mind is fully accessible,** with the entire brain processing one hundred million sensory messages every second. (See **Illustration 2-1** below.) Conversely, in the awakened state the **conscious mind uses less than ten percent of the brain's potential**, processing only a handful of information at any given time. (See **Illustration 2-2** below.)

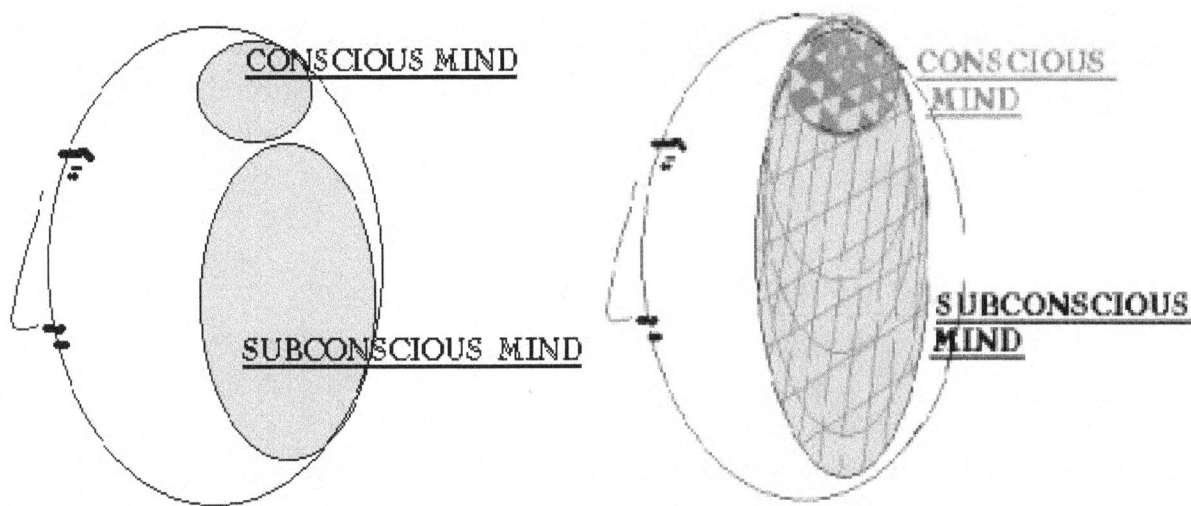

Illustration 2-1 (less than 10% of potential)   **Illustration 2-2** (fully accessible)

Note: In the state of hypnosis, the subconscious mind is fully accessible, utilizing the maximum amount of the brain's potential - insomuch that it even takes control of the conscious mind. According to scientists such as Carl Sagan, the subconscious possesses the incredible ability to process over a hundred million bits of information - in a mere second.

THE MIGHT OF MENTAL IMAGERY
The Mighty Law of Hypnosis

No matter which aspect of the mind, the mastery of it begins with your Mental Images. Every positive image brings a positive result. Every image brings to the fore its corresponding counterpart. Since every image brings a corresponding reaction, you can successfully influence the conscious mind through the subconscious mind.

Our Mental Images, far more proficient than our thoughts, control our lives. Induce positive visualization to take root in your subconscious, and you can take charge -- you can become master of your fate. You can obtain everything your heart desires.

In conjunction with Mental Images, since hypnotism produces organic responses, every negative thought must be counteracted by a positive thought. In this manner, you are bound to hypnotize yourself into a life of success, gratification and joy. This is The Mighty Law of Hypnosis!

THE CONCEPTION OF MENTAL THOUGHT
The Principle Rule of Mental Power

The person, who knows and applies the power of suggestion through the subconscious mind, becomes the master of the conscious mind -- thereby achieving <u>all that is desired</u>. This is The Principle Rule of Mental Power.

THE SUBJECTS' PERCEPTIBILITY

Spontaneous Test
Do you: - - - - - - - - (yes or no)
1. Practice relaxation exercises such as yoga, meditation or prayer? ___
2. Feel you are able to relax at any time, even if you are tense? ___
3. Make use of a schedule or routine to go to sleep? ___
4. Live in an imaginary world often taking you far from reality? ___
5. Have an extravagant imagination? ___
6. Have the ability to create mental images or visualizations? ___
7. Become strongly impressed by pleasant events or images? ___
8. Become thoroughly engrossed when you follow a movie? ___
9. Feel your emotions are spontaneous but disappear quickly? ___
10. Give more credence to your heart than to your intellect? ___
11. Become irritated or impatient when you have to wait? ___
12. Let your impulses rule over you? ___
13. Let yourself become easily intimidated? ___
14. Become easily influenced, according to your own point of view? ___
15. Let yourself become distracted when you work? ___
16. Have a passive attitude regarding responsibility and decisions? ___
17. Let impressive appearances of your neighbor influence you? ___
18. Feel comfortable with human contact? ___
19. Have absolute confidence in trusting certain people? ___
20. Believe subliminal messages have a strong influence? ___
21. Focus on the past, present, or future, rather than all three? ___
22. Make critical judgments at the time you learn something new? ___
23. Feel stronger about touching rather than seeing what you learn? ___
24. Prefer to write new ideas down rather than dreaming them up? ___
25. Prefer to control interactions rather than let others take over? ___

Susceptibility Test

The <u>Susceptibility Test</u> is performed using one of two simple inductions, as described below. First, have the subject sitting and facing straight ahead and, without moving the head, lift the **eyes up to the eyebrows** and slowly close them. Just before the eyelids close, take note of how much of the **iris** shows.

Carefully observe the "**Iris Test**" as follows: If little or none of the **iris** shows, it means the subject is very susceptible, and capable of the deepest trance -- the more of the **iris** that shows the less susceptible to being hypnotized. Most people reveal about half the **iris** showing, and are likely candidates for hypnosis. People with the **majority** of the **iris** showing are either likely to be mentally disturbed, or they simply cannot be readily hypnotized, if at all.

Note: **<u>Generally, all words in Italics are the spoken words</u>**.

Proceed with this induction: (with subject standing or sitting)

I would like to know if you are able to relax. Place your wrist in my hand – let me have the weight. (Let the arm fall, then try the other hand.) *Now, the other hand.* (Let the arm fall, then continue.) *Okay, I'm going to draw some circles around your body with my hands. Nothing to fear . . . They're called Mesmer Passes, or Halos to help you relax.*

Make gentle passes with the hands about six inches away from the body. The idea is to create a feeling of warmth, to relieve tension, and to basically gain the subjects trust.

Or, proceed with this very effective induction: (with subject sitting)

I'd like you to place your eyes up to your forehead and, when you feel like it, close them. Everything will go very well. Now, breathe calmly, regularly. Good, nothing can distract you. As I count from three down to zero, I'd like you to imagine yourself floating on your back, as if you are in a swimming pool. 3 . . . 2 . . . 1 . . . 0.

You welcome this pleasant imaginary sensation as you concentrate on floating. As you continue to focus on floating, I'm going to lift your left arm and concentrate on stroking your hand. On the count of three I'm going to put your hand down and it will float right back up to where it is now. As you open your eyes you will find something amusing about this.
1 . . . 2 . . 3 . . . Open your eyes.

(If this induction doesn't work, don't worry; try another approach. The fact that this procedure doesn't take effect, either means the subject has some resistance, or is not readily susceptible to this process. Or, without discouraging the subject, simply proceed with **Testing *The Trance Zone*** or the **Hypnosis Illustration** listed in **Chapter Four**.)

Concentration Test

The Concentration Test is not only a way of testing the subject's frame of mind, but of a way to Perform the test as described below:

Proceed with this simple test: (with subject sitting)

I'd like you to concentrate on the number 8, and remember it when I ask you at the end of this soup riddle:

Once upon a time, there were 15 boys who were instructed to sit down and eat bowls of soup. 6 boys that were being served chose Pea soup, while the other boys chose Carrot soup. Since 9 boys had Carrot soup, how many boys had Pea soup? (The answer would be 6.) What was the number I gave you to remember? (The answer should be 8.)

(Note: If the subject doesn't come up with the right answer, don't make an issue of it. Simply explain that the subject may be nervous. Sometimes, it could mean the subject is tense, or has some resistance to becoming hypnotized. Without discouraging the subject, simply proceed with any of the hypnosis procedures. In instances where the subject is extremely forgetful, look for reasons or indications of confusion, stressful conditions, or a possibility of mental illness.)

HYPNOSIS DEFINED:
HYPNOTIST INDUCED HYPNOSIS (posthypnotic suggestion)

(Note: **Posthypnotic Suggestions** are the messages, key words, or triggers induced by the hypnotist to the subject in the hypnotic state.)

The word **hypnosis** comes from the Greek word, Hypnos, meaning sleep, to sleep, or to lull to sleep. In actuality, hypnosis is not of the sleep state, but rather of a trance-like daydream state, where the senses are awake and fully aware. If the subject does go to sleep, the hypnotic session is over - until awakened.

Webster's New World Dictionary defines **hypnosis** as "A trance-like condition usually induced by another person, in which the subject is in a state of altered consciousness and responds, with certain limitations, to the suggestions of the hypnotist." It defines hypnotize as "to spellbind."

Mosby's Medical Dictionary defines **hypnotism** as "A trance-like state, resembling normal sleep, during which perception and memory are altered, resulting in greater susceptibility to suggestion." Another definition states: "**hypnosis** is relaxation with an agenda."

The American Heritage Dictionary defines the term, subliminal as "Below the threshold of conscious perception." Therefore, by definition, the act of **hypnosis is a subliminal process**.

SELF-HYPNOSIS DEFINED:
SUBJECT INDUCED HYPNOSIS (autosuggestion)

(Note: **Autosuggestions** are the messages, or words induced by the subject to induce the self-hypnotic state, herein called self-hypnosis.)

Webster's New World Dictionary refers self-hypnosis to autohypnosis and defines it as "The act of hypnotizing oneself or the state of being so hypnotized."

Actually, through **autosuggestion** the subject makes suggestions to the self, effecting the mind, thoughts, and bodily functions, thereby becoming hypnotized.

When the subject performs hypnosis on the self, the process is called self-hypnosis or the act of **self-hypnotism. Self-hypnotic suggestion, self-hypnosis, or autosuggestion** is that state of hypnosis induced by the subject.

Note that when the subject induces hypnosis on the self, the subject cannot cause an arm or limb to become cataleptic (rigid), while the hypnotist can. The reason for this has to do with the hypnotist's power over the subject, which raises a question. If the subject is always in control of the session, how can he allow the hypnotist to take such control over his subconscious mind?

The answer is that the subject has a choice of giving the power over to the hypnotist, benefiting by years of professional experience, or to choose not to engage in such an enriching process. Or the subject can choose to practice and become an exceptional self-hypnotist. The subject should also consider whether the benefits of becoming hypnotized outweigh one's own talent and creative ability at mastering this complex phenomenon. On the other hand, the subject can realize that the only control, ever, is the self, and that no one has the power to overcome anyone else's mind. However, the synergy derived from duality has tremendous credence, with much to be gained from the chemical reactions and concerted interrelations between the hypnotist and the subject's subconscious mind.

PART TWO

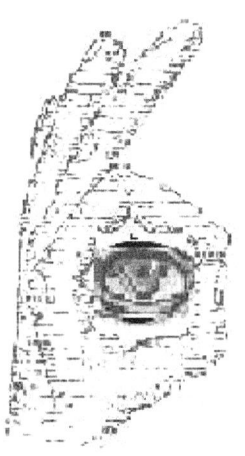

CHAPTER THREE
3

THE TRANCE ZONE
THE CONCEPT BEHIND THE BOOK

---

3   HYPNOSIS
THE TRANCE ZONE:

There are opportunities
That your mind cannot
      Yet construe,
But which make way into your life
And as if by some majestic rapture,
    Touch and influence you.

CHAPTER THREE
3

THE TRANCE ZONE
THE CONCEPT BEHIND THE BOOK

THE TRANCE ZONE TECHNIQUE
THE PSYSIOLOGY OF *THE TRANCE ZONE:*

The Trance Zone is the life force, the true spirit of the soul within the physical body -- in short; it is the superlative energy of the subconscious mind. This is the majestic state of hypnosis. Upon reaching this subconscious state the feeling becomes one of splendor, as if subjected to a majestic spell between the conscious mind and the spirit. It is that special, deepened trance state between the **Alpha** and **Theta** brain waves.

Being under the influence of hypnosis is to become charmed -- it is tantamount to that of the Cobra, where the snake charmer casts a spell and causes it to respond from within a basket. Yet, the Cobra is not responding to the music, for it cannot hear -- the snake is being charmed by the snake charmer's flute assimilating the movement of a pendant. Because of being highly focused on the flute, the Cobra cannot help but become hypnotized. This is the basis of all hypnotism.

The Trance Zone, state of hypnosis is not that of the sleep state, but of a false, facsimile of sleep, called the trance state. This is the state where the mind, in its entirety, is most accessible. Because the conscious mind is judgmental and obstinate, it is restrictive compared to the subconscious. ***The Trance Zone* is that state where the subconscious operates, fully free from conscious intervention.**

When reaching *The Trance Zone* state of hypnosis, many changes occur within the body. As the subject relaxes, the breathing becomes calm, the temperature goes down, the pulse rate slows, and the blood pressure falls. There may be signs of rapid eye movements as the mind shifts from consciousness to the subconscious state. The deeper the trance, the more unencumbered the body, and the more uninhibited the mind becomes.

At some deepened state, the adrenaline, metabolism, visual perception and intuition becomes increased, whereby the feeling of being in "the groove," or in "the arousal-state" kicks in, as many athletes have reported when being in "the zone." Then, hypnosis becomes organic, in nature, and everything seems to be functioning as though everything was right.

At best, a state of euphoria will ensue, where mind, body and spirit feel so harmonious nothing becomes impossible to achieve. At worst, the state of total relaxation occurs, leaving the subject with the feeling that some kind of magic has been performed, some kind of vacation has been provided. In essence, all this is due to the natural release of endorphins and enkephalins.

The Trance Zone Concept 33

The Trance Zone is that altered state of mind where the **Brain Waves** of the **Alpha State** and **Theta State** vibrate between 4 and 14 CPS. It is that unique place between the conscious and the sleep state, where the mind can reach its highest state of enchantment. It is that trance state of hypnosis; that place deep within us, where hallucination, amnesia, and fantasy take over the conscious mind, thereby subconsciously becoming realized as truth. Asleep or awake, the mind's state of awareness is measured in brain waves from approximately 1/2 to 40 CPS, or **Cycles Per Second**. (See **Illustration 3-1** below.)

The **Delta State** is reached when the brain waves become as low as ½ - 1 CPS at its deepest sleep state, increasing only to 4 CPS. The **Beta State** is reached when the mind is in its conscious, awakened state where the vibrations measure from about 14 CPS to as high as 40 CPS, or more. (Waves vibrating in the higher registers most likely would indicate stress, high anxiety or a virus invading the immune system.)

States of Mind	Brain Waves -- Cycles Per Second
Delta State - Deep Sleep State	½ to 4 CPS
Theta State - Subconscious Deep Trance State	4 to 7 CPS
Alpha State - Subconscious Daydream State	7 to 14 CPS
Beta State - Conscious State, the Awake State	14 to 40 CPS

Illustration 3-1

(Note: Rapid Eye Movement (REM) sometimes occurs during the Alpha state. However, it is not an indication that a trance has been induced, it is merely the indication of a shift from the conscious to the subconscious state.)

THE PSYCHOLOGICAL TOOLS *

Listed below, are descriptions of the psychological tools suggested in order to induce hypnosis in ***The Trance Zone.*** They are listed below in the following order: **the hypnotic eye; eyes up to the eyebrows; deep yawn; inhale through the nose; the observing eye**, and **Hypnotic WORDS**. Other tools include **subliminal sounds, multifaceted crystals, and The Might of Mental Imagery**.

* the hypnotic eye

This posturing of the fingers is commonly perceived as a sign representing perfection. Holding the hand in the air, indicating with the encircled fingers has been used to represent many kinds of expression, including to show that everything is okay; to stress a point; or to demonstrate confidence. It has also been used to demonstrate security, or an attempt to express one's feelings. I consider it as "the Eye to The Supernatural Spirit."(See **Illustration 3-2** below.)

After creating this powerful hypnotic sign, I became amazed to see how many times people have used it on television to express themselves. At first, it seemed coincidental - but I don't really believe in coincidences. It is my firm belief that every idea becomes a universal consciousness -- that people can become subconsciously influenced through some form of telepathy. So, it doesn't surprise me that this placing of the fingers together in this manner has caught on.

Ever since I discovered the extreme power of **_The Trance Zone,_** I have become excited about this symbol's profound effectiveness. In realizing that the fingers subconsciously represent an extension of the subconscious inner spirit, or higher self, I have found the use of **"the hypnotic eye"** to be a very majestic way of inducing hypnosis.

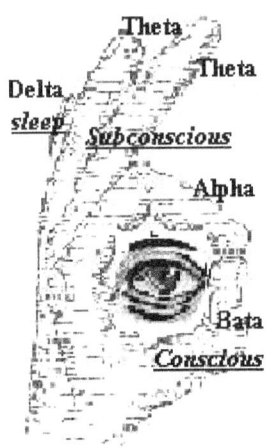

Illustration 3-2 -- the hypnotic eye

As if designated for this purpose, it is interesting that **Alpha**, the subconscious, represented by the first finger, forms the position of dominance, while **Beta**, the conscious, represented by the thumb, constitutes the subordinate power. The leverage of **Alpha** becomes even more pronounced because of the **middle finger** representing the deep subconscious state of **Theta**, right behind it.

What a coincidence that the last two fingers, the fourth finger and the pinkie, representing the varied sleep states of **Delta**, are farthest from the conscious state. The significance of this formation is quite mysterious, but I have found that there is no question regarding its unlimited effectiveness.

Forming **"the hypnotic eye"** is a powerful tool (see **Illustration 3-2** above), which aids in the process of hypnosis, in addition to providing an opening to supernatural intervention. Acting in concert with the **eyes up to the eyebrows, inhale through the nose,** and the **deep yawn,** placing the thumb and first finger together enables either the hypnotist or the subject to "Go Into" **_The Trance Zone._**

One use of **"the hypnotic eye"** is to establish an association between the action of the fingers and lifting the **eyes up to the eyebrows**. This action serves as a trigger, transforming the psychosomatic/emotional conscious state into the subconscious trance state.

Other uses of **"the hypnotic eye"** are to gain a highly concentrated state of focus. This is accomplished by placing the fingers together as shown above and then by visualizing a supernatural third eye within the circle. The extraordinary powers of this action are explained in the examples given below.

The Trance Zone Concept   35

(1.) <u>**Fo**cusing to memorize</u> reading material, or documents, by placing "<u>**the hypnotic eye**</u>" over the paper to be memorized.

PRACTICE EXERCISE: (see **Illustration 3-2** above.)
By drawing the encircled fingers over words and focusing, you can study the pages as if using a magnifying glass. In focusing in this manner the text becomes intensified, eventually bringing total recall. Simply place "<u>**the hypnotic eye**</u>" over the printed page, or document and take an imaginary "snapshot" for as long as it takes to get the required results. Even pictures, objects or complex scenes can be memorized in the same way. This may have to be repeated many times, but with practice you could inevitably develop a photographic memory.

(2.) <u>**Fo**cusing to create a particular desire, result or need</u> by concentrating on "<u>**the hypnotic eye**</u>." For example: place the fingers together as in **Illustration 3-2** above and say the words, *I have so much money, I am financially independent.*

To manifest a particular desire, focus on the center of "<u>**the hypnotic eye**</u>" while creating tension with the fingers and concentrating on the need. Focus on the Illustration below until you can associate it with the vision you have created in you mind.

Then "Go Into" *The Trance Zone* and focus on the visualization while keeping "<u>**the hypnotic eye**</u>" at your side.

PRACTICE EXERCISE: (See **Illustration 3-3** below.)
The **Illustration** below shows a number of ways to focus on quitting a bad habit, for example, **The Desire To Quit Smoking** is one way. You may concentrate on words, the pack of cigarettes, or the thought of quitting. To augment this process, acquire a small crystal ball, place it inside the fingers that form "<u>**the hypnotic eye**</u>," and focus on attaining the desired result. Try to choose a clear, multifaceted crystal ball or one that is smooth; preferably blue, in color. Light up some frankincense during the ritual to produce even more effective results.

Note! Whether it is a yacht, money, a job, or love, the principle is the same. This works exceptionally well when closing the eyes and imagining your ideal dream.

   $50,000

Quit Smoking   **Possessions**   **Love**   **Money**

Illustration 3-3

(3.) **Focusing** to induce instant hypnosis by placing "**the hypnotic eye**" above the forehead.

PRACTICE EXERCISE:
As the subject, stare at "**the hypnotic eye**" using either hand, and place it above the forehead. Then lift the **eyes up to the eyebrows** and close them.
Nearly automatically, this will induce the trance state. This should be reinforced be saying, ***This is how I 'Go Into' The Trance Zone.***

(See **Illustration 3-2** above)

(4.) **Focusing** to induce instant hypnosis by placing "**the hypnotic eye**" above the subject's forehead.

PRACTICE EXERCISE:
As the hypnotist, have the subject stare at "**the hypnotic eye**" using either hand, and place it above the subject's forehead. Then have the subject lift the **eyes up to the eyebrows** and close them. Nearly automatically, this will induce the trance state. This should be reinforced by saying: *"This is how you 'Go Into' **The Trance Zone**."*

(See **Illustration 3-2** above.)

PRACTICE EXERCISE:
Have the subject stare at "**the hypnotic eye**."
Then say aloud, *lift the **eyes up to the eyebrows** and close them.*
With either hand, form "**the hypnotic eye**" and place it above the subject's forehead. Then say aloud: *"This is how you 'Go Into' **The Trance Zone**."*

(See **Illustration 3-2** above.)

(5.) **Focusing** to radiate love using "**the hypnotic eye**" over the subject's body to induce hypnosis for influencing love, as well as providing healing powers.

PRACTICE EXERCISE:
After placing "**the hypnotic eye**" near or over the subject's body, imagine the center having a laser beam whereby focusing intensifies the powers of personal magnetism, reciprocal love, and healing, as well as performing hypnotism.

(See **Illustration 3-2** above.)

Note: Focusing on "**the hypnotic eye**" is the key to unleashing the power of the subconscious mind. Whenever you call upon this image, hidden knowledge will be brought to light. As you look deeper and deeper within your spirit, you draw wisdom from the depths of your subconscious mind. All knowledge is there for you. All channels of guidance are opened to you, especially spiritual guidance. Everything you want to know is revealed. Everything is made clear; everything is exposed. Your will, as well as Thy will, will be done - and thus it is laid out before you.

With practice, using these procedures will not only improve the powers of hypnosis, but they will enhance all aspects of mind, body and spirit.

Whether the hypnotist or the subject, the most important thing to bear in mind is this:
What the subconscious mind can believe, the mind can conceive.

(6.) <u>F**o**cusing to recall past incidents and make mental notes</u> simply by forming "**the hypnotic eye.**"

   PRACTICE EXERCISE: (See **Illustration 3-4** below.)
 To recall the details of a movie, make a note of the information then lift the **eyes up to the eyebrows** and close them. Form "**the hypnotic eye,**" focus, and then open your eyes. Because all information, including activity, sounds and visual images remain in the subconscious, you will able to recall practically every detail you focus upon.

   For an example, see the breakdown as listed below:
Main Issue or Subject - (the center of the "**eye**"): Filing cabinet A = *Classic movies;*
Events - (first finger): <u>Drawer #1</u> = *Gone With The Wind*;
Facts - (thumb): <u>Drawer #2</u> = *Tragic Love and War Story;*
Place - (middle finger): <u>Drawer #3</u> = *The South*;
Persons - (fourth finger): <u>Drawer #4</u> = *Clark Gable and Olivia DeHaviland;*
Details - (pinky): <u>Drawer #5</u> = *War between the North and South.*

 Use this process long enough; believe in it strong enough and it <u>will</u> happen because it becomes registered, subconsciously, as if it were true. In fact, this process can be used as a **memory filing cabinet** to gather details for a book, or for any other collective cause. This theory is based on Dr. Carl Jung's concept of the "collective unconscious." When facts are assigned subconsciously, they become permanent addresses in the matrix of the human mind.

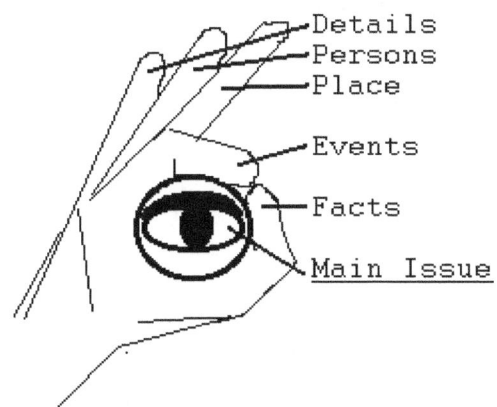

Illustration 3-4
<u>Use for total recall within the matrix of the mind.</u>

(7.) **Focusing** to ward off evil forces by forming "**the hypnotic eye**," and using the fingers to recite prayers. Note: By moving the thumb of the hand from the first finger and then back to the thumb, this becomes an extremely powerful method. The connection between the hand, fingers, and "**the hypnotic eye**" induces a very strong relationship with the protective, supernatural spirit.

PRACTICE EXERCISE:

Using the fingers as prayer beads is an ideal way to meditate, or to concentrate on relaxing. For an even greater effect read prayers aloud, as holy words become very powerful tools against evil influences. An excellent way to use this method would be to go to the bible and read the verses of **Ephesians 6: 10 - 18**. (See **Illustration 3-5** below.) Appropriately, I call the following set of prayers, *__The Whole Armor of God.__*

For the most effective results, be sure to follow these instructions to the letter: While placing the thumb and first finger together *__recite verse 10__* concentrating on the thumb; then *__recite verse 11__* while concentrating on the first finger.

Then continue, placing the thumb and middle finger together *__recite verse 12__* while concentrating on that middle finger.

Then, placing the thumb and ring finger together *__recite verse 13__* while concentrating on that ring finger. Then, placing the thumb and pinky together *__recite verse 14__* while concentrating on that pinky.

Then, returning the thumb to the ring finger *__recite verse 15__* while concentrating on that ring finger. Returning the thumb to the middle finger *__recite verse 16__* while concentrating on that middle finger. Finally, returning the thumb to the first finger *__recite verse 17__* while concentrating on that same first finger; and *__recite verse 18__* while concentrating on the thumb.

After completing this cycle of spiritual prayers, you can rest assured that you will be able to relax, no matter what the problem. Then, sit back and watch the demons vacate the premises!

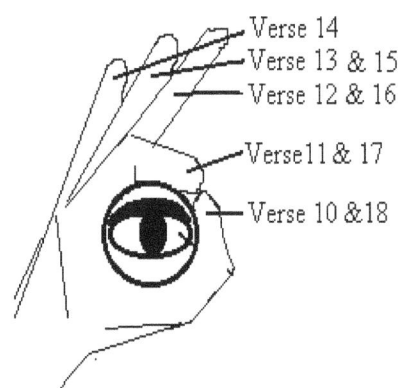

Illustration 3-5
Use for memorizing details for total recall

For an example of reciting and memorizing the above passages, see the sequence of prayers listed below:

Thumb & First Finger - (Concentrating on the Thumb):
> *Verse 10: "Finally, my brethren, be strong in the Lord, and in the power of His Might"*

Thumb & First Finger - (Concentrating on the First Finger):
> *Verse 11: "Put on the whole armor of God, that you may be able to stand against the wiles of the devil."*

Thumb & Middle Finger - (Concentrating on the Middle Finger):
> *Verse 12: "For we wrestle not with flesh and blood, but against principalities; against powers; against rulers of darkness of this world; against spiritual wickedness in high places.*

Thumb & Ring Finger - (Concentrating on the Ring Finger):
> *Verse 13: "Wherefore take unto you The Whole Armor of God, that you may be able to withstand in the evil day, and having done all to stand."*

Thumb & Pinky Finger - (Concentrating on the Pinky Finger):
> *Verse 14: "Stand therefore having your loins girt about with truth; and having on the breastplate of righteousness.* (Notice that this finger is only touched once.)

Thumb & Ring Finger - (Concentrating on the Ring Finger):
> *Verse 15: "And your feet shod with the preparation of the Gospel of peace."*

Thumb & Middle Finger - (Concentrating on the Middle Finger):
> *Verse 16: "Above all, taking the shield of faith, wherewith you shall be able to quench all the fiery darts of the wicked."*

Thumb & First Finger - (Concentrating on the First Finger):
> *Verse 17: "And take the helmet of salvation, and the sword of the spirit, which is the word of God:"*

Thumb & First Finger - (Concentrating on the Thumb):
> *Verse 18: "Praying always in the Spirit, and watching there for all Saints."*

* the observing eye

This eye formed the same way as "**the hypnotic eye**" as shown above, except that the fingers are stretched out, forming a narrow "eye." Mainly, it is used as an alternative to augment the **Majestic Trance Spells** found in later chapters on self-hypnosis. (This narrowing of the eye depicts the Egyptian, Horus, son of Osiris and Isis.)

* eyes up to the eyebrows

Lifting the **eyes up to the eyebrows** and closing them triggers the conscious mind into the subconscious state. It is as if the eyes receive subconscious messages because they are parked within the synapse centers of the matrix of the brain.

* **deep yawn**

The reason for the **deep yawn** is, not only because it is contagious, but also because it aids in triggering the brain's subconscious activity. Yawning is a very effective way of relaxing both the body and mind in preparation to going into hypnosis.

* **inhale through the nose**

Focusing on **inhale through the nose** instructs the conscious mind to let go, allowing better transformation to the subconscious state. Since brain cells die at the rate of millions per second, this form of breathing enables the oxygen to replenish the brain cells at a more intensified rate. When breathing, think of breathing between the eyes. Sometimes, merely getting a person to smile during this time can make a great difference regarding attitude.

* **Hypnotic WORDS**

The keys to all hypnotic inductions are the **Hypnotic WORDS**, and the soothing, positive, reassuring manner in which they are executed. They have a specific energy and can be a very powerful influence on people, affecting their truths. **Hypnotic WORDS** delivered in the right rhythm and tones have an astonishing impact consciously. But when bypassed by the conscious mind, which restricts and edits, they become even more profound in the altered, subconscious state. Since you have been mesmerized through advertising, commercials, social interactions, and other means, negative messages have become imprinted within your subconscious.

Transforming these self-defeating messages is the task of the hypnotist. The objective is to alter, reverse, or eradicate the condition so that you, the subject, will become free of the psychologically damaging influences. While the mind, through repetitious bombardment, has accepted the notion that it may be prone to failure in all endeavors, the hypnotist can induce suggestions and, virtually, reverse the infliction.

Through the hypnotist's voice, the **Hypnotic WORDS** can be delivered with such an infiltrating impact the subconscious mind could literally enable you to change the course of your life for the best. Practice speaking aloud, discovering the right timbre and cadence of your voice, and you will have discovered the foundation of a good hypnotist.

* <u>subliminal sounds</u>

In concert with the hypnotist's WORDS, **<u>subliminal sounds</u>** serve equally well as they pacify the emotions; becoming formidable tools in penetrating the subconscious mind. Subliminal sounds (or background sounds), played or recorded during the hypnotic trance aid in inducing the hypnosis. The sounds of a ticking clock or a metronome, musical instruments, animal calls, running water, ocean waves, and singing voices are all very effective means of soothing us and summoning the power of the subconscious mind. A great example of this is when a mother sings her child to sleep. The short, soothing song, classified as a "lullaby" has pacified many a baby to the point of falling asleep in its mother's arms -- a perfect example of a subconscious induction, and how it affects the mind. Other incidents, such as falling asleep during plays, operas, and movies are all reactions to subliminal inducements. Dozing off behind the wheel due to staring at the white line is another subliminal inducement -- a classic state of trance.

* <u>multifaceted crystals</u> (and other methods of focus)

Through using transparent, **<u>multifaceted crystals</u>**, either in hand or spinning above the subject, going into ***<u>The Trance Zone</u>*** becomes very easy. Since the main requirement of hypnosis is focus, the crystal is able to command full attention. Other instruments for attaining focus include the pendulum; a swinging watch, a spinning disk, or the manipulation of the hand – even a mere spot can provide the focus point for a successful hypnotic induction.

* <u>The Might Of Mental Imagery</u>

No matter which aspect of the mind, the mastery of it begins with your Mental Images. Every positive image brings a positive result. Every image brings to the fore its corresponding counterpart. Since every image brings a corresponding reaction, you can successfully influence the conscious mind through the power of the subconscious mind. **<u>The Might Of Mental Imagery</u>**, far more proficient than our thoughts, controls our lives. Allow positive **visualizations** to take root in your subconscious, and you can become master of your fate. You **<u>can</u>** obtain everything your heart desires. Since hypnotism produces organic responses, every negative thought must be counteracted by a positive thought. In this manner, you are bound to hypnotize yourself into a life of success, gratification and joy.

The person who exercises and applies the **power of suggestion** through the subconscious mind becomes somewhat of a master. Having transformed to that certain suggestion actually empowers one to achieve **<u>all that is desired</u>**.
This is The Principle Rule of <u>The Might of Mental Imagery</u>.

CHAPTER FOUR
4

THE TRANCE ZONE
REACHING
THE INITIAL STATE
OF
HYPNOSIS

---

4 <u>HYPNOTISM</u>
<u>INDUCTIONS:</u>

The hypnotist hypnotizes the subject, whereby the subject becomes hypnotized through posthypnotic suggestions. When the hypnotist performs hypnosis on the subject -- it is called hypnotism.

Of <u>The Trance State</u> I could reasonably say:
"Feed the subconscious mind enough optimism and it will flourish alive and well; feed it excessive negative, pessimistic thoughts and it will degenerate, inevitably to expire. I conclude that, for the hypnotherapist, the use of hypnosis is paramount in supplanting optimistic attitudes; it works equally well in providing treatment for disease and despair."

Edward J. Longo

CHAPTER FOUR
4

THE TRANCE ZONE
REACHING THE INITIAL STATE
OF HYPNOSIS

REACHING *THE TRANCE ZONE*
Penetrating The Subconscious Mind

Visualization - The Way Of Bringing Ideals, Dreams, And Desires Into Reality.

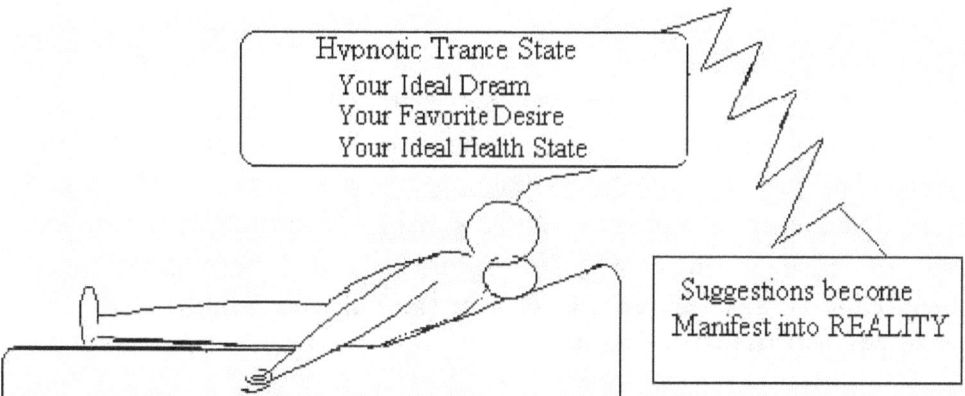

Because the conscious mind is by-passed, the subconscious readily accepts everything it receives as the TRUTH. When properly administered through hypnosis, all suggestions manifest into REALITY through supernatural powers of the subconscious mind.

Below is the general procedure in order to "Go Into" **The Trance Zone**. With the understanding that the trance script should either be memorized, or taped in the "first person," follow the instruction below to experience what it may be like to enter the trance state. Note: Brief as this may seem, some persons will be able to go right into the trance state. The best way to gain this remarkable uplifting experience is to simply proceed without skepticism, or doubt that this is really possible.

The Trance Zone Prone Position Above: With the eyes closed and up to the eyebrows, take in a deep yawn with the hand forming "The Hypnotic Eye" at your side. This becomes the eye to your subconscious mind, which you can call upon any time you wish to "Go Into" the hypnotic trance state.

THE TRANCE ZONE INDUCTION:
TO "GO INTO" *THE TRANCE ZONE*

The Initial Procedure - (induced by the hypnotist)
To "Go Into" ***The Trance Zone***, induce the hypnosis as follows:
First, have the subject form "**the hypnotic eye**," by placing the thumb and first finger together and place it at either side.
Then, have the subject lift the **eyes up to the eyebrows**, close them, and give a **deep yawn**.
Next have the subject recite: *This is how I "Go Into"* ***The Trance Zone.***

Now, instruct the subject **inhale through the nose** and exhale *while counting down from 30 by 2's, relaxing the body more and more while going into the hypnotic state. (*Due to the many variations, counting down is optional.)

This is how *The Trance Zone* is induced. This is the initial procedure used to "Go Into" every hypnotic trance. (Continue with the hypnosis.)

TESTING *THE TRANCE ZONE* INDUCTION

To demonstrate the effectiveness of hypnosis, form "**the hypnotic eye**" with both hands and interlock the centers, that is, the thumb and first finger of one hand encircling the thumb and first finger of the other. Now, lift the **eyes up to the eyebrows** and **try to pull them apart** while thinking and saying, *"I cannot pull my fingers apart."* You will never be able to pull them apart as long as you firmly commit to believing you cannot.

To prove this, continue thinking you cannot pull them apart, while saying, *"I can pull my fingers apart."* As long as you are thinking you cannot, you will not be able to pull them apart, because your thought has generated a contrary, subliminal message to your subconscious. The principle is the same if you reverse the process. While thinking, *"I can pull my fingers apart,"* you will be able to – even though you say, *"I cannot pull my fingers apart."* **(Irrefutably, the subconscious is the dominant power over the conscious mind!)**

(See "Hypnosis Demonstration" in Chapter 7)

(Note: The **Induction Tests** listed below are optional, and should be used with discretion.)

1ST INDUCTION TEST (with the subject sitting)
HYPNOTIST:

Have the subject "Go into" ***The Trance Zone***, as described previously then continue with the hypnotic suggestions.

*I'd like you to form "**the hypnotic eye**" and place your hand at your side. This is the eye to your subconscious, which puts you into **The Trance Zone**. Now, I'd like you to lift your **eyes up to the eyebrows** and, when you feel like it, close them. Keeping your eyes up take in a **deep yawn**, and recite: This is how I "Go Into"* ***The Trance Zone.***

(continue)

1ST INDUCTION TEST (continued)

In that wide opening to your subconscious, you are listening intently to my voice. Under hypnosis, you can speak to me if I ask you to. I'm now going to ask you to deepen your own hypnosis by remembering the order of the numbers when I count from 10 to 1 in this order: 10, 9, 8, 7, 6, 4, 3, 2, 1. I also ask you to say the words <u>deeper I go</u>, between my counts. By saying this you will go deeper into hypnosis 10, 9, 8, 7, 6, 4, 3, 2, 1. Good going. Now repeat the numbers as you just heard me count them. If you wish to add <u>deeper I go</u> with them, that's okay.

(This procedure tests the depth of the hypnotic state. If the subject remembers to leave out the 5, proceed with the hypnosis - if not, repeat the count down. Then proceed with the hypnosis using any of the inductions, and bring the subject out and back to normal.

(Note that, part of the hypnotist's obligation is to guide the subject into the trance state by offering helpful hypnotic suggestions, and by verbally painting colorful pictures. Aside from experience and creative talent, the hypnotist's voice is, perhaps, the most powerful of all the tools.)

2ND INDUCTION TEST (with the subject sitting)
HYPNOTIST:

Have the subject "Go into" ***The Trance Zone***, as described previously then continue with the hypnotic suggestions.

I'd like you to form "**the hypnotic eye**" and place your hand at your side. This is the eye to your subconscious, which puts you into **The Trance Zone**. Now, I'd like you to lift your **eyes up to the eyebrows** and, when you feel like it, close them. Keeping your eyes up take in a **deep yawn,** and recite: This is how I "Go Into" **The Trance Zone**.

In that wide opening to your subconscious, you are listening intently to my voice. As you are resting comfortably you will notice that your eyes are closed tight, very tight. They are stuck so tight you are not able to open them. In a moment I will ask you to try to open them - you will not be able to do so. You will find they are sealed tight, they are stuck firmly together. You may be able to manage the muscle groups around your eyes, but not your eyelids. No matter how hard you try, you will be unable to open your eyes.

When I count down from 3 to zero, you will find it impossible to open your eyes and you will go deeper into hypnosis. 3... Your eyelids are sealed tight, 2... They are stuck tight, 1... They are stuck firmly together, Zero... Try, but you are unable to open them. Stop trying, and go deeper into hypnosis.

(The procedure below tests the depth of the hypnotic state. If the subject's arm becomes comatose, proceed with the hypnosis - if not, repeat the process or try another technique. Then proceed with the hypnosis using any of the hypnotic inductions.)

3RD INDUCTION TEST (with the subject sitting)
HYPNOTIST:

Have the subject "Go into" ***The Trance Zone,*** as described below, and then continue with the hypnotic suggestions.

*I'd like you to form "**the hypnotic eye**" and place your hand at your side. This is the eye to your subconscious, which puts you into **The Trance Zone**. Now, I'd like you to lift your **eyes up to the eyebrows** and, when you feel like it, close them. Keeping your eyes up take in a **deep yawn,** and recite: This is how I "Go Into" **The Trance Zone**."*

In that wide opening to your subconscious, you are listening intently to my voice. I am now going to take your arm by the wrist and hold it up. As I lock it at the elbow and lock it at the shoulder, you acknowledge this. Then, as I give it a tug, your whole arm remains stiff and rigid as a wooden log. In a moment, I will ask you to lower your arm. You will not be able to do so. Any downward movement will cause your arm to bounce back up . . . (repeat the words as you test this) *Bounce back up.*

As I count to three, I'd like you to try to lower your arm. But even though you try you will not be able to lower your hand or your arm. 1 . . . your arm is stiff and rigid as a wooden log, 2 . . . stiff and rigid, it remains like a wooden log, 3 . . . try to lower it. You can't. Try harder, you can't. Try harder, You cannot. Stop trying. Okay, unlock your elbow (you do it); unlock your shoulder (you do it). Good, place your arm in your lap and go deeper into hypnosis.

(The procedure below provides an example of reaching the depth of the hypnotic state. If the subject becomes relaxed, proceed with the hypnosis - if not, repeat the process differently. Then proceed with the hypnosis.)

HYPNOSIS INDUCTION

HYPNOTIST: (with the subject sitting or lying)

Have the subject "Go into" **The *Trance Zone*,** as described below, and then continue with the hypnotic suggestions.

*I'd like you to form "**the hypnotic eye**" by placing the thumb and forefinger of either hand together, and place your hand at your side. This is the eye to your subconscious, which puts you into **The Trance Zone**. Now, I'd like you to lift your **eyes up to the eyebrows** and, when you feel like it, close them. Keeping your eyes up take in a **deep yawn,** and recite: "This is how I go into **The Trance Zone**."*

In that wide opening to your subconscious, you are listening intently to my voice. Now, I'd like you to <u>inhale through the nose</u> and exhale through the mouth, while I count down from 30 by 2's, relaxing your body more and more while going into the hypnotic state. 30 . . . 28 . . . 26 . . . 24 . . . 22 . . . 20 . . . 18 . . . 16 . . . etc. Now, imagine yourself rising up into the sky where you manifest three giant screens in front of you. Visualize yourself in the <u>middle screen</u> in your present condition. Include your feelings, attitude and state of mind.

In the <u>left screen</u> envision a disgusting picture of yourself approaching a lake, wearing dirty clothing, and carrying a suitcase. After walking toward a motorboat, you climb aboard, drive it out to a raft in the middle of the lake, and climb onto it. Suddenly, you open the suitcase, spilling the contents onto the raft, and begin reexamining the paraphernalia. Picture those discarded contents as being everything negative in your life -- all the excess baggage, including, the headaches, tension, guilt, paranoia, illness, addiction to alcohol, drugs, or cigarettes, or any other agony you wish to get rid of.

The important thing is to unload everything that bothers you or interferes with your life right here on the surface of this raft -- see it all; acknowledge it. Okay -- now set a match to everything, get into the motorboat and watch it burn. Stay with it; watch the flames rise, watch your addiction go up into bright flames and turn to ashes. Watch your anger disappear -- everything, every little thing that bothers you -- as they turn into ashes and vanish. Brother, are you relieved!

Finally, in the <u>right screen</u> picture yourself all cleaned up, feeling as happy and worry free as you possible can. Enlarge the picture, along with your emotions. If those feeling turn into a giggles, go with it, laugh out loud, it will do you good. Along with feeling positive about yourself, become reassured that all your worries are gone, that all your ills have faded. (continue)

HYPNOSIS INDUCTION (continued)
HYPNOTIST: (continued)

Now, in the wide opening to your subconscious mind acknowledge all that has happened, and that everything is now resolved -- there is nothing left to fear, nothing to be sick or tired, or depressed about. All is better, it is all over -- the pain, the confusion, the discomfort, and it is all over.

In conclusion, recall the <u>left screen</u> one last time and make it disappear before your eyes. What you see remaining is the vision you have of the <u>right screen</u>. Hold that vision and remember it every time you check yourself in the mirror. Remember what you see, because every time you look in the mirror you will look better and better -- and positively better. As you do so, know that you are totally capable of coping with your newly discovered strengths and powers over your life.

When I count from 1 to 5 you will remember everything that happened in your trance. Every part of you will feel better than ever before. 1 . . . 2 . . . you feel alert and refreshed, 3 . . . 4 . . . you are alert and alive; you will open your eyes feeling alert, refreshed and fully alive. 5 . . . open your eyes.

HYPNOSIS INDUCTION -- FOR INDUCING HOPE
HYPNOTIST: (with the subject lying down)

Have the subject "Go into" **The Trance Zone,** as described below, and then continue with the hypnotic suggestions. Note: During this process, it is highly suggested that you have some soft, relaxing music playing in the background.

*I'd like you to form "**the hypnotic eye**" by placing the thumb and forefinger of either hand together, and place your hand at your side. This is the eye to your subconscious, which puts you into **The Trance Zone**. Now, I'd like you to lift your **<u>eyes up to the eyebrows</u>** and, when you feel like it, close them. Keeping your eyes up take in a **deep yawn,** and recite: "This is how I go into **The Trance Zone**." In that wide opening to your subconscious, you are listening intently to my voice. I'd like you to <u>inhale through the nose</u> and exhale through the mouth, while I count down from 30 by 2's, relaxing your body more and more while going into the hypnotic state. 30 . . . 28 . . . 26 . . . 24 . . . 22 . . . 20 . . . That's very good, your breathing is deep, relaxed. 18 . . . 16 . . . 14 . . . 12 . . . 10 . . . 8 . . . 6 . . . 4 . . . 2 . . . 0. Very good . . . Now, as you keep listening intently to my voice know that because of over-activity, troubles, and regressive thoughts, the conscious mind tends to override the subconscious. In doing so, it acts in stifling your mind, interfering with your natural capabilities.*

(continue)

HYPNOSIS INDUCTION -- FOR INDUCING HOPE (continued)
HYPNOTIST: (continued)

To alleviate these problems, I'm going to ask that you go deeper into that wide opening to your subconscious, where you feel safe, unaffected by worldly influences. As you lie there completely relaxed and tranquil, imagine rising above the earth and settling into a large, soft, white cloud. It is a moonlit night, and the cloud is completely illuminated, holding you spellbound within its magnificent splendor.

Imagine being completely enveloped by the illumination of this cloud, as you become totally absorbed in the power of its vast whiteness. Within these surroundings, have this become your ideal place of serenity, of solitude, of comfort where you feel a complete detachment from the world. Here, you are completely protected and removed from all your problems. Here, is the place where you can experience nothing but total peace and serenity.

Now, in all your calmness in that wide opening to your subconscious, you are listening closely to all my words. Every minute of every day, you get better and better. You get calmer and calmer with each passing moment; and with each moment, you feel more and more positive about yourself. As you listen intently to this message, you realize that all your faults, all your weaknesses, and all your failure have just become meaningless. What is now meaningful to you is that you have life, a life that is so unique and so wonderful you can now begin to appreciate it more.

From this moment forward, you will begin to appreciate your blessings. You will not only realize how great it is to be living, but you will come to appreciate your surroundings. Suddenly, you will appreciate the air you breathe, the trees you see, and the flowers you smell. From this moment forward, the foods you taste, the wonderful music you hear will take on a new meaning. Right now, you can imagine all this, and you now feel your senses becoming aware, invigorating you, and knowing that this is important to every aspect of your life.

As you keep listening to my words, you acknowledge that all is love, and that love becomes everything through living day by day in a positive fashion. Know that, even at this very moment, you feel a great appreciation of life and that you are something more precious than you have ever imagined. Yes, you are not only precious to yourself; you are very precious to those around you. You see, with this renewed you the world will have a greater chance of becoming a better place to live.

HYPNOSIS INDUCTION -- FOR INDUCING HOPE (continued)
HYPNOTIST: (continued)
Now, as you leave that place and come down from that cloud, you arrive here with a renewed sense of life, a rejuvenated spirit, and a completely restored sense of hope. You feel completely relaxed and at peace with everything around you. As for your problems, they have become the least of you concerns. What you are concerned with, now, is how to live your life to its fullest, completely free of negativity and conflicting emotions.

When I count from 1 to 5 you will remember everything that happened in your trance. Every part of you will feel better than ever before. 1 . . . 2 . . . you feel alert and refreshed, 3 . . . 4 . . . you are alert and alive; you will open your eyes feeling alert, refreshed and fully alive. 5 . . . open your eyes.

HYPNOTIST'S INDUCTION
EXTENSIVE COMBO TRANCE -- INSOMNIA
Note: the following trance may be used for self-hypnosis by changing it into the "first person." (for example, change "You are" to "I am.")

THE BLUE AURA OF DHARMA
HYPNOTIST (induce the hypnosis as follows - with subject lying or sitting)
I'd like you to lift your <u>eyes up to the eyebrows</u>, and close them. Give a <u>deep yawn,</u> and form "<u>the hypnotic eye</u>" by placing your thumb and forefinger together. Now, <u>recite</u>, "This is how I Go Into <u>The Trance Zone.</u>"

Concentrate as you, <u>inhale through the nose</u> and exhale counting down from 30 by 2's, relaxing the body more and more until reaching 0. Count down with me slowly, evenly as I begin: 30 . . . 28 . . . 26 . . . 24 . . . 22 . . . 20 . . . 18 . . . 16 . . . 14 . . . 12 . . . 10 . . . 8 . . . 6 . . . 4 . . . 2 . . . 0.

You are lying comfortably with your eyes still closed; your arms and legs are flexible, relaxed. Now, concentrating on being loose and free, and with your hand still forming "<u>the hypnotic eye,</u>" imagine yourself as being surrounded with a blue aura. As you concentrate, this blue aura begins to glow blue -- more and more glowing blue. Taking in deep breaths through your nose and exhaling through your mouth, let your entire body relax while lying in this comfortable position. While you imagine your blue aura, watching it as it continues to glow, you feel it getting warmer and warmer until you sense a rush of energy surging throughout your body.

(continue)

This energy is a positive and healing energy. This powerful, relaxing energy overcomes you to the point you feel a tremendous confidence in yourself. Let yourself go. Let yourself be . . . Let whatever happens happen because terrific things are taking place. Still concentrating on this blue aura, you feel that your mind is free of all worry, free of daily problems and headaches. As you lie, free of tension, you rejoice in the sense of well being that your blue aura brings you, which envelops you from head to foot. Feel and experience this wonderful sensation, which spreads more and more throughout your body.

You feel protected, secure and full of high esteem as the sensation forms a permanent place in your subconscious. Your subconscious is registering all my words. Wider and wider, this opening has become. The gentle words of my voice are being deeply engraved there as you listen intently to these suggestions. You are listening very intently as I proceed, confidently. Now that you are a free spirit capable of conquering any problem and unafraid of doing anything you desire, you now imagine yourself entering your dream world. Deeper and deeper, you enter freely into your dreams. You are unafraid, protected, and delighted at being far away from reality and the responsibilities and burdens that go along with your daily activities.

In this wonderful state of peace, you have an opening to your subconscious -- wider and wider this opening is becoming. Your subconscious is registering all my words. The gentle words of my voice are being deeply engraved there as you listen intently to my suggestions. You are listening very intently as I proceed with care. Listen closely to these words as I say them to you: You feel peaceful; you feel very quiet emotionally. You feel calm physically, and you enjoy the peace, the quiet, and the calm that exudes from within you.

As you listen to my voice, your entire body becomes more relaxed, more and more. While your muscles become free of tension, my voice is going deeper into that opening to you subconscious. Now that you are totally relaxed and feeling completely free of tension, imagine all your worries, frustrations, and hostilities leaving your body permanently.

Imagine that all that negativity is flowing out of your lungs and pores like poisonous gases, leaving you feeling completely refreshed, recharged and rejuvenated. Right now, know in your mind that you fully and freely release all grudges held from the past. Fully and freely loosen and let go of all anger, resentment and pent-up emotional disorders. Feel the relief of unloading all this excess baggage from your mind. From this day forward your load is finally light. Your burdens are light and all your worries and problems have just become trivial.

(continue)

Continue to breathe slowly and calmly. Let your body relax more and more each time. Relaxing, relaxing; going deeper and deeper into hypnosis. As you are resting comfortably, you will notice that your eyes are closed tight, very tight. They are stuck so tight you are not able to open them. Your eyes are stuck together so tight they feel as if they are sealed with a mudpack. In a moment I will ask you to try to open them - you will not be able to do so. You will find they are sealed tight, they are stuck firmly together. You may be able to manage the muscle groups around your eyes, but not your eyelids. No matter how hard you try, you will be unable to open your eyes until I bring you out of this deep trance.

When I count down from 3 to zero, you will find it impossible to open your eyes and you will go deeper into hypnosis. 3 . . . Your eyelids are sealed tight, 2 . . . They feel stuck tight with mud, 1 . . . They are stuck firmly together, Zero . . . Try, but you are unable to open them. Stop trying, and go deeper into hypnosis.

In that wide opening to your subconscious, you are listening intently to my voice. Perhaps you already know about your subconscious mind's extraordinary powers of self-healing, and how the right side of your brain controls the functioning of your entire body. The right side of your brain, the subconscious mind, knows how to regulate your breathing even while you are sleeping. And it knows how to regulate your circulatory system and how to carry the right nutrients to all the parts of your body that need them.

This brilliant part of your mind also knows how to instruct every cell in your body to heal itself, to improve your mind so that you become healthier and sound-minded, cell by cell. And I don't know how fast your body is healing itself now, but your mind knows just how to accelerate the healing that is already taking place in your body. Yes, your subconscious has the intelligence and the power to heal anything inside of you on an intercellular basis. It is doing this effectively even as I speak.

And I don't know if you are already feeling certain sensations in your body, signaling that the healing process has already started, but you can be sure that while you are in this deep, resting trance state, your body is already healing itself. You enjoy feeling relaxed, knowing your body can accelerate and improve your immune system even now, as you enjoy this rest. Know for sure that you can rely on your inner self; that you can count on that part of you in your subconscious that knows exactly what to do, and exactly how to do it. While your body has a tremendous ability to heal itself, the subconscious mind actually serves as the regulator of every possible function. Not only does your subconscious have the ability to perform all the healing you need, it has the capability to initiate peaceful rest and recuperation whenever you decide to fall asleep.   *(continue)*

Your subconscious mind is capable of extraordinary recouping powers, and endless capacities, even while you enjoy this peaceful state. You know that, and you continue to allow your body to rejuvenate while you relax and enjoy feeling peaceful. That deep place in your subconscious mind acknowledges all this and remembers the need to recall everything when you come out of this trance. And even after you come out of this exhilarating trance state, you can trust your ability to initiate peace and relaxation whenever it is needed. When you go to bed at night, you take delight in the fact that sleeping serves to replenish your entire body, hour after hour, cell by remarkable cell.

Imagine a large softgel *containing a liquid tranquilizer being lodged in the upper portion of your brain. Let it become loose and slowly travel down the head, and settle into the back of your neck. Now, let the softgel dissolve, allowing the liquid tranquilizer to flow down your throat and settle there. Think of the softgel as being like a Tylenol, or liquid capsule. Feel the liquid dissolving into your throat. And now, allow the liquid tranquilizer to settle into every part of your body starting from your throat, and seeping down to the bottom of your feet. Feel its tranquilizing effect as it seeps down your chest and arms. Feel its loosening and healing effects as it seeps into every muscle, every ligament and into every joint.*

Imagine every part of your body *becoming so relaxed it seems like jelly. Allow this liquid tranquilizer to relieve every pain, every arthritic condition, every restrictive feeling in your body. Allow this tranquilizer to balance your entire nervous system, your complete immune system, as you focus on allowing your mind to come to complete rest. You are free of all worry, free of all tension as you drift off into your hypnotic trance. Deeper and deeper you go into this deep trance state; deeper and deeper you go into hypnosis. The deeper you go into hypnosis, the deeper you go into this trance state. Deeper and deeper, you drift off into your beautiful, restful hypnotic trance.*

Imagine every part of your body *becoming so relaxed it seems like jelly. Allow this liquid tranquilizer to relieve every pain, every arthritic condition, every restrictive feeling in your body. Allow this tranquilizer to balance your entire nervous system, your complete immune system, as you focus on allowing your mind to come to complete rest. You are free of all worry, free of all tension as you drift off into your hypnotic trance. Deeper and deeper you go into this deep trance state; deeper and deeper you go into hypnosis. The deeper you go into hypnosis, the deeper you go into this trance state. Deeper and deeper, you drift off into your beautiful, restful hypnotic trance.*

(continue)

Even after you come out of this trance, you will remember that the "<u>the hypnotic eye</u>" is the key to unleashing the power of your subconscious mind. Whenever you call upon this image hidden knowledge is brought to light. As you look deeper and deeper within your spirit, you draw wisdom from the depths of your subconscious mind. All knowledge is there for you. All channels of guidance are opened to you, especially spiritual guidance. Everything you want to know is revealed. Everything is made clear; everything is exposed.

As far as any problems with sleeping are concerned, you are confident all is resolved. Any bouts with insomnia are finally over. Struggling in order to find peaceful sleep is a thing of the past. Now, whenever you lay down for the night, you realize that sleeping is the way your body recuperates. You also know that sleep is inevitable because it is nature's way of replenishing your strength and your state of mental balance. Whenever you decide to fall asleep your sleep is deep and unencumbered. Whenever you awaken, there is complete rest and complete relief from all kinds of stress. Your will, as well as Thy Will be done - and thus, it is laid out before you.

Focusing on this subconscious state, know that you have permission to become anyone you wish to be, accomplish anything you wish to accomplish. With your newly formed identity, you envision yourself as the person you have always dreamed you could be. In this state of subconscious, you will always remember how great it felt to have your imagination make you over. Your subconscious mind has already allowed you to feel better about yourself. And as you awaken, you will remember everything that happened during this trance.

As I slowly begin to count from 1 to 5, you will become better and better upon each count. 1 . . You are feeling terrific knowing that deep sleep comes whenever you need it; 2 . . You remember everything that happened in this trance state; 3 . . You feel happy that your life is changed for the better; 4 . . You are totally relaxed, fully aware, and functioning perfectly normal, 5 . . You are awake and feeling better than ever before. Finally, you are healthy, alert, and fully alive.

Note: Generally, sentences appearing in ***italics*** throughout this manual represent the ***voice***, or WORDS, of the subject or hypnotist.

Both the WORDS of the SUBJECT and the WORDS of the HYPNOTIST are always shown in ***italics***. The main difference between the dialog of the SUBJECT and the HYPNOTIST is that the subject's WORDS are always shown in the "first person.")

SELF-HYPNOSIS INDUCTION

SUBJECT INDUCED SELF-HYPNOSIS: (self-hypnotic autosuggestion)

Using the information you have so far, become seated comfortably and "Go Into" ***The Trance Zone***. You can do this by memorizing the words, or by first taping this and then listening to it with full concentration. Imagine everything as colorful and vivid as you possibly can. Do not become disappointed if it doesn't seem like you went into a trance -- although you probably will. Hypnotism takes a lot of Practice, Patience and Persistence - the three P's of any successful endeavor.

(Note: In the event that you wish to use any of the hypnotist's inductions for self-hypnosis, be sure to change the wording to the "first person." The following illustration is an example of this. Imaginative variations of this illustration can be used to alter situations, resolve problems, and alleviate pain and sickness. Other creative variations can aid in achieving practically anything you desire.)

The example below is a typical self-hypnotic induction.

SUBJECT:

First, form "**the hypnotic eye**" by placing the thumb and forefinger of either hand together, and place it at your side. This is the eye to your subconscious.

Then, lift your **eyes up to the eyebrows**, close them, and give a **deep yawn**.

Then, recite: *This is how I "Go Into"* ***The Trance Zone****, where only good things happen.*

Now, recite: *While I begin* counting down *from 30 by 2's until reaching zero, I* inhale through the nose*, and exhale through the mouth, relaxing the body more and more.*

Then begin counting: from 30 by 2's until reaching zero. 30 . . . 28 . . . 26 . . . 24 . . . 22 . . . 20 . . . 18 . . . 16 . . . 14 . . . 12 . . . 10 . . . 8 . . . 6 . . . 4 . . . 2 . . . 0.

In that wide opening to my subconscious, I am listening intently to my voice. I am resting, calm, relaxed, my eyes are closed and my arms and legs are flexible. I am free of tension, nothing distracts me as I feel myself being drawn along, breathing slowly, regularly. I am quite relaxed as I feel this wonderful peacefulness envelop my being. In this state of peace I acknowledge that opening to my subconscious. This opening grows wider, more and more. My words are settling into my subconscious, are taking root there.

I now submit to the following commands: So far I have been using only a small fraction of my mind, my conscious mind. I have been using less then five percent of my true potential because of using only my conscious mind. Now, using the power of the subconscious, I use more and more of my true power -- now, I am using the full power of my subconscious mind. (continue)

SELF-HYPNOSIS INDUCTION
SUBJECT INDUCED SELF-HYPNOSIS: (continued)

Every minute of every day my mind gets better and better in every positive way. Every minute of every day, my mind continues developing to its fullest potential -- it is better in every possible way.

As I sit here completely focused on creating an oil painting, I pick up my brush, repeatedly execute bright colors, and imagine painting a City skyscraper. The lines are concise, the dimensions, proportionate, and the environment, including several persons standing in the scene. After I complete my work I place it inside a frame, hang it on my wall and name it, "Views by Architectural Design." Then, I step back and admire the great job I've done.

When I count to five I will open my eyes feeling alert and refreshed. Every part me you will feel better than ever before. One, two . . . I feel alert and refreshed, three, four . . . I am alert and alive. Five, I open my eyes.

Again, **never,** during **any stage** of the hypnotic trance, is there any danger of not being able to "**Come Out**" of ***The Trance Zone***. At worst, you will merely take a short nap and wake up naturally, feeling **completely normal** – and **not** under the hypnotist's power.

PART THREE

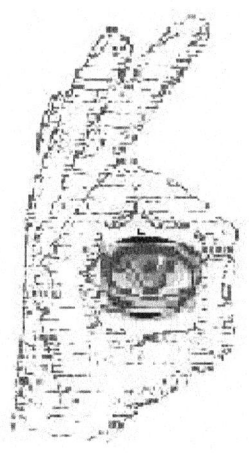

CHAPTER FIVE
5

UNLEASHING THE POWER OF YOUR SUBCONSCIOUS MIND

5   PROGRAMMING
REPROGRAMMING:

Negative thoughts cause pessimistic behavior patterns, just as pessimistic behavior patterns cause negative thoughts. People say, "sticks and stones shall break your bones, but names shall never hurt you." Well, words can stick in your head; thoughts can stick in your mind. Negative things your parents, your friends, your enemies, and even total strangers have told you can become etched in the subconscious mind.

Like a recording, it plays, on and on, whether you are aware of it, or not. Things you wouldn't dream of thinking consciously can be sitting there undermining your thoughts, sabotaging your very ideals. The consequences can result in inner conflicts, turmoil and, sometimes, utter confusion.

Whether being a victim of temptation, alcoholism, smoking, or gambling, reprogramming the mind, the thoughts, or the habitual behavior can alter these, as well as other addictive personality traits.

. . . . . . Edward J Longo

CHAPTER FIVE
5

UNLEASHING THE POWER OF YOUR SUBCONSCIOUS MIND

REPROGRAMMING THE SUBCONSCIOUS MIND
ALTERING THE BELIEF SYSTEM

Holding The Elephant Captive

In a sense, our minds can hold us captive. Because of conditioning, our beliefs can become set, depriving us of all hope, of even attempting to change our ways. Conditioning can go both ways – it can either hold us captive, or it can release us from our bondage. And one way to become released from bondage is to practice repetition so positive that the mind will come to believe it is so.

When wild elephants are captured in Africa they are fenced off and left there for a certain period of time. After a form of brainwashing, they become tamed. Then, upon being taken to a circus, for example, they are shackled to the ground by one leg for long periods. In time, they grow accustomed to it, with the understanding and acceptance that they cannot break loose from the chain that held them for so long. Through repetition, they come to believe they cannot escape their bondage. Weighing in at several tons, it is obvious to anyone, that with one simple tug the elephant could be off and running. But these elephants don't know this – they have become conditioned to believe it is not possible, so they give up trying. And so, we too, tend to give up when things seem fruitless – when we cannot seem to break away from the chain that binds us. That chain <u>can be broken</u>; the chain that holds <u>us</u> down is <u>our belief system</u>, or more appropriately, our <u>conscious mind</u>. And the way it can be broken is, not by brainwashing, but by brain conditioning, sending positive suggestions directly to the subconscious mind through hypnosis.

Negative thoughts cause pessimistic behavior patterns, just as pessimistic behavior patterns cause negative thoughts. People say, "sticks and stones shall break your bones, but names shall never hurt you." Well, words can stick in your head; thoughts can stick in your mind. Negative things your parents, your friends, your enemies, and even total strangers have told you can become etched in the subconscious mind. Like a recording, it plays, on and on, whether you are aware of it, or not. Things you wouldn't dream of thinking, consciously, can be sitting there, undermining your thoughts, sabotaging your very ideals. The consequences can result in inner conflicts, turmoil, utter confusion and oftentimes, mental illness.

THE MIND CAN ACTUALLY CHANGE THE BRAIN!

"**The mind can change the brain**," according to psychiatrist Jeffrey Schwartz in a Newsweek article on February 26 1996. During the month of February, Dr. Schwartz and four UCLA colleagues reported in the Archives of General Psychiatry that the mind can be at least as powerful as medicine when it comes to remodeling the brain. Behavioral modification, (altering the way a person behaves,) and cognitive therapy, (altering the way a person thinks,) can alter the biology of their brains.

It is true that a leopard can't change its spots – just as a person cannot change the color of the skin. But as human beings, we can adjust our thinking, which in turn <u>alters our</u> <u>behavior</u>, which leads to a change in our personality. Inevitably, this person, along with all the characteristics, identities, individualities, mannerisms, dispositions and traits becomes subject to some form of physiological change. Actors do this all the time.

In order to induce a positive message into the subconscious, the old message must be removed. Since the undesirable old message is not automatically erased by the desired new message, it must be nullified by inducing a positive message. In the following example, the positive fresh message or image serves to replace the fixated, stale message:

Your old feelings, attitudes and fixations about smoking have now been dismissed. They are now erased and extracted from your subconscious, so that they are replaced only by positive confirmations.

Repeat after me: As far as my health and my breathing, I have but one desire - and that is, that I breathe clean, fresh air, rather than saturating my system with smoke. Throughout the day, I shall breathe only the fresh air given to me naturally, unencumbered by needing to have filthy objects in my mouth and sucking on them.

The **first principle** in attempting to alter negative behavior is to realize that we are all creatures of habit. Since positive habits are far more beneficial than bad habits, the key is to initiate a positive habit strong enough to overcome the bad habit. This can be accomplished by **developing new patterns,** or by selecting a habit so effective and enjoyable that it acts to overpower the undesirable bad habit.

The **second principle** in order to affect a change is to "**rename**" the habit - for instance, call being addicted to cigarettes "I am having a nicotine urge," rather than an attack. (Verbalizing the truth sometimes makes the best medicine.)

The **third principle**, provided the case is true, is to attribute the urge to a "biochemical imbalance in the brain" and begin developing new patterns. (Admitting that the problem is chemical, rather than having a mental weakness, is closer to the truth, relieving unnecessary guilt - then the impetus to change becomes easier.)

The **fourth principle** in order to affect change is to "**refocus**" on some positive, constructive activity for fifteen minutes. This engages another part of the brain and alters the brain circuits that initially caused them to become stuck.

(Between **developing new patterns**, "**renaming**" and "**refocusing**" it is possible that the mind can rewire neural synapses that cause phobias and depression.)

PHYCHOLOGICAL ADJUSTMENT

Everyone develops habits, but most are positive, while others are negative. The problems arise when our negative, or bad, habits control us -- for they begin inducing demoralizing, and abusive, self-defeating traits. Whether falling into patterns of negative conditioning, or self destruction -- reprogramming our thoughts can be successfully used to alter the defeatist personality. Through the application of **PSYCHOLOGICAL ADJUSTMENT**, you will learn how to actually alter your personality traits. This can be achieved by practicing the following:

ALTERING THOUGHT PATTERNS:

Without realizing it, people become so set in their way of thinking they never realize that changing their attitude is an option. Sometimes, it is possible to influence a subject's thought process by making direct, helpful suggestions during the hypnotic induction. Below are some examples.

Alter The Thought
Just when you think it is time to quit; that's the ideal time to begin.
Why not learn to become the head, instead of the tail.

Change The Focus
To break a negative bad habit, replace it with a positive good habit.
Life is hard by the yard; by the inch it's a cinch.

Build Self-confidence
Everything is all right now; everything will continue to be all right.
First, love yourself, and then you will be able to give love, as well as accept it.

Instill Motivation
To accomplish a goal, find a believable reason for it.
Acknowledging that life is but a breath is seeing a life more precious.

Induce Belief
What the subconscious mind can believe, the mind can conceive.
Know that changing the word can't to can do, all things become possible.

Create Hope
With the new beginnings of today, come the opportunities of tomorrow.
Every minute of every hour, you are better because of having this power.

Develop A Positive Attitude
You cannot decrease your age, but you can behave as being younger.
Everything you do is right, because it comes from the best within you.

PHYSIOLOGICAL ADJUSTMENT

Whether being a victim of temptation, alcoholism, smoking, or gambling - reprogramming the mind, thoughts, or habitual behavior can be successfully used to change the addictive personality. Through the application of **PHYSIOLOGICAL ADJUSTMENT**, you will learn how to alter personality traits of the spirit, mind and body. To begin adjusting your life, consider the following alterations:

ALTERING PERSONALITY TRAITS:
PHYSIOLOGICAL ADJUSTMENT can be achieved through **Unleashing The Power Of The Subconscious, The Subconscious Genie Within,** and **Accessing The Fountain Of Energy,** as described below.

UNLEASHING THE POWER OF THE SUBCONSCIOUS:
THE SPIRIT - the internal and external subconscious energy

The Spirit is the all-knowing, all encompassing power of our being, our very soul. Feed your spirit prayer and affirmations and you will receive inspirational thoughts, and countless blessings. Through **The Spirit**, you can not only learn to develop inspirationally, but you can learn to grow emotionally as well – in important ways, such as compassion, understanding and, most of all, love. When you learn to live in **The Spirit**, you will become entirely alive, living within the powers of your subconscious, supernatural mind.

The examples shown below are illustrations of the use of self-hypnosis. This is an extremely effective way to unleash the power of the subconscious mind. After taping the following induction lie back, "Go Into" The Trance Zone, and listen to your own words until satisfactory results are accomplished.
(Note: At the end of the trance, you may choose to further the hypnosis, or you may choose to proceed to "Come Out" of the trance, as described at the end of this chapter.)

SUBJECT: (self-hypnotic induction)
*The image I have formed of "**the hypnotic eye**" is the key to unleashing the power of my subconscious mind. Whenever I call upon this image, hidden knowledge will be brought to light. As I look deeper and deeper within my spirit, I draw wisdom from the depths of my subconscious mind.*

All knowledge is there for me. All channels of guidance are opened to me, especially spiritual guidance. Everything I want to know is revealed to me. Everything is made clear; everything is exposed. My will, as well as Thy Will, will be done – and thus it is laid out before me.

Note: Both the *words* of the SUBJECT and the *words* of the HYPNOTIST are always shown in *italics*. The main difference between the dialog of the SUBJECT and the HYPNOTIST is that the subject's *words* are always shown in the "first person."

THE SUBCONSCIOUS GENIE WITHIN
THE MIND - the internal conscious and subconscious energy

The Mind, as the fundamental organ of human life, comes complete with its supernatural compliment, called the subconscious. Together, they form the most complete organism of all the species on earth. Through this unique formulation of organs, glands, circulatory and nervous systems there is nothing that can't be accomplished. With all its brain cells, synapses, and intuitiveness, this combination has conquered every obstacle, in order to reign supreme. With that being said, it should mean that every individual has the same chance of becoming effective. However, not all individuals are able to make use of this amazing facility. Through bypassing the conscious mind and going into the hypnotic state, you have the opportunity of altering your mind, so that you can attain whatever it is you desire. And, when it comes down to bad habits, you won't have a great struggle with quitting smoking, or any other addiction. All this will make more sense as you gain more experience and begin to know yourself as a perfect and complete human being. Finally, as you regain your self-esteem you will feel all those negative gremlins fading by the wayside.

Dream Fulfillment During Sleep

The standard practice regarding dreams is to interpret them <u>after</u> they occur. However, to my surprise, I have discovered that if a person would set up a dream fulfillment request prior to going to sleep, that request would become actualized during the dream state. Then, upon awakening, the person would remember everything the dream revealed. The request could be as simple as asking for a solution to a specific problem, or of asking to live an experience that would bring a certain kind of fulfillment; sexual or financial gratification, for example. As you can imagine, this technique could produce rewarding results, having a remarkable, positive effect on one's self-esteem. Go into a trance and discover the Genie within you. Whether a spirit-guide, a vision, a mediator, or a God; seek, and you shall find.

SUBJECT: (self-hypnotic induction)

I imagine a large softgel containing a liquid tranquilizer being lodged in the upper portion of my brain. I Let it become loose and slowly travel down the head, and settle into the back of my neck. Now, I let the softgel dissolve, allowing the liquid tranquilizer to flow down my throat and settle there. I feel the liquid dissolving into my throat. And now, I allow the liquid tranquilizer to settle into every part of my body starting from my throat, and seeping down to the bottom of my feet. I feel its tranquilizing effect as it seeps down my chest and arms. I Feel its loosening and healing effects as it seeps into every muscle, every ligament and into every joint.

I Imagine every part of my body becoming so relaxed it seems like jelly. I Allow this liquid tranquilizer to relieve every pain, every arthritic condition, every restrictive feeling in my body. I allow this tranquilizer to balance my entire nervous system, my complete immune system, as I focus on allowing my mind to come to complete rest.

ACCESSING THE FOUNTAIN OF ENERGY
THE BODY - the internal chemical energy

The Body is the fountain from which we draw our natural source of energy. Because the energy provided by our body is so accessible, we expend it foolishly, making ill use of its astonishing power. In addition to mental and spiritual inspiration, we must keep it supplied with nutrition and exercise.

Feed the body the proper nutrition and it will keep up the pace; refurbish it with exercise and it will beget the stimulation necessary to instill determination, as well as endurance. In addition to implementing the exercises given in **Chapter 14**, the following induction will aid in activating the endocrine glands, which cause the body to become relaxed, receptive and supple.

Below is an illustration of the use of self-hypnosis. It is an extremely effective way to unleash the power of the subconscious mind. After taping the following induction lie back, "Go Into" *The Trance Zone*, and listen to your own words until satisfactory results are accomplished.

SUBJECT: (self-hypnotic induction)

I understand that, due to the conflicts between my accountability and accomplishments, tension builds up causing much discomfort and despair -- even disease. To alleviate these pressures, I begin by stretching all my fingers open wide. As I continue stretching my fingers, I open my mouth very wide and give a deep yawn. Even more, I stretch my fingers and stretch my jaws open wider. Taking another deep yawn, I close my fists then stretch my fingers, close my fists and stretch my fingers.

Now I relax all my muscles and take deep breaths as if allowing the oxygen to flow into the muscles of my jaw, shoulders, hands, legs and feet. I focus on this deep breathing until I feel tingling in different parts of my body. I really feel this happening. I feel the oxygen rejuvenating my body and spirit, replenishing my stamina. My entire body feels loose and my mind is so clear I feel all the stress leaving my being.

As I go into a deep state of hypnosis, I imagine going into an even deeper hypnotic trance. Using my imagination, I find the words to put my body in such a hypnotic trance, everything I can imagine, becomes possible. I see this, feel this, and experience the results as my wishes, desires and most magnificent dreams come true.

When I count to five, I will open my eyes feeling alert, refreshed and alive. 1, 2, every part of me is better than ever before, 3, I am feeling alert and refreshed, 4; I am alert, refreshed and fully alive. 5, now, I open my eyes.

Unleashing The Power 65

Note: In order to "Come Out" of any trance, merely stop the session and open your eyes. Counting from 1 to 5 is a good way to "Come Out" of a self-hypnotic trance because it conditions you to becoming alert at the end of a session. If you happen to fall asleep, that is okay too; you will awaken automatically, most likely retaining the messages in your subconscious. The reason it is best to stay awake during the trance state, is to ensure that the subconscious does receive the messages.

THE HYPNOSIS POWER - It Boils Down To This:

Most people are skeptical about hypnosis because they don't understand it - the same way they fear everything they have never tried before. Once you understand and incorporate the power of the subconscious mind, even your most desirable dreams will manifest, as if by magic.

Trying to accomplish the same feats by way of the conscious state could take a lifetime. *In essence, people should be more skeptical of the limits of the conscious mind, rather than to fear the unlimited power of the subconscious mind.* The subconscious mind is that place where all things become manifest into reality. The prerequisite is that you believe that all things are possible - and then allow the positive and mystifying powers of the supernatural take their course. Finally, realize that through the powers of the subconscious, Nothing Is Really Impossible . . . *EjL*

Penetrating The Subconscious Mind

Perhaps the most important thing to bear in mind regarding accessing the hypnotic state is this: In order to **penetrate the subconscious mind**, reaching a complete state of serenity allows the incoming messages to take hold more effectively. The more the subject is able to relax, the longer positive suggestions will endure. Reaching the state of tranquility also serves to disarm the conscious mind, thus allowing the subconscious to override all unnecessary censoring. This is one of the reasons exercise is stressed so frequently. (See the exercises in Part Eight.)

Empowering The Subconscious Mind

Suggestions such as: *I will not think of an apple with a worm inside*, causes just the opposite affect. First, because *I will not* relates to the future in a negative sense; the subconscious only acknowledges the present, and it acknowledges suggestions in a positive sense. Secondly, the statement, *an apple with a worm inside,* evokes a **vision** of a *rotten apple with a worm inside.* This is because the subconscious overlooks the negative term, *not*.

The hypnotist, always looking on the brighter, positive side, would be wiser to choose to state: *I can see an apple with its rosy colors*.

To see examples of the various trances to be performed by the HYPNOTIST proceed to *The Trance Zone* Hypnosis Induction Techniques as described in the following chapter.

(**Note: Posthypnotic Suggestions** are the messages, key words, "CUES," or triggers induced by the hypnotist to the subject in the hypnotic state. They can even work during self-hypnosis, executed by the subject. The aim is to have them carry over to the awakened state, or to be used as a signal to return to the hypnotic state. **Self-hypnotic suggestion, self-hypnosis, or autosuggestion** is that state of hypnosis induced by the subject.)

True Testimonials Given By Subjects

Insomnia

My name is Gary. I'm a nationally syndicated publicist. I've had bouts with insomnia all of my life--that's well over 60 years. My problem was that I could only get little more than an hour-and-a-half of sleep without being awakened. This interrupted sleep pattern has never really kept me from functioning, but it has played havoc on my nervous system. Perhaps that is why people associate problems of this nature as "Chinese torture." where victims have been reported being tortured using drops of water to keep prisoners awake. I certainly felt like that. Thankfully, after confiding in this gentle man, Edward Longo, my symptoms have begun to subside. I am happy to report that I am now capable of getting more than four hours of uninterrupted sleep. This is my story.
Gary Stevens - New York City

Hypnosis and Certification

To whom it may concern:
In the fall of 2000, I received some very helpful therapy through hypnosis sessions with Edward J Longo. A short period later, I received more progressive therapy while I studied the Hypnotherapy Course using the techniques based on his hypnosis manual, The Trance Zone.
After receiving my Certification through The Trance Zone Hypnotherapy Course, I was also able to become certified by the American Board of Hypnotherapy (ABH) as a certified hypnotherapist, complete with a valid Certificate Number. Since your training was so thorough, I was pleased when I was able to qualify without needing any additional training or testing.

Positive Attitude

In the past, I've always had trouble concentrating and making up my mind. It seemed I always depended on other people for direction. Then Mr. Longo said the following: "You've been accustomed to being led by others for too long, Carol. You've been behaving as if you were in a rowboat, being hopelessly led about without any oars. Well, it's time you began to take control. Grab a hold of your oars, place them in the water, and begin rowing until you reach your goals. Resolve to take control of your life beginning right now." Soon, aided with this simple analogy, and followed by affirmative, guided imagery, my whole attitude began to change for the best.
Carol Negrette - Snowy Lane, Utah

CHAPTER SIX
6

HYPNOSIS INDUCTION > TECHNIQUES <

6   HYPNOSIS
APPLICATION:

By utilizing the instructions and practicing the applications of **The Trance Zone,** *you can gain access to your programming. The secret to tapping the depths of your mind is to go into the subconscious, where the true source of power rules.*

This is where you can unleash the power of your subconscious mind, and change negative habits of thought and action into what you desire them to be. This is how you can alter your programming for the better.

. . . Edward J. Longo

CHAPTER SIX
6

HYPNOSIS INDUCTION TECHNIQUES
(with examples, in steps)

Due to the affects parents have on us in early childhood, the influences of society, and negativity from friends and associates, we often become undermined with suggestions of incompetence and failure. Subconsciously, that subliminal tape recording of years past kicks in and plays derogatory messages over, and over, sabotaging your mind. In essence, your conscious mind becomes the very part of you that criticizes, edits, and judges everything, thereby limiting your capabilities.

It is through the subconscious mind that you gain the key to insight, self-esteem and success. The subconscious is the intrinsic substance of the mind - it is the mother lode; the more powerful part of you; that stronger part of your individuality that is really the dominant force.

Through the practice of hypnosis you will gain access to knowledge and human understanding, the likes of which millions of people, including most doctors and psychologists, will never acquire. Ultimately, through the application of self-hypnosis, there is no limit to what you can achieve - you can even become a virtual genius, provided you spend enough time, effort and perseverance.

The use of hypnosis is not some form of hocus-pocus. It is one of the most powerful, effective ways to gain access to that supreme part of you that, probably, has never been programmed properly. Hypnosis has been used by psychiatrists during World War II to treat wounded soldiers - it was used in addition to banish the combat traumas that caused hysterical paralysis, as well as amnesia. Ever since 1958, when the American Medical Association approved the use of hypnosis, it has been used successfully to treat phobias, addiction, insomnia, pain, depression, and neurological problems.

Hypnotism is still being widely practiced by psychiatrists, surgeons, doctors, and hypnotherapists alike to treat disease - and because its effect is organic, hypnosis is truly a marvel of mind over mind. When used properly, it can be used as a tool to investigate past lives, probe into the problems of the psyche, and even traverse and envision what the future has in store. The act of hypnotism is not a mere mental process. Hypnosis has turned out to become a supernatural phenomenon that continues to behoove the average person, even to this day. Becoming hypnotized is definitely the wave of the future, where more and more people want to grow intellectually, as well as psychologically, and physiologically. Finally, health, wealth and the pursuit of happiness can be achieved by all who dare to do so.

Here, the Induction Techniques may vary, depending on the subject's needs, and how you decide to treat the problem. Some hypnotists use a spinning wheel, or a pendulum, while others use flickering lights. Still, other hypnotists use the snap of a finger to induce posthypnotic suggestions, while others use a certain touch. All of these techniques are acceptable and okay to use. However, I have found the techniques listed below to be highly effective, while they quickly find a direct path to the subconscious.

(Note: The hypnotist's inductions may be recorded for the subject's use of at home.)

THE TRANCE ZONE **INDUCTION TECHNIQUES**

TO "GO INTO" *THE TRANCE ZONE*

The Initial Procedure - (induced by the hypnotist, the subject sitting or lying)
To "Go Into" ***The Trance Zone:***

First, have the subject form "**the hypnotic eye,**" by placing the thumb and first finger of either hand together, and place it to the side.

Then, have the subject lift the **eyes up to the eyebrows,** close them, and give a **deep yawn.**

Next, recite: *This is how you "Go Into"* ***The Trance Zone.***

Continue with the hypnotic suggestions.

(**This is how *The Trance Zone* is initially induced. The intention behind repeating this is to have it act as a posthypnotic suggestion, a subconscious trigger to "Go Into" the hypnotic trance more easily.**)

The Hypnotic Eye Technique (with the subject sitting or lying)

(NOTE -- For the hypnotist: as an alternate method, place a multifaceted crystal between your fingers within "**the hypnotic eye**" and slowly raise it up to the subject's head. The eyes will close very rapidly.)

To have the subject "Go Into" ***The Trance Zone*** proceed as follows:

EXAMPLE INDUCTION
HYPNOTIST (induce the hypnosis, as follows):

*I'd like you to place your thumb and forefinger of either hand together, form what we'll call, '****the hypnotic eye,*** *' and place it at your side. This is the eye to your subconscious. Now, I'd like you to lift your **eyes up to the eyebrows** and, when you feel like it, close them. Keeping your eyes up, take in a **deep yawn**.*

Very good . . . That is how you "Go Into" ***The Trance Zone****, where only good things happen. Now, I'd like you to **inhale through the nose** and exhale through the mouth while counting down from 30, by 2's. I'll begin with you . . . 30, 28, 26, 24, 22 . . . continue counting down slowly. Good, breathe slowly and calmly. Just let your body relax more and more each time. That's right, inhale through your nose. Exhale as we keep counting . . . 20, 18, 16 . . . etc.*

Proceed with the hypnosis by inducing any of the posthypnotic suggestions.

Squeeze The Ball Technique (with the subject sitting or lying)
To have the subject "Go Into" ***The Trance Zone*** proceed as follows:
First, have the subject hold a soft rubber ball in either hand and focus the eyes on it while squeezing very tightly.
Then, have the subject lift the **eyes up to the eyebrows,** close them, and give a **deep yawn.**
Next recite: *This is how you "Go Into"* ***The Trance Zone.***
Then, have the subject continue to squeeze the ball until the need is felt to release the pressure. As the subject releases the pressure, suggest that letting the ball fall also allows the arm to fall, along with the entire body. Suggest that every part of the body fall into a relaxed position.

EXAMPLE INDUCTION
HYPNOTIST (induce the hypnosis, as follows):

As I place this rubber ball into your hand, I would like you to focus your eyes on it while squeezing it as hard as you can. Stare at it while you concentrate and give it your complete attention. Now, I'd like you to lift your **eyes up to the eyebrows** *and close them, still squeezing the ball. That's it -- now give a* **deep yawn.** *Very good . . . This is how you "Go Into"* ***The Trance Zone***, *where only good things happen.*

Okay, let up the pressure very slowly until you feel your fingers release it. As you release the ball and let it fall out of your hand, imagine your entire body falling with it. Good. Breathe slowly and calmly, and let your body relax more and more. That's right, keep relaxing---

Now, I'd like you to **inhale through the nose** *and exhale through the mouth, while counting down from 30, by 2's. I'll begin with you . . . 30, 28, 26, 24, 22 . . . continue counting down slowly. Good, breathe slowly and calmly. Just let your body relax more and more each time. That's right, inhale through your nose. Exhale through your mouth as we keep counting, 20, 18, 16, 14, 12, 10 . . . relaxing and counting, etc.*

(Note: From here, you may choose to extend the hypnosis by inducing any of the posthypnotic suggestions. Generally, you would finish the session as described below in order for the subject to "Come Out" of the trance. See more about this at the end of this chapter.)

To have the subject "Come Out" :)
That's very good. Now, when I count to five, you will open your eyes feeling alert, refreshed and alive. 1, 2, every part of you is better than ever before, 3, you are feeling alert and refreshed, 4, you are alert, refreshed and fully alive. 5 . . . it's time to open your eyes.

Split Screen Technique (with the subject sitting or lying)

To have the subject "Go Into" ***The Trance Zone*** proceed as follows:

First, instruct the subject to lift either arm, as if a balloon was attached, and have it rise. Then suggest that the arm fall, as if it were heavy as lead.

Then, have the subject lift the **eyes up to the eyebrows,** close them, and give a **deep yawn.**

Next recite: *This is how you "Go Into"* ***The Trance Zone.***

Now, have the subject **inhale through the nose**, and exhale counting down from 30 by 2's, relaxing the body more and more, until reaching 0.

Finally, ask the subject to imagine rising up into a blue sky and floating there, feeling light and free of earthly problems. Then, suggest that the subject imagine three giant screens, and describe in detail, the image of the present self in the **middle screen.** Then have the subject visualize the image of the negative self, including all problems, in the **left screen;** and then the image of the positive self with all the problems resolved in the **right screen.**

EXAMPLE INDUCTION
HYPNOTIST (induce the hypnosis, as follows):

*I'd like you to lift your right arm, as if a balloon was attached to your elbow, and have it rise. Hold it there. Good... Now let your arm fall as if it were heavy as lead. I'd like you to lift your **eyes up to the eyebrows** and close them, still squeezing the ball. That's it -- now give a **deep yawn.***

*Okay, this is how you "Go Into" **The Trance Zone**, where only good things happen. Now, I'd like you to **inhale through the nose** and exhale through the mouth, while counting down from 30, by 2's. I'll begin with you... 30, 28, 26, 24, 22... continue counting down slowly. Good, breathe slowly and calmly. Just let your body relax more and more each time. That's right, inhale through your nose. Exhale as we keep counting, 20, 18, 16... relaxing... etc.*

*When you're ready, I'd like you to imagine rising up into a blue sky and floating there, feeling light and free of all earthly problems. Now, imagine three giant screens, one in the middle, one on the left, and one on the right. Visualize the image of you present self in the **middle screen**. And then, visualize the image of your negative self, including all your problems, in the **left screen.** Now, visualize the image of your positive self with all your problems resolved in the **right screen.** Try it again. Try to imagine everything as clear as possible, making the negative look bleak, and making your positive self look as bright and colorful as you would like yourself to become.*

(Note: From here, you may choose to extend the hypnosis by inducing any of the posthypnotic suggestions. Generally, you would finish the session as described above, as well as at the end of this chapter, in order for the subject to "Come Out" of the trance.)

Spinning Crystal Technique (with the subject sitting or lying)

To have the subject "Go Into" ***The Trance Zone*** proceed as follows:

First, ask the subject to focus on a spinning multifaceted crystal as you suspended it on a string, above the subject's eyes.

Then, instruct the subject to keep staring, and then lift the **eyes up to the eyebrows,** close them, and give **deep yawn**. (Note: As an alternative, this may be done holding a multifaceted crystal within "**the hypnotic eye**" of your own hand, lifting it above the subject's eyes.)

Next recite: *This is how you "Go Into"* ***The Trance Zone.***

Now, have the subject **inhale through the nose**, and exhale counting down from 30 by 2's, relaxing the body more and more, until reaching zero.

EXAMPLE INDUCTION
HYPNOTIST (induce the hypnosis, as follows):

*With your eyes wide open, watch the crystal intently as it spins above you. Don't take your eyes off it. Your eyes continue to remain transfixed as you focus on the details of the spinning crystal. Whenever you feel like it, lift your **eyes up to the eyebrows,** close them and give **deep yawn**.*

Okay, this is how you "Go Into" ***The Trance Zone***, *where only good things happen. Now, I'd like you to **inhale through the nose** and exhale through your mouth, while I begin counting down from 30, by 2's. 30, 28, 26, 24, 22, 20 . . . As I continue counting down slowly, you go deeper into hypnosis. 18, 16, 14, 12, 10. . That's right, inhale through your nose, exhale through your mouth, 8, 6, 4, 2, 0. Good, breathe slowly and calmly. Let your body relax more and more each time. Relaxing, relaxing, going deeper and deeper into hypnosis.*

(Note: From here, you may choose to extend the hypnosis by inducing any of the posthypnotic suggestions. Generally, you would finish the session as described above, as well as at the end of this chapter, in order for the subject to "Come Out" of the trance.)

The brief examples described above are intended to serve as an introduction to the different types of **Techniques** used to induce the trance state. It is up to each individual to find the appropriate combination that will be most effective for each situation. While the **Techniques** listed above are incomplete, the **Technique** listed below is a full, in-depth trance developed for the purpose of inducing a much deeper trance state. Although the thoughts may seem too complex, and even redundant, the subconscious mind will sift through the information, make the appropriate adjustments, and come up with its desired resolution. The messages should be delivered slowly, in a monotone voice, making sure the emphasis is directed toward the goal or problem at hand. Where some words may be eliminated, others should be introduced and directed toward accomplishing the proper results. Don't forget that the idea is to deliberately distract the conscious mind by having it lose focus, thereby allowing the subconscious mind to take over.

(This condition, whether associated with hypnosis, or not, occurs naturally every day.)

Liquid Tranquilizer Technique (with the subject sitting or lying)

To have the subject "Go Into" ***The Trance Zone*** proceed as follows:

First, ask the subject to focus on a spinning multifaceted crystal as you suspended it on a string, above the subject's eyes.

Then, instruct the subject to keep staring, and then lift the **eyes up to the eyebrows,** close them, and give **deep yawn**. (Note: As an alternative, this may be done holding a multifaceted crystal within "**the hypnotic eye**" of your own hand, lifting it above the subject's eyes.)

Next recite: *This is how you "Go Into"* ***The Trance Zone.***

Now, have the subject **inhale through the nose**, and exhale counting down from 30 by 2's, relaxing the body more and more, until reaching zero.

EXAMPLE INDUCTION -- DEEP STATE
HYPNOTIST (induce the hypnosis, as follows):

*I'd like you to form "**the hypnotic eye**" and place it at your side. This is the eye to your subconscious. Now, I'd like you to lift your **eyes up to the eyebrows** and, when you feel like it, close them. Keeping your eyes up, take in a **deep yawn**.*

Very good -- that is how you "Go Into" ***The Trance Zone****, where only good things happen. As I begin counting down from 30 by 2's, I'd like you to **inhale through the nose** and exhale through your mouth. 30, 28, 26, 24, 22, 20 . . . Good, breathe slowly and calmly. 18, 16, 14, 12, 10 . . . That's right, inhale through your nose. Just let your body relax more and more each time. 8, 6, 4, 2, 0 . . . In that wide opening to your subconscious, you are listening intently to my voice.*

You are lying comfortably. Your eyes are closed. Your arms and legs are flexible, relaxed. Continue breathing evenly, inhaling through your nose and exhaling through your mouth. With each breath, you sink deeper and deeper and deeper into a relaxed state of mind. You no longer want anything. Become passive as you listen to my voice. Let yourself go. Let it be . . . Let it happen. Nothing bothers or distracts you. Nothing bad or unusual is going to happen.

Your head is clear. Your mind is free of all problems. You rejoice in this sense of peace and well being that envelops you from head to foot. Feel this wonderful relaxation which spreads more and more throughout your body. Feel the new looseness and weightlessness of your body. In this wonderful state of peace, you have an opening to the subconscious -- wider and wider this opening is becoming.

Your subconscious is registering all my words. The gentle words of my voice are being deeply engraved there as you listen intently to my suggestions. You are listening very intently as I proceed with care. Good, breathe slowly and calmly. Let your body relax more and more each time. Relaxing, relaxing, going deeper and deeper into hypnosis.

As you are resting comfortably, you will notice that your eyes are closed tight, very tight. They are stuck so tight you are not able to open them. Your eyes are stuck together so tight they feel as if they are sealed with a mudpack. In a moment I will ask you to try to open them - you will not be able to do so. You will find they are sealed tight, they are stuck firmly together. You may be able to manage the muscle groups around your eyes, but not your eyelids. No matter how hard you try, you will be unable to open your eyes until I bring you out of this deep trance. When I count down from 3 to zero, you will find it impossible to open your eyes and you will go deeper into hypnosis. 3 . . . Your eyelids are sealed tight, 2 . . . They feel stuck tight with mud, 1 . . . They are stuck firmly together, Zero . . . Try, but you are unable to open them. Stop trying, and go deeper into hypnosis.

In that wide opening to your subconscious, you are listening intently to my voice. Perhaps you already know about your subconscious mind's extraordinary powers of self-healing, and how the right side of your brain controls the functioning of your entire body. The right side of your brain, the subconscious mind, knows how to regulate your breathing even while you are sleeping, and knows how to regulate your circulatory system, how to carry the right nutrients to all the parts of your body that need them.

This brilliant part of your mind also knows how to instruct every cell in your body to heal itself, to improve, to feel more comfortable and to be healthy and sound, cell by cell. And I don't know how fast your body is healing itself now, but your mind knows just how to accelerate the healing that is already taking place in your body. Yes, your subconscious has the intelligence and the power to heal anything inside of you on an intercellular basis.

You may have read or heard, or perhaps you know from your own experience that athletes need to take great care in order for their bodies to grow strong, and recuperate from overwork. And as you rest your body now, like an athlete rests, your body can become stronger and healthier, revitalizing your nerves, your blood, and even your brain cells. And although the aging process is always causing deterioration, it doesn't have to follow that your vision, your memory or your legs have to become weakened.

And I don't know if you have already felt certain sensations in your body, signaling that the healing process has already started, but you can be sure that while you are in this deep, resting trance state, your body is already healing itself. You can enjoy feeling relaxed, knowing your body can accelerate and improve your immune system even now, as you enjoy this rest. Know for sure that you can rely on your inner self; that you can count on that part of you in your subconscious that knows exactly what to do, and exactly how to do it.

Perhaps you remember a time when you had a cut that was so deep you felt it wouldn't heal, or perhaps you had a bout with the flu. You probably went to a doctor for treatment, but then even as you slept and played and worked, your body did all the healing. While your body has a tremendous ability to heal itself, the subconscious mind actually serves as the regulator of every possible part, every possible function. Not only does your subconscious have the ability to perform all the healing you need, it has the capability to initiate peaceful rest and sleep when called upon.

Your subconscious mind is capable of extraordinary recouping powers, and endless capacities, even while you enjoy this peaceful state. You <u>know</u> that, and you can continue to allow your body to rejuvenate while you relax and enjoy feeling peaceful. That deep place in your subconscious mind acknowledges all this and remembers the need to recall everything when we are through. And even after you come out of this exhilarating trance state, you can trust your ability to initiate peace and relaxation whenever it is needed. When you go to bed at night, you take delight in the fact that sleeping serves to replenish your entire body, hour after hour, cell by remarkable cell.

Imagine a large softgel *containing a liquid tranquilizer being lodged in the upper portion of your brain. Let it become loose and slowly travel down the head, and settle into the back of your neck. Now, let the softgel dissolve, allowing the liquid tranquilizer to flow down your throat and settle there. Feel the liquid dissolving into your throat. And now, allow the liquid tranquilizer to settle into every part of your body starting from your throat, and seeping down to the bottom of your feet. Feel its tranquilizing effect as it seeps down your chest and arms. Feel its loosening and healing effects as it seeps into every muscle, every ligament and into every joint.*

Imagine every part of your body *becoming so relaxed it seems like jelly. Allow this liquid tranquilizer to relieve every pain, every arthritic condition, every restrictive feeling in you body. Allow this tranquilizer to balance your entire nervous system, your complete immune system, as you focus on allowing your mind to come to complete rest. You are free of all worry, free of all tension as you drift off into your hypnotic trance. Deeper and deeper you go into this deep trance state; deeper and deeper you go into hypnosis. The deeper you go into hypnosis, the deeper you go into this trance state. Deeper and deeper, you drift off into your beautiful, restful hypnotic trance.*

Imagine a large softgel *containing a liquid tranquilizer being lodged in the upper portion of your brain. Let it become loose and slowly travel down the head, and settle into the back of your neck. Now, let the softgel dissolve, allowing the liquid tranquilizer to flow down your throat and settle there. Feel the liquid dissolving into your throat. And now, allow the liquid tranquilizer to settle into every part of your body starting from your throat, and seeping down to the bottom of your feet. Feel its tranquilizing effect as it seeps down your chest and arms. Feel its loosening and healing effects as it seeps into every muscle, every ligament and into every joint.*

Imagine a large softgel *containing a liquid tranquilizer being lodged in the upper portion of your brain. Let it become loose and slowly travel down the head, and settle into the back of your neck. Now, let the softgel dissolve, allowing the liquid tranquilizer to flow down your throat and settle there. Feel the liquid dissolving into your throat. And now, allow the liquid tranquilizer to settle into every part of your body starting from your throat, and seeping down to the bottom of your feet. Feel its tranquilizing effect as it seeps down your chest and arms. Feel its loosening and healing effects as it seeps into every muscle, every ligament and into every joint.*

Imagine every part of your body *becoming so relaxed it seems like jelly. Allow this liquid tranquilizer to relieve every pain, every arthritic condition, every restrictive feeling in you body. Allow this tranquilizer to balance your entire nervous system, your complete immune system, as you focus on allowing your mind to come to complete rest. You are free of all worry, free of all tension as you drift off into your hypnotic trance. Deeper and deeper you go into this deep trance state; deeper and deeper you go into hypnosis. The deeper you go into hypnosis, the deeper you go into this trance state. Deeper and deeper, you drift off into your beautiful, restful hypnotic trance.*

Personal Magnetism rules the world. In order for you to realize the power of this statement, you should know there are adjustments to be made in your life. Since everything indicates that great magnetic forces develop in persons who know how to purify their bodies through love and healthful living, it is to your enrichment to do the same. Beginning right now, agree to accept temperance in all things - from moderation in food consumption, to a simple diet, to strategic physical exercise, to calmness and kindness, to evenness of mind. This is already accepted subconsciously - it happened when I stated that Personal Magnetism rules the world.

As I go into that wide opening to your subconscious, I see that all the traits of Personal Magnetism have become stored there. This enables you to make use one of the most powerful tools the mind can possess any time you wish. Even now, know that golden opportunities want to come to you, know that friends, strangers, even your enemies want to help you. Anything and everything is now virtually yours for the asking. The ease with which you are able to influence those around you to gain love, admiration, opportunities and wealth may seem amazing, but at this very moment all the above have become possible through the power of your Personal Magnetism and the powers of your subconscious mind.

*A habit is something you repeat; the more you repeat it, the more it wants to stay with you, and since we are creatures of habit, they will eventually overtake your subconscious mind. The only difference between a bad habit and a good habit is that the bad habit overtakes you in a **negative**, harmful way, while the good habit overtakes you in a **positive**, joyous way. The surest way to quit a bad habit is to increase the period of time away from it - the longer the period, the farther away the unwanted habit becomes until eventually the body and mind no longer craves it. This is mental conditioning.*

Another way to quit a bad habit is to break the cycle and replace it with a habit that is better for you. The most effective approach to this is to initiate the new habit exactly at the times the bad habit kicks in with its craving. Eventually the mind will become tricked into thinking it is getting the old habit, while it is, in face, getting a sort of transfusion of recouping power, rather than the degenerative, life-sapping energy.

In order to induce a positive message into the subconscious, the old message must be removed. Your old unwanted messages are now about to become replaced by new messages. Your old message is now being voided as I state the following positive messages. Your old feelings, attitudes and fixations about smoking have now been dismissed. They are now erased and extracted from your subconscious so that they are replaced by the following positive confirmations:

As far as your old habits go, that wide opening to your subconscious is now open to resolving your bad habits through the supernatural powers above. You now let go of all desires, and cravings that cause you despair, grief, and feelings of unnecessary guilt. Through the supernatural powers that rein above, you now release all your unwanted habits. You can now breathe freely, because instead of these bad habits you so truly want to get rid of, you find you have the inner power to resist and overcome them. Instead of these unwanted habits, you are now able to connect to that resourceful place in your subconscious that enables you to lead a healthy, wholesome, and psychologically sound, balanced life.

In order that your dreams become fulfilled, listen carefully as I plant these thoughts deep within that brilliant, manifestation compartment of your mind: As far as your finances go, that wide opening to your subconscious is now open to receiving money. Through the supernatural powers above, you now agree to allow and accept abundance in every way into every aspect of your life. Now, money is able to flow into your life; enough so that it will fulfill all your needs; enough so that you are able to receive more abundantly than ever before. Your subconscious mind acknowledges this matter and agrees in kind to be receptive in every possible way.

As far as love goes, that wide opening to your subconscious is now open to receiving love, along with all the touching, embracing and sharing that goes along with it. Through the supernatural powers above, you are now capable to allow and accept love in every form. You are now open to receiving love from the special compatible person or persons you have been longing for. Now, love is able to flow into your life, enough so that it will fulfill all your romantic and sexual needs; enough that you receive love more readily, and expeditiously than ever before.

Your subconscious mind has recorded this and will remember everything that has been said. Before I bring you out of this trance, allow a brief pause as a way thanking God for the infinite riches flowing into your life.

When I count to five, you will open your eyes feeling alert, refreshed and alive. 1, 2, every part of you is better than ever before, 3, you are feeling alert and refreshed, 4, you are alert, refreshed and fully alive, 5 - it's time to open your eyes.

TO "COME OUT" OF *THE TRANCE ZONE*:

There are several ways a trance may be terminated when administering self-hypnosis: It can either be terminated by, say, counting from 1 to 5, or it may happen naturally, by falling asleep during the trance. There is, absolutely, no danger or reason to worry about coming out of a trance, because you <u>do not</u> go to sleep. The trance state is not a sleep state, but rather the completely relaxed state of mind, prior to going into the normal sleep state.

The worse thing the subject could do is fall asleep while being hypnotized by a hypnotist, albeit taking a short nap and then awakening automatically within a short period is harmless in itself; the session will have been wasted. More than likely, the hypnotist will not allow the subject to doze off, because the trance, as well as the session will have become terminated.

During the session, the subject always has the control to interrupt the trance at any time, or the hypnotist may choose various methods of terminating the trance. Some of the hypnotist's methods include counting, snapping the fingers, giving posthypnotic suggestions, touching, or other harmless procedures.

<u>To have the subject "Come Out"</u>
ANOTHER EXAMPLE:

That's very good. The way you are feeling refreshed now is the way you can always expect to feel. Your subconscious mind has recorded this and will remember everything that has been said. Before I bring you out of this trance, allow a brief pause as a way thanking God for the infinite riches flowing into your life.

Now, upon the count of five, you will open your eyes feeling alert, refreshed and free of tension. 1 . . . 2 . . . every part of you is better than ever before. 3 . . . you are feeling alert and refreshed. 4 . . . you are alert, refreshed and feeling fully alive. 5 . . . open your eyes.

<u>Again, never is there a danger of not being able to "Come Out" during any stage of the hypnotic trance.</u>

PART FOUR

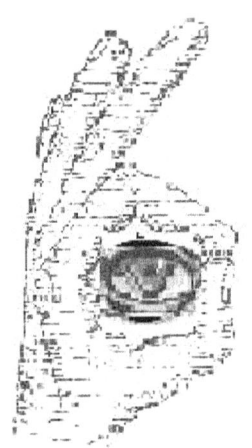

Part Four

CHAPTER SEVEN
7

HYPNOSIS INDUCTION
> ILLUSTRATIONS <

7   HYPNOSIS
       ILLUSTRATIONS:

When thoughts and words are said and done
   There can always be room for improvement;
Whether in the bathroom or under the sun -
   As long as it initiates a positive inducement.

. . . EjL

CHAPTER SEVEN
7

HYPNOSIS INDUCTION ILLUSTRATIONS
(with examples)

As a hypnotist, practice memorizing and performing the Illustrations below on your subjects. Imagine seeing the results of them fulfilling their dreams, their hearts desires. Although it is best to perform the inductions from memory there are so many it would be very difficult. Select your favorites, and practice memorizing them until you are ready for more. Another point to consider is that, since the subject's eyes will be closed, you could actually read the inductions from printed pages, or cards.

However, don't rely too heavily on cold readings - review the following **Illustrations** and practice reading them aloud before initiating them. It is important that your voice flows rhythmically when performing all hypnotic inductions. In practicing the examples as demonstrated below, you will eventually be able to develop your own personalized inductions. Whenever applicable, it is best to use the "Come Out" procedure after every hypnosis session. (See the method above.)

If you are practicing self-hypnosis, there is not much to memorize. Simply tape your preferred inductions (it is best to record them in the "first person"), and listen to them repeatedly, using headphones.

Whether Hypnotist or Subject the following "**Hypnosis Demonstration**" should be very convincing in regard to testing the powers of the subconscious mind:

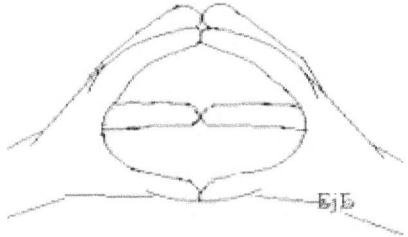

Hypnosis Demonstration

Place both hands together, spreading and placing the fingertips together, forming a hollow sphere. Focusing intently on the center while gently pressing the fingertips against each other, imagine a cylindrical fireball inside. Concentrate on having this fireball between your hands getting hotter, and hotter. As you feel the heat warming your hands press your fingertips together as hard as possible. Now, while **concentrating 100 percent on exerting full pressure**, mentally think it as you say audibly "*I want to pull my hands apart*."

You will find this impossible! The reason is that you cannot exert two opposing forces in a positive direction. The lesson is that, where the positive force is strongest, the negative power becomes weakest. This is one of the best examples of how the subconscious can be programmed to overcome negativity, yes, even illness. *"Find the positive force that overcomes the conflicting, negative weakness and you have discovered the key to positive change"* . . . EjL

THE TRANCE ZONE **INDUCTION ILLUSTRATIONS**
The **Illustrations** below have been designed to give inductions that are more specific - while the previous **Techniques** explain more about procedure.

Typical Induction Illustration (with the subject sitting or lying)
(An extended version of **The Hypnotic Eye Technique** described previously.

First, have the subject "Go Into" **The Trance Zone** as described in the previous chapter. (It is repeated below for your convenience and for better understanding of its use:)
   HYPNOTIST (induce the hypnosis, as follows):
  *I'd like you to form "**the hypnotic eye**" and place it at your side. This is the eye to your subconscious. Now, I'd like you to lift your **eyes up to the eyebrows** and, when you feel like it, close them. Keeping your eyes up, take in a **deep yawn**.*
  *Very good -- that is how you "Go Into" **The Trance Zone**, where only good things happen. As I begin counting down from 30 by 2's, I'd like you to inhale through your nose and exhale through your mouth. 30, 28, 26, 24, 22, 20 . . . Good, breathe slowly and calmly. 18, 16, 14, 12, 10 . . . That's right, inhale through your nose. Just let your body relax more and more each time. 8, 6, 4, 2, 0 . . . In that wide opening to your subconscious, you are listening intently to my voice.*
  You are lying comfortably. Your eyes are closed. Your arms and legs are flexible, relaxed. Continue breathing evenly, inhaling through your nose and exhaling through your mouth. With each breath, you sink deeper and deeper and deeper into a relaxed state of mind. You no longer want anything. Become passive as you listen to my voice. Let yourself go. Let it be . . . Let it happen. Nothing bothers or distracts you. Nothing bad or unusual is going to happen.
  Your head is clear. Your mind is free of all problems. You rejoice in this sense of peace and well being that envelops you from head to foot. Feel this wonderful relaxation which spreads more and more throughout your body. Feel the new looseness and weightlessness of your body. In this wonderful state of peace, you have an opening to the subconscious -- wider and wider this opening is becoming. Your subconscious is registering all my words. The gentle words of my voice are being deeply engraved there as you listen intently to my suggestions. You are listening very intently as I proceed with care.

  Proceed with the hypnosis using any of the hypnotic inductions.

  (Note: From here, you may choose to extend the hypnosis by inducing any of the posthypnotic suggestions. Generally, you would finish the session having the subject "Come Out" of the trance. This has been covered in the previous chapter.)

The Falling Backwards Illustration (with the subject sitting)

First, have the subject "Go Into" ***The Trance Zone.*** Then induce the hypnosis.

HYPNOTIST:

*Very good -- that is how you "Go Into" **The Trance Zone**, where only good things happen. With your eyes still closed, your arms and legs are flexible, relaxed. Now, I'd like you to **inhale through the nose** and exhale through your mouth as you count down from 30 to 0 by twos. As you do so, let yourself fall backwards, inching very slowly as you count. Let all your muscles relax as you sink farther and farther.*

Let yourself go as you continue counting. Let yourself be . . . Let whatever happens happen, because nothing bad is about to take place. Your mind is free of all worry and problems. As you sit, free of worry, you rejoice in the sense of peace and well being that envelops you from head to foot. Feel and experience this wonderful relaxation which spreads more and more throughout your body.

My words are sinking even farther, and as you listen closely to my voice, you willfully allow my words into an opening to your subconscious. With each breath, you sink deeper and deeper, and deeper into your subconscious state of mind. Wider and wider this opening is becoming. Your subconscious is registering all my words. The gentle words of my voice are being deeply engraved as you listen intently to my suggestions. You are listening very intently as I proceed with care.

Proceed with the hypnosis using any of the hypnotic inductions.

Oxygen As An Elixir Illustration (with the subject sitting)

First, have the subject "Go Into" ***The Trance Zone.*** Then induce the hypnosis.

HYPNOTIST:

*Very good -- that is how you "Go Into" **The Trance Zone**, where only good things happen. Now, I'd like you to **inhale through the nose** and exhale through your mouth. Keep doing that for a while as you listen intently to my voice. In that wide opening to your subconscious, you are listening intently to my voice.*

You are sitting comfortably with your eyes still closed; your arms and legs are flexible, relaxed. I'd like you to keep breathing in and out continuously. As you are doing this, think of the incoming oxygen as an elixir, a magic potion that cleanses you inside and out. And as you exhale imagine all your ailments, frustrations, and worries actually leaving your body. Think of all negativity, doubts and fears leaving through your pores.

(continue)

Oxygen As An Elixir Illustration   (continued)

Each time you inhale think of the oxygen as being a bright white mist coming into your spirit, cleansing you of all your impurities, all your ailments. Now, imagine the white mist becoming an even stronger bright blue mist. And now imagine this bright blue mist becoming a powerful healing potion. Every time you breathe in, make the blue mist give off more energy, have it become more splendid.

It is now the most wonderful feeling you've felt in a long time. Your mind is free of all worry, free of daily problems and headaches. Feel and experience this wonderful sensation which spreads more and more throughout your body. Your subconscious is registering all my words. Wider and wider this opening has become. The gentle words of my voice are being deeply engraved as you listen intently to my suggestions. You are listening very intently as I proceed with care.

Proceed with the hypnosis using any of the hypnotic inductions.

The Blue Aura Of Dharma Illustration (with the subject sitting)
DEEPER STATE OF TRANCE

First, have the subject "Go Into" **The Trance Zone.** (See **Illustration 2** below).

HYPNOTIST:

*Very good -- that is how you "Go Into" **The Trance Zone**, where only good things happen. In that wide opening to your subconscious, you are listening intently to my voice. You are sitting comfortably with your eyes still closed; your arms and legs are flexible, relaxed. Gracefully and freely, I'd like you to lift both arms and imagine yourself as an angel, wings and all. Now, imagine yourself as being surrounded with a blue aura. And as you concentrate, this blue aura begins to glow more and more bluer. Taking deep breaths let your entire body relax, but still keeping your arms in a comfortable, raised position.*

Soon, while your blue aura continues to glow, it gets warmer and warmer until you feel a rush of energy surging throughout your body. This energy is a positive and healing energy; it is such a powerful energy it overcomes you to the point you feel a tremendous confidence in yourself. And, keeping this feeling of confidence, know your self worth; know that you are loved and precious. Now, I would like you to lower your arms and let yourself go.

Let yourself be . . . Let whatever happens happen, because great things are taking place. Your mind is free of all worry, free of daily problems and headaches. As you sit, free of worry, you rejoice in the sense of well being that your blue aura brings to you, which envelops you from head to foot. Feel and experience this wonderful sensation which spreads more and more throughout your body.

(continue)

The Blue Aura Of Dharma Illustration (with the subject sitting)

You feel protected, secure and full of high esteem as the sensation forms a permanent place in your subconscious. Your subconscious is registering all my words. Wider and wider, this opening has become. The gentle words of my voice are becoming deeply engraved as you listen intently to my suggestions. You are listening very intently as I proceed with great care.

Now that you are a free spirit, capable of going anywhere you wish, unafraid doing anything you desire, I'd like you to imagine yourself flying on the back of a huge white eagle. Higher and higher, you soar freely among the clouds on those thick, soft, protective feathers. You are unafraid because you are fully protected by this eagle. You are happy, and delighted at being far away from planet earth, far away from reality, far away from the boredom and the burdens that go along with all your daily functions.

Then, focusing and returning to the world below know that you have permission to become anyone you wish to be, accomplish anything you wish to accomplish. With your newly formed identity, envision yourself as the person you always dreamed you could be. In that wide opening to your subconscious mind, you will remember how great it feels when your imagination takes over, how it can make you feel better about yourself. When you come out of this, you will remember everything and make use of it in every aspect of your life.

Very good, rest and relax. As I count from one to five, you will become awake and fully alert, feeling better and healthier than ever before. One, two, three, four . . . You are fully alert and functioning better than ever before . . . Five, you are wide awake and fully alive.

The Blue Aura Of Dharma Illustration 2 (with the subject sitting)
<u>EXTENSIVE COMBO TRANCE -- INSOMNIA</u>

First, have the subject "Go Into" **The Trance Zone** as follows, and induce the hypnosis.
<u>HYPNOTIST</u>

*I'd like you to lift your <u>**eyes up to the eyebrows**</u>, and close them. Give **<u>a deep yawn</u>**, and form "<u>**the hypnotic eye**</u>" by placing my thumb and forefinger together. Now, <u>recite</u>, "This is how I Go Into **The Trance Zone**."*

*Concentrate as you, <u>**inhale through the nose**</u> and exhale counting down from 30 by 2's, relaxing the body more and more until reaching 0. Count down with me slowly, evenly as I begin: 30 . . . 28 . . . 26 . . . 24 . . . 22 . . . 20 . . . 18 . . . 16 . . . 14 . . . 12 . . . 10 . . . 8 . . . 6 . . . 4 . . . 2 . . . 0.*

(continue)

The Blue Aura Of Dharma Illustration 2 (continued)

You are lying comfortably with your eyes still closed; your arms and legs are flexible, relaxed. Now, concentrating on being loose and free, and with your hand still forming "<u>the hypnotic eye</u>," imagine yourself as being surrounded with a blue aura. As you concentrate, this blue aura begins to glow blue -- more and more glowing blue. Taking in deep breaths through your nose and exhaling through your mouth, let your entire body relax while lying in this comfortable position. While you imagine your blue aura, watching it as it continues to glow, you feel it getting warmer and warmer until you sense a rush of energy surging throughout your body.

This energy is a positive and healing energy. This powerful, relaxing energy overcomes you to the point you feel a tremendous confidence in yourself. Let yourself go. Let yourself be . . . Let whatever happens happen because terrific things are taking place. Still concentrating on this blue aura, you feel that your mind is free of all worry, free of daily problems and headaches. As you lie, free of tension, you rejoice in the sense of well being that your blue aura brings you, which envelops you from head to foot. Feel and experience this wonderful sensation which spreads more and more throughout your body.

You feel protected, secure and full of high esteem as the sensation forms a permanent place in your subconscious. Your subconscious is registering all my words. Wider and wider, this opening has become. The gentle words of my voice are being deeply engraved there as you listen intently to these suggestions. You are listening very intently as I proceed, confidently. Now that you are a free spirit capable of conquering any problem and unafraid of doing anything you desire, you now imagine yourself entering your dream world. Deeper and deeper, you enter freely into your dreams. You are unafraid, protected, and delighted at being far away from reality and the responsibilities and burdens that go along with your daily activities.

In this wonderful state of peace, you have an opening to your subconscious -- wider and wider this opening is becoming. Your subconscious is registering all my words. The gentle words of my voice are being deeply engraved there as you listen intently to my suggestions. You are listening very intently as I proceed with care. Listen closely to these words as I say them to you: You feel peaceful; you feel very quiet emotionally. You feel calm physically, and you enjoy the peace, the quiet, and the calm that exudes from within you.

(continue)

The Blue Aura Of Dharma Illustration 2 (continued)

As you listen to my voice, your entire body becomes more relaxed, more and more. While your muscles become free of tension, my voice is going deeper into that opening to you subconscious. Now that you are totally relaxed and feeling completely free of tension, imagine all your worries, frustrations, and hostilities leaving your body permanently.

Imagine that all that negativity is flowing out of your lungs and pores like poisonous gases, leaving you feeling completely refreshed, recharged and rejuvenated. Right now, know in your mind that you fully and freely release all grudges held from the past. Fully and freely loosen and let go of all anger, resentment and pent-up emotional disorders. Feel the relief of unloading all this excess baggage from your mind. From this day forward your load is finally light. Your burdens are light and all your worries and problems have just become trivial.

Continue to breathe slowly and calmly. Let your body relax more and more each time. Relaxing, relaxing, and going deeper and deeper into hypnosis. As you are resting comfortably, you will notice that your eyes are closed tight, very tight. They are stuck so tight you are not able to open them. Your eyes are stuck together so tight they feel as if they are sealed with a mudpack. In a moment I will ask you to try to open them - you will not be able to do so. You will find they are sealed tight; they are stuck firmly together. You may be able to manage the muscle groups around your eyes, but not your eyelids. No matter how hard you try, you will be unable to open your eyes until I bring you out of this deep trance.

When I count down from 3 to zero, you will find it impossible to open your eyes and you will go deeper into hypnosis. 3 . . . Your eyelids are sealed tight, 2 . . . They feel stuck tight with mud, 1 . . . They are stuck firmly together, Zero . . . Try, but you are unable to open them. Stop trying, and go deeper into hypnosis.

In that wide opening to your subconscious, you are listening intently to my voice. Perhaps you already know about your subconscious mind's extraordinary powers of self-healing, and how the right side of your brain controls the functioning of your entire body. The right side of your brain, the subconscious mind, knows how to regulate your breathing even while you are sleeping. And it knows how to regulate your circulatory system and how to carry the right nutrients to all the parts of your body that need them.

(continue)

The Blue Aura Of Dharma Illustration 2 (continued)

This brilliant part of your mind also knows how to instruct every cell in your body to heal itself, to improve your mind so that you become healthier and more sound-minded, cell by cell. And I don't know how fast your body is healing itself now, but your mind knows just how to accelerate the healing that is already taking place in your body. Yes, your subconscious has the intelligence and the power to heal anything inside of you on an intercellular basis. It is doing this effectively even as I speak.

And I don't know if you are already feeling certain sensations in your body, signaling that the healing process has already started, but you can be sure that while you are in this deep, resting trance state, your body is already healing itself. You enjoy feeling relaxed, knowing your body can accelerate and improve your immune system even now, as you enjoy this rest. Know for sure that you can rely on your inner self; that you can count on that part of you in your subconscious that knows exactly what to do, and exactly how to do it. While your body has a tremendous ability to heal itself, the subconscious mind actually serves as the regulator of every possible function. Not only does your subconscious have the ability to perform all the healing you need, it has the capability to initiate peaceful rest and recuperation whenever you decide to fall asleep.

Your subconscious mind is capable of extraordinary recouping powers, and endless capacities, even while you enjoy this peaceful state. You know that, and you continue to allow your body to rejuvenate while you relax and enjoy feeling peaceful. That deep place in your subconscious mind acknowledges all this and remembers the need to recall everything when you come out of this trance. And even after you come out of this exhilarating trance state, you can trust your ability to initiate peace and relaxation whenever it is needed. When you go to bed at night, you take delight in the fact that sleeping serves to replenish your entire body, hour after hour, cell by remarkable cell.

Imagine a large softgel *containing a liquid tranquilizer being lodged in the upper portion of your brain. Let it become loose and slowly travel down the head, and settle into the back of your neck. Now, let the softgel dissolve, allowing the liquid tranquilizer to flow down your throat and settle there. Feel the liquid dissolving into your throat. And now, allow the liquid tranquilizer to settle into every part of your body starting from your throat, and seeping down to the bottom of your feet. Feel its tranquilizing effect as it seeps down your chest and arms. Feel its loosening and healing effects as it seeps into every muscle, every ligament and into every joint.*

(continue)

The Blue Aura Of Dharma Illustration 2 (continued)

Imagine a large softgel *containing a liquid tranquilizer being lodged in the upper portion of your brain. Let it become loose and slowly travel down the head, and settle into the back of your neck. Now, let the softgel dissolve, allowing the liquid tranquilizer to flow down your throat and settle there. Feel the liquid dissolving into your throat. And now, allow the liquid tranquilizer to settle into every part of your body starting from your throat, and seeping down to the bottom of your feet. Feel its tranquilizing effect as it seeps down your chest and arms. Feel its loosening and healing effects as it seeps into every muscle, every ligament and into every joint.*

Imagine every part of your body *becoming so relaxed it seems like jelly. Allow this liquid tranquilizer to relieve every pain, every arthritic condition, every restrictive feeling in you body. Allow this tranquilizer to balance your entire nervous system, your complete immune system, as you focus on allowing your mind to come to complete rest. You are free of all worry, free of all tension as you drift off into your hypnotic trance. Deeper and deeper you go into this deep trance state; deeper and deeper you go into hypnosis. The deeper you go into hypnosis, the deeper you go into this trance state. Deeper and deeper, you drift off into your beautiful, restful hypnotic trance.*

Even after you come out of this trance, you will remember that "<u>the hypnotic eye</u>" is the key to unleashing the power of your subconscious mind. Whenever you call upon this image hidden knowledge is brought to light. As you look deeper and deeper within your spirit, you draw wisdom from the depths of your subconscious mind. All knowledge is there for you. All channels of guidance are opened to you, especially spiritual guidance. Everything you want to know is revealed. Everything is made clear; everything is exposed.

As far as any problems with sleeping are concerned, you are confident all is resolved. Any bouts with insomnia are finally over. Struggling in order to find peaceful sleep is a thing of the past. Now, whenever you lay down for the night, you realize that sleeping is the way your body recuperates. You also know that sleep is inevitable because it is nature's way of replenishing your strength and your state of mental balance. Whenever you decide to fall asleep your sleep is deep and unencumbered. Whenever you awaken, there is complete rest and complete relief from all kinds of stress. Your will, as well as Thy Will be done - and thus, it is laid out before you.

(continue)

The Blue Aura Of Dharma Illustration 2 (continue)

Focusing on this subconscious state, know that you have permission to become anyone you wish to be, accomplish anything you wish to accomplish. With your newly formed identity, you envision yourself as the person you have always dreamed you could be. In this state of subconscious, you will always remember how great it felt to have your imagination make you over. Your subconscious mind has already allowed you to feel better about yourself. And as you awaken, you will remember everything that happened during this trance.

As I slowly begin to count from 1 to 5, you will become better and better upon each count. 1 . . You are feeling terrific knowing that deep sleep comes whenever you need it; 2 . . You remember everything that happened in this trance state; 3 . . You feel happy that your life is changed for the better; 4 . . You are totally relaxed, fully aware, and functioning perfectly normal, 5 . . You are awake and feeling better than ever before. Finally, you are healthy, alert, and fully alive.

Behavior Modification Illustration (with subject sitting or lying)

First, have the subject "Go Into" ***The Trance Zone*** as follows:
HYPNOTIST:

*I'd like you to lift your **eyes up to the eyebrows**, and when you feel like it, close them. Give **a deep yawn**, and form "**the hypnotic eye**" by placing my thumb and forefinger together. Now, recite, "This is how I Go Into **The Trance Zone**."*

*Very good -- that is how you "Go Into" **The Trance Zone**, where only good things happen. In that wide opening to your subconscious, you are listening intently to my voice.*

Your arms and legs are flexible, relaxed. As I count down from 30 by 2's, continue breathing evenly, inhaling through your nose and exhaling through your mouth. 30, 28, 26, 24 . . . With each breath you sink deeper and deeper and deeper into a relaxed state of mind. 22, 20, 18, 16 . . . You no longer want anything. Become passive as you listen to my voice. Let yourself go . . . . 14 . . . 12 . . . 10 . . . 8 . . . 6 . . . 4 . . . 2 . . . 0.

Let it be . . . Let it happen. Nothing bothers or distracts you. Nothing bad or unusual is going to happen. Your head is clear. Your mind is free of all problems. You rejoice in this sense of peace and well being that envelops you from head to foot. Feel this wonderful relaxation which spreads more and more throughout your body. Feel the new looseness and weightlessness of your body.

(continue)

Behavior Modification Illustration (continued)

In this wonderful state of peace, you have an opening to the subconscious -- wider and wider this opening is becoming. Your subconscious is registering all my words. The gentle words of my voice are being deeply engraved there as you listen intently to my suggestions. You are listening very intently as I proceed with care. Listen closely to these words as I say them to you: You feel peaceful; you feel very quiet emotionally. You feel calm physically, and you enjoy the peace, the quiet, and the calm that exudes from within you.

As you are resting comfortably, you will notice that your eyes are closed tight, very tight. They are stuck so tight you are not able to open them. In a moment I will ask you to try to open them - you will not be able to do so. You will find they are sealed tight; they are stuck firmly together. You may be able to manage the muscle groups around your eyes, but not your eyelids. No matter how hard you try, you will be unable to open your eyes.

When I count down from 3 to zero, you will find it impossible to open your eyes and you will go deeper into hypnosis. 3 . . . Your eyelids are sealed tight, 2 . . . They are stuck tight, 1 . . . They are stuck firmly together, Zero . . . Try, but you are unable to open them. Stop trying, and go deeper into hypnosis.

As you listen to my voice, your entire body becomes more relaxed, more and more. While your muscles become free of tension, my voice is going deeper into that opening to you subconscious. Now that you are totally relaxed and feeling completely free of tension, imagine all your worries, frustrations, and hostilities leaving your body permanently.

Imagine that all that negativity is flowing out of your lungs and pores like poisonous gases, leaving you feeling completely refreshed, recharged and rejuvenated. Right now, know in your mind that you fully and freely release all grudges held from the past. Fully and freely loosen and let go of all anger, resentment and pent-up emotional disorders. Feel the relief of unloading all this excess baggage from your mind. From this day forward your load is finally light. Your burdens are light and all your worries and problems have just become trivial.

What has become important to you is your renewed spirit, and the good you see in everything. You understand that, due to the conflicts between accountability and accomplishment, tension builds up causing much discomfort and despair - even disease. To alleviate these pressures, begin by stretching all your fingers open wide. As you continue stretching your fingers, open your mouth wide and give a deep yawn. That's it - stretch your fingers, with your jaw open wide. Open and close your jaw, stretching . . . stretching. That's very good.

(continue)

Behavior Modification Illustration (continued)

Now relax all your muscles and take deep breaths as if allowing the oxygen to flow into the muscles of your jaw, shoulders, hands, legs and feet. Focus on this deep breathing until you feel tingling in different parts of your body. You feel this happening; you feel the oxygen rejuvenating your body and spirit, replenishing your stamina. Your entire body feels loose and your mind is so clear you feel all the stress leaving your being. Beginning this very moment all thoughts that come into your mind are positive.

You never have to worry about being inadequate, because you have found the peace and the power to take control of your emotions. No matter what pressures you face, you remain cool, calm and concentrated. Every minute of every hour, you feel better in every possible positive way because of unleashing this power.

You are motivated and rejuvenated; you are relaxed and totally optimistic every minute of every day. Now, I'd like you to imagine you are away on vacation. It is a lovely, sunny day at the beach in the Bahamas. As you return from a refreshing swim in the ocean you dry yourself off and place your towel down. Sitting right at the edge of the water where the sand is moist, you bask in the sun as you watch the sailboats passing by. Suddenly, you look up through your sunglasses and see me approaching you. You watch me stop to entice you to play a mental game where you have to draw numbers in the sand in order to become hypnotized. You readily agree, and you follow my procedure.

Using your finger to draw in the moist sand next to you, trace a square about the size of the length of your arm, from your fingertips to the end of your elbow. Carefully, in your imagination, draw a circle inside the square, having it touch all four sides of the square. Inside the circle, draw the open version of the number 4, making all four points touch the edge of the circle.

Even if you can't see all this, it's okay, because you can imagine you see it. And imagining is what this is all about. Now, using your fingers gently erase the 4. As you do this, I want you to be very careful not to break the circle. So, using the tip of your finger, I want you to erase the 4 – but only where it touches the circle at the four points. Do this slowly and calmly.

Now that you've done this, erase the rest of the 4 with your fingers. Then, trace the number 30 inside the circle, making it small enough to have room to work without damaging the circle. Now, erase the 30 and draw number 29; erase that number and draw number 28; erase that number, and so on.

(continue)

Behavior Modification Illustration (continued)

After I tell you to draw number 27, don't pay attention to my voice; just continue erasing and tracing lower numbers, concentrating on getting to zero. Okay, whenever you are ready, you can draw the number 27.

*You don't have to worry about paying attention to me, because your subconscious will hear and register everything I say as I continue talking. So, you don't have to be nervous, because your only focus is making these numbers. You just keep on making your numbers lower and lower until you get to the number zero. When you get to number zero, I want you to say the words, **deeper I go**, then begin again, starting at 30 and keep right on drawing your numbers and erasing them until reaching zero again. Just keep right on drawing your numbers and erasing them.*

One number *after the other, erase and draw, erase and draw, going deeper and deeper into hypnosis. Be neat as you work in the moist sand. As you keep working, try to avoid letting too much sand inside the circle. Try to keep the area smooth and your fingers clean, wiping them on your towel so that you get neat numbers each time. When you get to zero, the deeper you will go into hypnosis. The main thing to remember is that the lower the numbers, the deeper you go into hypnosis. Every time you get to zero, you will say the words, **deeper I go**. Then you will begin again, starting at 30 and keep right on drawing your numbers and erasing them until reaching zero again. As you keep tracing lower numbers, that wide opening to your subconscious brings you deeper and deeper into hypnosis. The lower you go, the deeper you go; the lower the number, the deeper you go into hypnosis, and the deeper the hypnosis becomes. Deeper and deeper.*

One number *after the other, erase and draw, erase and draw, going deeper and deeper into hypnosis. Be neat as you work in the moist sand. As you keep working, try to avoid letting too much sand inside the circle. Try to keep the area smooth and your fingers clean, wiping them on your towel so that you get neat numbers each time. When you get to zero, the deeper you will go into hypnosis. The main thing to remember is that the lower the numbers, the deeper you go into hypnosis. Every time you get to zero, you will say the words, **deeper I go**. Then you will begin again, starting at 30 and keep right on drawing your numbers and erasing them until reaching zero again. As you keep tracing lower numbers, that wide opening to your subconscious brings you deeper and deeper into hypnosis. The lower you go, the deeper you go; the lower the number, the deeper you go into hypnosis, and the deeper the hypnosis becomes. Deeper and deeper.*

(continue)

Behavior Modification Illustration (continued)

When I count to five, you will open your eyes feeling alert, refreshed and alive. 1, 2, every part of you is better than ever before, 3, you are feeling alert and refreshed, 4, you are alert, refreshed and fully alive, 5 -- open your eyes.

The key to developing hypnotic powers is practice, and then more practice.

The above methods are only some of the ways of inducing full-depth hypnosis. Other variations are to keep repeating the same trance script, or to create your own script using your own words. Still other variations can be designed for specific purposes, using the many suggestions or autosuggestions found throughout this book.

CHAPTER EIGHT
8

HYPNOTIST'S POSTHYPNOTIC SUGGESTIONS INDUCED TO THE SUBJECT

8 HYPNOSIS
INDUCTION:

Go where he will, the wise man is at home,
His hearth the earth, his hall the azure dome;
Where his clear spirit leads him, there's his road,
By God's own light illuminated and foreshadowed.
       ----Emerson

CHAPTER EIGHT
8

HYPNOTIST'S POSTHYPNOTIC SUGGESTIONS INDUCED TO THE SUBJECT

HYPNOTIST'S INDUCTIONS
POSTHYPNOTIC SUGGESTIONS:

Posthypnotic Suggestions are the "CUES," messages, key words, or triggers induced by the hypnotist to the subject in the hypnotic state. The purpose of the hypnotist's suggestions is to have them carry over, thus influencing the subject in the awakened state -- they are also used as a trigger to aid the subject in returning to the hypnotic state.

For example, the hypnotist can give the subject a word, such as "**golden nugget**," under hypnosis, and upon being given that command in the awakened state, the subject will return to the hypnotic state. Also, snapping the fingers three times, while the subject repeats, *"I can do"* three times under hypnosis can induce self-confidence when the command is executed in the awakened state. **Posthypnotic Suggestions** act as tools, in order to enable progressive treatment. In this instance, forming "**the hypnotic eye**" would enable the subject to rapidly "Go Into" ***The Trance Zone*** in subsequent sessions. Invariably, the subject's eyes will close very rapidly, inducing the trance.

Since all posthypnotic suggestions become effective when induced during the trance state, have the subject "Go into" ***The Trance Zone,*** and repeatedly give the subject the key words: *This is how you "Go Into"* ***The Trance Zone***. After a few visits, the subject will easily go into hypnosis.

EXAMPLE:
Have the subject encircle the thumb and forefinger to form "**the hypnotic eye**." Then have the subject place the **eyes up to the eyebrows,** close them, and give **deep yawn**. Then give the posthypnotic suggestion, which will become a "CUE", subconsciously, to go into the trance state.

HYPNOTIST:
This is how you "Go Into" ***The Trance Zone***. *Every time I give you this message, it will be easier for you to go into hypnosis. Now, forming "the hypnotic eye," go into your trance and then* ***go deeper into hypnosis***.

Then, proceed with any of combination of the posthypnotic suggestions – which are all actually forms of guided imagery and affirmations, for the purpose of improvement.

Note: To better serve the subject, these suggestions may be recorded for use at home.

To Gain Infinite Riches

Personal Magnetism rules the world. In order for you to realize the power of this statement, you should know there are adjustments to be made in your life. Since everything indicates that great magnetic forces develop in persons who know how to purify their bodies through love and healthful living, it is to your enrichment to do the same.

Beginning right now, agree to accept temperance in all things -- from moderation in food consumption, to a simple diet, to strategic physical exercise, to calmness and kindness, to evenness of mind. This is already accepted subconsciously -- it happened at the beginning of this induction, when I stated that Personal Magnetism rules the world.

As I go into that wide opening to your subconscious, I see that all the traits of Personal Magnetism have become stored there. This enables you to make use one of the most powerful tools the mind can possess any time you wish. Between your newly acquired knowledge of Personal Magnetism, doors to every imaginable scenario are now being opened to you. Already, you realize that some people sense you are the spiritual person they have been looking for, that you are a caring person of deep knowledge, wisdom and compassion. Even now, know that friends, strangers, even your enemies want to do favors for you, as well as offer you money and other golden opportunities.

Anything and everything is now virtually yours for the asking. The ease with which you are able to influence those around you to gain love, admiration, opportunities and wealth may seem amazing, but at this very moment all the above have become possible through the power of this Personal Magnetism, and the powers of your subconscious mind. Your subconscious mind has recorded this and remembers everything that has been said.

As I go into that wide opening to your subconscious, I see that your memory has been improved. And the ease with which you are able to influence those around you to gain love, admiration, opportunities and wealth may seem amazing, but at this very moment all the above have become possible through the powers of your subconscious mind.

Your subconscious mind has recorded this and will remember everything that has been said. Before I bring you out of this trance, allow a brief pause as a way thanking God for the infinite riches flowing into your life.

When I count to five, you will open your eyes feeling alert, refreshed and alive. 1 . . . 2 . . . every part of you is better than ever before, 3 . . . you are feeling alert and refreshed, 4 . . . you are alert, refreshed and fully alive, 5 . . . Open your eyes.

The Divine Wish Conception

Imagine a decorative water fountain with statues pouring water into a pool at its base. See yourself standing in front of it with a sparkling coin in your hand. While you stare at the coin and make your finest wish, you imagine your guardian angel approaching you, giving you a blessing. As you toss the coin high in the air, keep your eyes glued to it; watch it hit the water until it settles to the bottom of the pool. Focusing on the coin, make it grow large enough to see what you wished for appear larger-than-life.

Since you have envisioned all you wished for, concentrate and whisper these words to your Angel - repeat after me: <u>Thank you for fulfilling my wish . . . In my subconscious mind, I shall always remember this moment . . . I realize now, that if I believe strong enough, and have faith long enough, anything is possible.</u>

To Refrain From Overeating

Willfully, you will go on a five day fast. You will loose all desire to overeat. You will eat very slowly and stop eating as soon as the feeling of "fullness" registers its message. Soon you will desire to begin some form of exercise. As you do so, listen closely to the instinctive messages your body sends you -- feel its true vibrations. Your natural instincts will tell you exactly what your weight should be, and will adjust accordingly. From this day forward, you agree to let your body be the judge of how much you should eat, and let your emotions stand aside. As of right now, this is your well-deserved reality.

To Overcome Illness

You are coming into a very deep subconscious state. Your imagination is free and clear. Here, you are enabled to use the power of your imagination to help you attain whatever it is you need to accomplish. I command that part of your subconscious that is responsible to restore your original powers. Now, you are enabled to begin functioning perfectly, just as you were intended to do from the beginning.

I address all the cells of your being, and command them to restore your powers. I call attention to your healthy cells and instruct them to heal you and make you healthy. These commands to your cells give them permission to begin your healing process. The healing process is already working and, in a very short period, the affects shall take place accordingly, and dramatically. Your natural instincts will tell you exactly what is needed and will adjust accordingly. From this day forward, you agree to let any negative attitudes stand aside. As of right now, this is your well-deserved reality.

To Alleviate Pressure And Tension

You understand that, due to the conflicts between accountability and accomplishment, tension builds up causing much discomfort and despair - even disease. To alleviate these pressures, begin by stretching all your fingers open wide. As you continue stretching your fingers, open your mouth wide and give a deep yawn. That's it - stretch your fingers, with your jaw open wide. Now relax all your muscles and take deep breaths as if allowing the oxygen to flow into the muscles of your jaw, shoulders, hands, legs and feet. Allow this oxygen to alleviate tension and stress within all your muscles.

Focus on this deep breathing until you feel tingling in the muscles and joints of your entire body. You feel this happening; you feel the oxygen replenishing your body and spirit, rejuvenating your stamina. Your entire body feels loose, and your mind is so clear you feel all the stress leaving your being. As you go deeper into the state of hypnosis, your subconscious is acknowledging all my words. Beginning this very moment all thoughts that come into your mind are positive.

You never have to worry about being inadequate, because you have found the peace, the power and the inner strength to take control of your emotions. No matter what pressures you face, you remain cool, calm and fully concentrated.

To Instill Direction And Motivation

You call upon your creative powers in order to enable you to choose the right direction. You have the ability to concentrate on completing the project nearest your ideals, nearest your passion, your creativity, and your most deeply rooted inclinations. You now have the ability to summon the powers within you to motivate yourself. You now have enough motivation to become active in putting together your ideal project and completing it, concentrating on it day by day until you succeed.

Again, you have enabled the power within you to summon your innermost, abilities, to initiate your tremendous capacity for active energy. You have now initiated your total being in order that you heighten and manifest whatever powers are within you. You now feel very adequate, and ready to accomplish that innate desire within yourself. In your mind's eye you already know you have what it takes to get this completed. You know all this is true, and you readily accept it.

I repeat: You have now initiated your total being in order that you heighten and manifest whatever powers are within you. You now feel very adequate, and ready to accomplish that innate desire within yourself. In your mind's eye you already know you have what it takes to get this completed. You know all this is true, and you readily accept it - every possible, positive bit of it.

Overcoming Disease Cell by Wonderful Cell

Perhaps you already know that when you are in the deeply relaxed state as you are now, every nerve and every cell in your body is able to restore and rejuvenate itself. Deep within your subconscious, you know your body has the intelligence to heal itself, cell by wonderful cell, so that your nerves, joints, ligaments, muscles and organs improve and become healthier. When you are quiet and peaceful, as you are right now, realize that there is a part of you that knows what parts need restoration, and exactly what to do about it.

And I don't know when you will begin to notice the increase throughout your immune system -- maybe you already noticed that you are feeling deeply relaxed and that your symptoms and ailments are melting, floating away, disappearing. And you can continue to imagine and accept that all the areas of your body which need healing are healthy, strong, whole and pure. You remember which parts of your mind, body, and spirit needs restoration. Deep within you, you know that your subconscious knows exactly how to cure everything. You know your subconscious acknowledges this, and that you can consider all of it done.

Journey Away To Your Vacation

After taking a safe flight, miles away from home, you find yourself riding in a convertible along the French Rivera. Since you have been enjoying the afternoon basking on the beach, you pull into special garden café where you know they go to extremes to please their patrons. While being led to a private wooded area, you become overwhelmed with your surroundings: beautiful weeping willows with colorful lanterns suspended high among them, while waitresses pass back and forth serving drinks along the adjacent pool. And then you see the hammock being spread between the trees, especially for you. As you slip into the canvas with your full weight, you find yourself swinging side-to-side, smiling contently because you are being served your favorite drink. Suddenly, you realize everything is just as you always dreamed it would be.

To Improve Health And Fitness

You may have read or heard, or perhaps you know from your own experience that athletes need to take great care in order for their bodies to grow strong, and recuperate from overwork. And as you rest your body now, like an athlete rests, your body can become stronger and healthier, revitalizing your nerves, your blood, and even your brain cells. And although the aging process is always causing deterioration, it doesn't have to follow that your vision, your memory, your legs, or your muscles have to become weakened.

And I don't know if you have already felt certain sensations in your body, signaling that the healing process has already started, but you can be sure that while you are in this deep, resting trance state, your body is already healing itself. You can enjoy feeling relaxed, knowing your body can accelerate and improve your immune system even now, as you enjoy this rest. You know for sure that you can rely on your inner self; that you can count on that part of you in your subconscious that knows exactly what to do, and exactly how to do it. In fact, your subconscious is considering this as already being done.

To Induce Overall Healing

Perhaps you already know about your subconscious mind's extraordinary powers of self-healing, and how the right side of your brain controls the functioning of your entire body. The right side of your brain, the subconscious mind, knows how to regulate your breathing even while you are sleeping, and knows how to regulate your circulatory system, how to carry the right nutrients to all the parts of your body that need them.

This brilliant part of your mind also knows how to instruct every cell in your body to heal itself. Yes, your subconscious is able to improve your mind to feel more comfortable in order to become healthy and sound, cell by incredible cell. And I don't know how fast your body is healing itself now, but your mind knows just how to accelerate the healing that is already taking place in your body. You may remember back to a time in your life that you broke a bone and had to go to a doctor to have the bone set and a cast put on you. But your subconscious mind knows that it wasn't the doctor who healed you -- it was you and your body that ultimately healed you, cell by incredible cell. Yes, your subconscious has the intelligence and the power to heal anything inside of you on an intercellular basis.

Nature's Deep Sleep Tranquilizer

Imagine a large softgel *containing a liquid tranquilizer being lodged in the upper portion of your brain. Think of this as a liquid capsule as you allow it become loose and slowly travel down the head, and settle into the back of your neck. Now, let the softgel dissolve, allowing the liquid tranquilizer to flow down your throat and settle there. Feel the liquid dissolving into your throat. And now, allow the liquid tranquilizer to settle into every part of your body starting from your throat, and seeping down to the bottom of your feet. Feel its tranquilizing effect as it seeps down your chest and arms. Feel its loosening and healing effects as it seeps into every muscle, every ligament and into every joint.*

(continue)

Nature's Deep Sleep Tranquilizer   (continued)

Imagine every part of your body *becoming so relaxed it seems like jelly. Allow this liquid tranquilizer to relieve every pain, every arthritic condition, every restrictive feeling in you body. Allow this tranquilizer to balance your entire nervous system, your complete immune system, as you focus on allowing your mind to come to complete rest. You are free of all worry, free of all tension as you drift off into your hypnotic trance. Deeper and deeper you go into this deep trance state; deeper and deeper you go into hypnosis. The deeper you go into hypnosis, the deeper you go into this trance state. Deeper and deeper, you drift off into your beautiful, restful hypnotic trance.*

Imagine a large softgel *containing a liquid tranquilizer being lodged in the upper portion of your brain. Let it become loose and slowly travel down the head, and settle into the back of your neck Now, let the softgel dissolve, allowing the liquid tranquilizer to flow down your throat and settle there. Feel the liquid dissolving into your throat. And now, allow the liquid tranquilizer to settle into every part of your body starting from your throat, and seeping down to the bottom of your feet. Feel its tranquilizing effect as it seeps down your chest and arms. Feel its loosening and healing effects as it seeps into every muscle, every ligament and into every joint.*

Imagine every part of your body *becoming so relaxed it seems like jelly. Allow this liquid tranquilizer to relieve every pain, every arthritic condition, every restrictive feeling in you body. Allow this tranquilizer to balance your entire nervous system, your complete immune system, as you focus on allowing your mind to come to complete rest. You are free of all worry, free of all tension as you drift off into your hypnotic trance. Deeper and deeper you go into this deep trance state; deeper and deeper you go into hypnosis. The deeper you go into hypnosis, the deeper you go into this trance state. Deeper and deeper, you drift off into your beautiful, restful hypnotic trance.*

Imagine every part of your body *becoming so relaxed it seems like jelly. Allow this liquid tranquilizer to relieve every pain, every arthritic condition, every restrictive feeling in you body. Allow this tranquilizer to balance your entire nervous system, your complete immune system, as you focus on allowing your mind to come to complete rest. You are free of all worry, free of all tension as you drift off into your hypnotic trance. Deeper and deeper you go into this deep trance state; deeper and deeper you go into hypnosis. The deeper you go into hypnosis, the deeper you go into this trance state. Deeper and deeper, you drift off into your beautiful, restful hypnotic trance.*

To Overcome Insomnia

Perhaps you remember a time when you had a cut that was so deep you felt it wouldn't heal, or perhaps you had a bout with the flu. You probably went to a doctor for treatment, but then even as you slept and played and worked, your body did all the healing. While your body has a tremendous ability to heal itself, the subconscious mind actually serves as the regulator of every possible part, every possible function. Not only does your subconscious have the ability to perform all the healing you need, it has the capability to initiate peaceful rest and sleep when called upon.

To get to sleep, go deep into your trance and speak to your subconscious mind. Talk to it, just as if it has the power and understanding to listen to your requests – for it does, you know. All you have to do is ask that you be given the opportunity to sleep when it comes time to retire for the night. Repeated often enough at bedtime, you will be granted your request. Remember that Desire, Belief and Expectation are very necessary tools. In combination with exercise and proper nutrition, as well as proper ventilation, you will learn to apply these in order to overcome your bouts with insomnia.

Your subconscious mind is capable of extraordinary recouping powers, and endless capacities, even while you enjoy your peaceful sleep. You <u>know</u> that, and you can continue to allow your body to rejuvenate while you relax and enjoy feeling peaceful. That deep place in your subconscious mind acknowledges all this and remembers to initiate sleep at bedtime. And even after you come out of this exhilarating trance state, you can trust your ability to initiate sleep whenever it is needed. When you go to bed at night, you take delight in the fact that sleeping serves to replenish your entire body, hour after hour, cell by remarkable cell.

CESSATION OF BAD HABITS (Or Addictions)

Through the practice of hypnosis, it is feasible to break a bad habit, which is a negative, degenerative habit. This is accomplished by replacing it with a good habit, which becomes a positive, beneficial habit.

Everyone develops habits, but most are positive, while others are negative. The problems arise when our negative, or bad, habits control us -- for they begin inducing demoralizing, and abusive, self-defeating traits.

Whether falling into patterns of negative conditioning, or self-destruction -- reprogramming our thoughts can be successfully used to alter the defeatist personality. Through the application of **Psychological Adjustment**, you will learn how to actually alter your personality traits. (Refer to Part Three, Chapter 5.) This can be achieved by practicing the following inductions:

Note to the hypnotist, or the subject: The following trance script may be administered to any negative habit. For example: To quit smoking, merely replace the negative habit of "nail biting" with "quit smoking". (More on this below.)

Shedding Addiction

Your shoulders and arms are relaxed, your legs and feet are relaxed, and all your muscles are completely loose. As you continue to relax, there is a deep opening to your subconscious, which listens intently to my voice. You now have the courage to give up your negative habit of __(address the negative habit here)__ .

Just as a snake is able to sheds its skin, you have the ability to shed your disturbing, unwanted habit, never to be part of your behavior again. Your subconscious pays full attention to my words and stores them into your memory. The more you imagine the nasty addiction you want to get ride of, the more you think of it as becoming an additional layer of skin. Imagine all aspects of your addiction as becoming an imaginary blanket of skin covering you from head to foot.

Now, in your mind's eye, imagine placing everything about your addiction into this imaginary skin. As it builds up in this outer blanket, you concentrate more and more, until you feel that every trace of your addiction becomes accumulated within this imaginary skin. Still concentrating with your imagination, have this addiction built up to such a point you decide to cast the entire skin away from you. As you cast your skin away, think of casting it away physically as well as emotionally. In your mind's eye, you finally feel a great release -- all the discomfort that you once felt has left you.

When you think about the snake shedding its skin, you realize in making use of the idea, you can shed your addicted skin, permanently. You see and feel everything let go; every discomfort you've every known is being shed before your eyes. As you feel this happening, you look behind you and see the skin you shed on the ground, disintegrating before your eyes. Finally, as you confirm that the skin has vanished, you realize that you have become free at last. In your subconscious mind, you actually believe this has happened, and you acknowledge that your entire addiction is gone -- all of it -- gone away, never to trouble you again. Now, you feel glad to have such new, beautiful skin.

Once more: Finally, as you confirm that the skin has vanished, you realize that you have become free at last. In your subconscious mind, you actually believe this has happened, and you acknowledge that your entire addiction is gone -- all of it -- gone away, never to trouble you again. Now, you feel glad to have such new, beautiful skin.

To Quit Smoking - *The Tombstone Imagery*

Imagine walking into a graveyard carrying a sack over your shoulder. It is daylight and people witness your actions as you put down the sack, pick up a shovel and dig a small grave. With a smile on your face, you empty the contents on the ground in front of you. When cartons of your favorite cigarette pile up, along with hundreds of loose cigarettes, you take the shovel and toss the disgusting cigarettes into the grave. You imagine all the stinks, all the inconveniences and all the misery you felt before you quit smoking as you shovel the sand. You are happy, because all the misery of your gross smoking habit is buried along with those cigarettes. After you finish packing down the sand using the shovel, you walk away from the cemetery. When you turn to look back, you see the people smiling in approval. Chiseled into the tombstone are the words: "__Here lies the death of my ugly, bad habit -- Smoking__."

To Quit Smoking - *The Bulldozer Imagery*

Imagine getting into a bulldozer and digging a deep hole in the middle of a park. After filling a dump truck with a load of sand, you climb down from the bulldozer and empty all your cigarettes into the hole. Imagine tossing cartons of cigarettes into the hole -- everything related to your addiction, including the undesirable habit, the nasty smoke, the shortness of breath, the loss of control and the feeling of being possessed -- everything.

As you toss in the last cigarette dangling from your mouth, you pick up several boulders and, furiously, toss them down on top of the cigarettes. As you do so, you say verbally: **I'm fed up, and I'm not going to be possessed any longer!** *Now, you climb into the dump truck and pour the sand into the hole, stopping only after making sure it is completely filled.*

You are smiling and proud of yourself as you sit back and imagine the future: The spot where you are sitting is now covered with tall Birch and Maple trees. Hundreds of people are gathered there with you, celebrating breathing the fresh oxygen produced by the trees. In your subconscious mind, you record the details of this imagined, future event. As you take in deep breaths, you suddenly realize your breathing feels clean. The thought of being relieved of your cigarette addiction feels absolutely pleasing to you.

To Quit Nail Biting

Your shoulders and arms are relaxed, your legs and feet are relaxed, and all your muscles are completely loose. As you continue to relax, there is a deep opening to your subconscious, which listens intently to my voice. Your subconscious pays close attention to my words and records them into your memory.

*Imagine your body raising up to the blue sky, and settling on a fluffy white cloud. Resting on that cloud in the sky, imagine three giant screens. In the **middle screen**, imagine yourself in your current state lying on the couch down below. You are resting on the cloud in the blue sky looking at the screen, looking at yourself dressed, and completely relaxed. Now, make this **middle screen** become enlarged, and imagine yourself, including all the colors, as vivid as you can.*

*On the **left screen**, imagine the negative image of yourself. This negative image shows you sitting up **biting your disgusting nails** nervously, while you are being uncomfortably tense. Enlarge that screen showing yourself with a disgusted, uneasy look on your face. Suddenly, your attitude is that you are entirely fed up with **biting your nails**. While you feel thoroughly discouraged because you can't beat the habit, you turn and go to the screen on the right.*

*On this **right screen** is the same large image of yourself in the sitting position, but with your hand removed from your face. Now, you see a smile on your face as you look at your hands and see clean, healthy fingernails. Your attitude is that you are happy that to have kicked the habit, that you have become permanently **relieved of biting your nails**. The feeling of relief is overwhelming, because you feel confident the habit is gone forever. And in the wide opening to your subconscious, you acknowledge this, and see that this is in your best interest. The image of being **free from biting your nails** makes you feel great. The air is clean all around you, and you take in the fresh air. You acknowledge that this is the way to feel, this is the way to be. You feel good about having a healthy outlook on life.*

*Momentarily, you notice that the **left screen** has completely vanished. And now, with the **right screen** becoming much more enlarged, you see yourself with a very happy smile on your face.*

*You whisper to yourself: **I'm glad you let go of me, you disgusting habit, because, I too, have let go of my need to bite my nails.** You are delighted that you let it go! You are delighted that the desire has left you for good. And you are **totally** relieved that the urges that left you feeling possessed, as well as distressed and stressed out, have gone by the wayside.*

FULL-DEPTH COMBINED INDUCTION

As you may have concluded, achieving successful results generally takes a bit more than half an hour. To fulfill the subjects' needs you will have to perform many helpful suggestions, much guided imagery, and a lot of encouragement. In addition to solving various psychological problems, or emotional conflicts, the following inductions were combined in order to resolve the subject's needs.

Fulfilling The Subjects' Needs

HYPNOTIST: (with the subject sitting or lying)

Have the subject "Go into" ***The Trance Zone,*** as described below, then continue with the hypnotic suggestions.

*I'd like you to form "**the hypnotic eye**" by placing the thumb and forefinger of either hand together, and place your hand at your side. This is the eye to your subconscious, which puts you into **The Trance Zone**. Now, I'd like you to lift your **eyes up to the eyebrows** and, when you feel like it, close them. Keeping your eyes up take in a **deep yawn,** and recite: "This is how I go into **The Trance Zone**."*

*Very good -- that is how you "Go Into" **The Trance Zone**, where only good things happen. In that wide opening to your subconscious, you are listening intently to my voice.*

Your arms and legs are flexible, relaxed. As I count down from 30 by 2's, continue breathing evenly, inhaling through your nose and exhaling through your mouth. 30, 28, 26, 24 . . . With each breath you sink deeper and deeper and deeper into a relaxed state of mind. 22, 20, 18, 16 . . . You no longer want anything. Become passive as you listen to my voice. Let yourself go . . . . 14 . . . 12 . . . 10 . . . 8 . . . 6 . . . 4 . . . 2 . . . 0.

Let it be . . . Let it happen. Nothing bothers or distracts you. Nothing bad or unusual is going to happen. Your head is clear. Your mind is free of all problems. You rejoice in this sense of peace and well being that envelops you from head to foot. Feel this wonderful relaxation which spreads more and more throughout your body. Feel the new looseness and weightlessness of your body.

In this wonderful state of peace, you have an opening to the subconscious -- wider and wider this opening is becoming. Your subconscious is registering all my words. The gentle words of my voice are being deeply engraved there as you listen intently to my suggestions. You are listening very intently as I proceed with care. Listen closely to these words as I say them to you: You feel peaceful; you feel very quiet emotionally. You feel calm physically, and you enjoy the peace, the quiet, and the calm that exudes from within you.

(continue)

Fulfilling The Subjects' Needs (continued)

In that wide opening to your subconscious, you are listening intently to my voice. Perhaps you already know about your subconscious mind's extraordinary powers of self-healing, and how the right side of your brain controls the functioning of your entire body. The right side of your brain, the subconscious mind, knows how to regulate your breathing even while you are sleeping, and knows how to regulate your circulatory system, how to carry the right nutrients to all the parts of your body that need them.

This brilliant part of your mind also knows how to instruct every cell in your body to heal itself, to improve, to feel more comfortable and to be healthy and sound, cell by incredible cell. And I don't know how fast your body is healing itself now, but your mind knows just how to accelerate the healing that is already taking place in your body.

As you are resting comfortably, you will notice that your eyes are closed tight, very tight. They are stuck so tight you are not able to open them. In a moment I will ask you to try to open them - you will not be able to do so. You will find they are sealed tight; they are stuck firmly together. You may be able to manage the muscle groups around your eyes, but not your eyelids. No matter how hard you try, you will be unable to open your eyes.

When I count down from 3 to zero, you will find it impossible to open your eyes and you will go deeper into hypnosis. 3 . . . Your eyelids are sealed tight, 2 . . . They are stuck tight, 1 . . . They are stuck firmly together, Zero . . . Try, but you are unable to open them. Stop trying, and go deeper into hypnosis.

As you listen to my voice, your entire body becomes more relaxed, more and more. While your muscles become free of tension, my voice is going deeper into that opening to you subconscious. Now that you are totally relaxed and feeling completely free of tension, imagine all your worries, frustrations, and hostilities leaving your body permanently.

Imagine that all that negativity is flowing out of your lungs and pores like poisonous gases leaving you feeling completely refreshed, recharged, and rejuvenated. Right now, know in your mind that you fully and freely release all grudges held from the past. Fully and freely loosen and let go of all anger, resentment and pent-up emotional disorders. Feel the relief of unloading all this excess baggage from your mind. From this day forward your load is finally light. Your burdens are light and all your worries and problems have just become trivial.

(continue)

Fulfilling The Subjects' Needs   (continued)

You may remember back to a time in your life that you broke a bone and had to go to a doctor to have the bone set and a cast put on you. But your subconscious mind knows that it wasn't the doctor who healed you -- it was you and your body that ultimately healed you, cell by amazingly incredible cell. Yes, your subconscious has the intelligence and the power to heal anything inside of you on an intercellular basis.

You may have read or heard, or perhaps you know from your own experience that athletes need to take great care in order for their bodies to grow strong, and recuperate from overwork. And as you rest your body now, like an athlete rests, your body can become stronger and healthier, revitalizing your nerves, your blood, and even your brain cells. And although the aging process is always causing deterioration, it doesn't have to follow that your vision, your memory or your legs have to become weakened.

And I don't know if you have already felt certain sensations in your body, signaling that the healing process has already started, but you can be sure that while you are in this deep, resting trance state, your body is already healing itself. You can enjoy feeling relaxed, knowing your body can accelerate and improve your immune system even now, as you enjoy this rest. Know for sure that you can rely on your inner self; that you can count on that part of you in your subconscious that knows exactly what to do, and exactly how to do it.

Perhaps you remember a time when you had a cut that was so deep you felt it wouldn't heal, or perhaps you had a bout with the flu. You probably went to a doctor for treatment, but then even as you slept and played and worked, your body did all the healing. While your body has a tremendous ability to heal itself, the subconscious mind actually serves as the regulator of every possible part, every possible function. Not only does your subconscious have the ability to perform all the healing you need, it has the capability to initiate peaceful rest and sleep when called upon.

Your subconscious mind is capable of extraordinary recouping powers, and endless capacities, even while you enjoy your peaceful trance. You <u>know</u> that, and you can continue to allow your body to rejuvenate while you relax and enjoy feeling peaceful. That deep place in your subconscious mind acknowledges all this and remembers to call upon this information. And even after you come out of this exhilarating trance state, you can trust your ability to initiate healing whenever it is needed. When you go to bed at night, you take delight in the fact that sleeping serves to replenish your entire body, hour after hour, cell by remarkable cell.

(continue)

Fulfilling The Subjects' Needs   (continued)

Now, breathing in deeply, take in full breaths as if you can picture the oxygen filling your lungs. As you continue to breathe deeply, imagine the oxygen as a magic healing vapor. The deeper you breathe, the deeper this healing vapor circulates into your entire body. The more oxygen you take in, the more you feel the effect of its healing powers. Visualize a clear picture of this healing vapor going into your lungs and circulating throughout your nervous system.

__Imagine a large softgel__ containing a liquid tranquilizer being lodged in the upper portion of your brain. Let it become loose and slowly travel down the head, and settle into the back of your neck. Now, let the softgel dissolve, allowing the liquid tranquilizer to flow down your throat and settle there. Feel the liquid dissolving into your throat. And now, allow the liquid tranquilizer to settle into every part of your body starting from your throat, and seeping down to the bottom of your feet. Feel its tranquilizing effect as it seeps down your chest and arms. Feel its loosening and healing effects as it seeps into every muscle, every ligament and into every joint.

__Imagine every part of your body__ becoming so relaxed it seems like jelly. Allow this liquid tranquilizer to relieve every pain, every arthritic condition, every restrictive feeling in you body. Allow this tranquilizer to balance your entire nervous system, your complete immune system as you focus on allowing your mind to come to complete rest. You are free of all worry, free of all tension as you drift off into your hypnotic trance. Deeper and deeper you go into this deep trance state; deeper and deeper you go into hypnosis. The deeper you go into hypnosis, the deeper you go into this trance state. Deeper and deeper, you drift off into your beautiful, restful hypnotic trance.

__Imagine every part of your body__ becoming so relaxed it seems like jelly. Allow this liquid tranquilizer to relieve every pain, every arthritic condition, every restrictive feeling in you body. Allow this tranquilizer to balance your entire nervous system, your complete immune system, as you focus on allowing your mind to come to complete rest. You are free of all worry, free of all tension as you drift off into your hypnotic trance. Deeper and deeper you go into this deep trance state; deeper and deeper you go into hypnosis. The deeper you go into hypnosis, the deeper you go into this trance state. Deeper and deeper, you drift off into your beautiful, restful hypnotic trance.

(continue)

Fulfilling The Subjects' Needs (continued)

Imagine a large softgel containing a liquid tranquilizer being lodged in the upper portion of your brain. Let it become loose and slowly travel down the head, and settle into the back of your neck. Now, let the softgel dissolve, allowing the liquid tranquilizer to flow down your throat and settle there. Feel the liquid dissolving into your throat. And now, allow the liquid tranquilizer to settle into every part of your body starting from your throat, and seeping down to the bottom of your feet. Feel its tranquilizing effect as it seeps down your chest and arms. Feel its loosening and healing effects as it seeps into every muscle, every ligament and into every joint.

Imagine every part of your body becoming so relaxed it seems like jelly. Allow this liquid tranquilizer to relieve every pain, every arthritic condition, every restrictive feeling in you body. Allow this tranquilizer to balance your entire nervous system, your complete immune system as you focus on allowing your mind to come to complete rest. You are free of all worry, free of all tension as you drift off into your hypnotic trance. Deeper and deeper you go into this deep trance state; deeper and deeper you go into hypnosis. The deeper you go into hypnosis, the deeper you go into this trance state. Deeper and deeper, you drift off into your beautiful, restful hypnotic trance.

As I go into that wide opening to your subconscious, I see that your memory has been improved. And the ease with which you are able to influence those around you to gain love, admiration, opportunities and wealth may seem amazing, but at this very moment all the above have become possible through the powers of your subconscious mind.

Your subconscious mind has recorded this and will remember everything that has been said. Before I bring you out of this trance, allow a brief pause as a way thanking God for the infinite riches flowing into your life.

When I count to five, you will open your eyes feeling alert, refreshed and alive. 1 . . . 2 . . . every part of you is better than ever before, 3 . . . you are feeling alert and refreshed, 4 . . . you are alert, refreshed and fully alive, 5 . . . Open your eyes.

PART FIVE

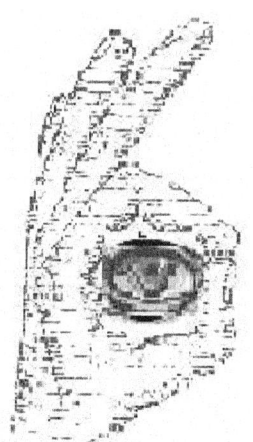

CHAPTER NINE
9

MANIFESTATIONS OF THE HIGHEST KIND

9   TRANSFORMATION
VISUALIZATION:

The hands can become a direct link between the subconscious and the supernatural and atomic forces of the universe. So, be transformed by the renewal of your mind: that you may prove what is the perfect and complete will of God. This becomes obvious in the following quotation from the bible:

You will make your prayer to Him, and he will hear you;
And you will pay your vows.
You will decide on a matter, and it will be established for you,
And light will shine on your ways.

Job 22: 27-28

CHAPTER NINE
9

MANIFESTATIONS OF THE HIGHEST KIND

One of the basic understandings of the **Stanislavski Method** of acting, is that the fingertips can be developed to such a degree they can become the actor's eyes. In "**Method**" acting, this serves to extend the actor's emotions and kinetic senses. To the blind person, the fingertips record the Braille and transform the meanings directly into visual images. With the use of the hands the blind are, sometimes, capable of sensing what emotions are coming through – merely by touching the person's face.

In a documentary called *The Ring of Fire* shown on PBS television, they filmed a man actually igniting newspapers with the electricity produced from his bare hands and fingers. Sometimes when we pray, we place our hands together and, with great faith, witness a miracle.

In demonstrating the powers of transformation, I cite the following example of metamorphosis: A larva produced by the caterpillar develops its cocoon from its worm-like pupa stage. Suddenly, one morning at the dawning of light, it transforms from its larva into its imago and manifests into an amazingly colorful, flying insect. Through a natural, though somewhat mysterious process, the caterpillar has transformed into a Monarch butterfly. This is, perhaps, the most dramatic example of transformation, in that the physical body has become completely changed. But remember: Its **spirit** has also been changed in the process. It is not surprising that it flies thousands of miles, freely demonstrating its colorful, black and orange wing patterns.

Obviously, we are not about to change our bodies completely – but we can change everything else about us by virtue of self-improvement, especially by renewing the **spirit**. This can be accomplished with creative mind-body techniques, using the hands to heal patients of physical and mental disorders. Used in concert with hypnosis, great strides can be accomplished within the mind-body research community. Within the contents of this chapter, you will learn to implement a highly effective, innovative way to treat patients through a process called the ***Trance-FormationVisualizer*** ™.

TRANCE MANIFESTATIONS

Illumination Therapy ™

    Because of its relative association to ***The Trance Zone*** ™, I have devised an effective posturing of the hands, called the ***Trance-FormationVisualizer*** ™ for the purpose of establishing a direct line of communication with the supernatural, spiritual forces. Obviously, I have based the name on the power of transformation, as well as the vivid visualizations that occur during the trance state.

    To alleviate any skepticism, place the fingers together as shown below in **Illustration 5-1** and press firmly. While positioning the hands in this manner, apply firm pressure, fingers-to-fingers, creating a cage-like sphere. Then, stare and concentrate on the inside of your hands until you begin to feel the nerves responding. When you feel this energy keep pressing and concentrating until you can actually feel the warmth traveling from your hands up into your arms. Imagine that your hands are getting warmer and warmer until you feel the heat traveling from your palms up into your arms, elbows, shoulders, and into your entire body, from your head to your feet.

    However, skeptical, don't give up trying. With a little practice, you will be able to imagine this happening. You will become amazed at how much your hands respond to your conscious and subconscious thoughts. Remember the expression, "cold hands; warm heart?" Well, people with cold hands generally have poor circulation, or some other chemical imbalance. Practicing this exercise could be of great help, along with looking into proper diet and physical exercise.

    At some point, when you have made this high-intensity connection, focus on this energy field you have created within the sphere and begin to imagine visualizing what you need, or wish to see in your mind's eye. This is where **IMAGERY** comes into play. By utilizing the power of this ***Trance-FormationVisualizer*** ™ you will be able to create images, perform cures, overcome addictions, conquer your worst fears, or even summon prosperity. You can even begin to speak to this transformer to the degree you receive surprisingly positive answers when you ask to be allowed to see visual solutions to your problems. After all, thinking in images is something we inherited from our ancestors.

    The possibilities are endless. In developing this transformer as a tool, one could feasibly develop a photographic memory by placing it over the subject to be memorized, or create a desirable condition, even to envision people or places using it as a crystal ball or television screen. With practice, one could even develop enough intensity to become a psychic. All this can be accomplished simply by activating your imagination. The secret is to practice developing the energy field until the sphere becomes spiritually electrifying, as well as supernaturally charged.

    And, speaking of possibilities, this concept could become something of a revelation in regard to mind-body healing. Since the 1970's, a process called therapeutic touch, or TT, has been taught at more than 80 universities. This process, mentioned above, could be practiced as **Illumination Therapy™**, or **IT**, by developing the energy field, opening the hands and illuminating different parts of the patient's body.

Illumination Therapy ™ (ontinued)

If the healer practicing **Illumination Therapy** ™, could focus on the sphere as pulling in laser-like, illuminated light from the universe, the results would be so effective it would stagger the imagination. Used in combination with hypnosis, there are no limitations as to the benefits to humanity. As I said, the uses of the *Trance-FormationVisualizer* ™ are endless.

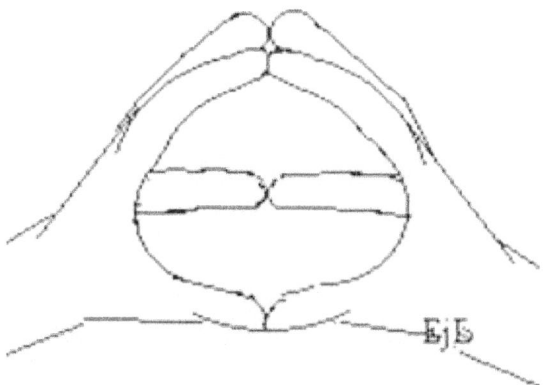

TRANCE-FORMATION VISUALIZER™ -- Illustration 9-1
(This is IT!)

This is that special hypnotic zone where dramatic changes actually take place within your psyche. It is that special state of mind, that magical place, where ideals, desires, and dreams become transformed into reality.
*(If nothing else, using **Illumination Therapy**™ on yourself with your eyes closed creates one of the deepest states of tranquility known -- and without prescriptions!)*

When placing the hands together to form the *Trance-FormationVisualizer,* it functions as a transformer producing the power of transformation, as well as visualizing the past, present, or future. The use of visualization can also become a powerful tool in influencing the mind through thoughts or pictures, thereby transforming the body from sickness to splendid health. (See **Illustration 9-2** below.

(Note: The healer, the hypnotist, or the subject can prepare to enhance the power of the hands by massaging them in a special way. First massage the fingers, one-by-one, increasing the blood flow; then slowly press each hand backwards at the wrist, loosening the tension; next, flip the hand over and pull each finger inside toward the wrist, loosening up the muscles and tendons. Finally, interweave the fingers between both hands, squeezing and manipulating until all the joints become free of tension – and then rub the hands together, stimulating them.)

118 *The Trance Zone*

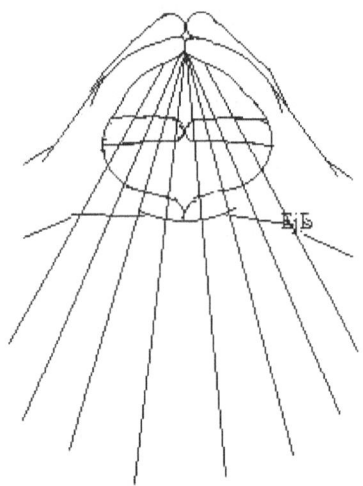

Illustration 9-2 (This is IT!) -- *Trance-Formation Visualizer ™*
To put **Illumination Therapy™ (IT)** into practice, focus as described above and think of a white spiritual light coming in through your subconscious mind.

While concentrating on the subject, think of this illuminating light beaming down, creating energy as it passes through the body, and into the hands. Then, focusing on the sphere with full intensity, transform that energy down and into the subject's body. As you do this, focus intently on the **vital organs**, curing the subject of any ailments or disorders.
(See **Illustration 9-3** below.

Illustration 9-3 (This is also IT!)

USING The Trance-Formation Visualizer™
Or Illumination Therapy™

EXAMPLE -- 1:
HYPNOTIST – AS HEALER

Have the subject "Go Into" ***The Trance Zone.***

Then recite: *This radiant, pure light within me is energizing and transforming your whole being in such positive ways multitudes of miracles are taking place mentally, physically and emotionally. This inner, illuminated light has created within you a sound mind and body, and is curing you of all disease and disorders. As you concentrate on feeling the warmth of my hands, think only of tranquility as you continue to breathe deeply, steadily, and evenly. As you listen to my voice, you are confident, having the knowledge that you are in good hands – hands that have very effective healing powers.*

Know that I am here to activate, stimulate and rejuvenate all the elements of you mind, body and spirit. Concentrate on this knowledge as you breathe deeply, having the incoming oxygen replenish your entire immune system, your entire being. Know that my energy is flowing through me to you, in order that you become well. Know this, believe it, and accept it as a gift to you coming from above.

EXAMPLE -- 2:
HYPNOTIST – AS HEALER

Have the subject "Go Into" ***The Trance Zone.***

Then recite: *As you continue breathing deeply and calmly, you know in your heart that your ideal state of mind is that of calmness and tranquility. In this peace that encompasses your whole being, you feel almost as if time has stopped. All worries are put aside, all tension and pain has left your body. In that wide opening to your subconscious, you feel you are in complete control of the healing powers of your own immune system, as well as all your vital organs. In this state of tranquility, your subconscious mind prevents any disease from disrupting your mental or physical health.*

EXAMPLE -- 3:
SUBJECT – SELF-HYPNOSIS (HEALING using the *Trance-Formation Visualizer*)

Subject Recite: *Through the powers of this illuminating light flowing through me, I command my subconscious to become free of smoking and all the undesirable things that go with it. I command my subconscious mind to free me of being possessed by this disgusting and depressing need to smoke. By the power of this illuminating light flowing through me, I now release all the binds that once held me hostage.*

7 SECRETS OF ATTRACTING LUCK

"If it be not now, yet it will come. Being ready is all." – William Shakespeare
In other words:
"If it is not already here, it will come. <u>Being ready is everything</u>. "EjL

As described all throughout this book, you already possess the power of releasing the unlimited potential within you. By applying the principles contained in this book, you already possess the key to unlocking the doors that have held you captive. The only limitations are those which lie within the mentality of the person creating, or denying them.

The **<u>7 Secrets Of Attracting Luck</u>** have been revealed so that you may have a full understanding of what it takes to develop a sound mind and body, as well as to reverse bad luck, or to turn chance into opportune luck. They are listed below in the order of prioritization. The first thing to do is to establish a **Method** of approaching the issue. Then, muster the **Motivation** to apply **Meditation** and **Matriculate** it by altering the **Mentality** and acquiring **Magnetism**, and in time, things will **Manifest** far beyond your wildest expectations.

But, before beginning to apply the knowledge of these secrets, follow the procedures as described below. First, learn to focus on hands, either with the eyes open or closed. Lift the hands above the head and run them down your body to get the feel of how your illuminated light affects you. Then, imagine the subject you wish to influence and focus, applying positive thoughts regarding the desired outcome, whether to mesmerize, or bring change.

However, before expecting to receive the appropriate outcome, you must first learn to <u>apply</u> the **<u>7 Secrets Of Attracting Luck.</u>**. For example, to have the number **<u>7</u>** become lucky for you, hold the hands over a sheet of paper with the number enlarged and focus, influencing it with your positive thoughts. Or, to become lucky at winning, or lucky in love, focus on the sphere as if it were a crystal ball and visualize the intended results. **(See Illustrations 9-1 and 9-2 above)**

Perhaps the most important thing to do is to develop and practice your own way to focus on the sphere, pulling in laser-like, illuminated light from the universe. Remember, a little prayer definitely helps.

<u>Illumination Therapy</u> ™

***<u>"You will decide on a matter,
and it will be established for you,
and light will shine on your ways."</u>***

Using the concept of the ***Trance-Formation Visualizer*** on yourself (as in the above **EXAMPLE 3,)** "Go Into" ***The Trance Zone*** and experiment with its power. Study, apply, and practice the **7 Secrets Of Attracting Luck** as listed below and, before you know it, a life filled with fortunate experiences will manifest before you – in real life. (Note: After going into the trance, it is no longer necessary to keep the eyes closed. With little practice, you will be able remain in the trance state while focusing on the sphere.)

To demonstrate another example -- after energizing the hands, lift and hold the ***Trance-Formation Visualizer*** overhead. Then concentrate on drawing supernatural power from above while reciting: *Since I am through with facing poverty, Infinite riches are flowing freely into my life. Each and every day I am growing more and more prosperous.* While doing this, visualize as vividly as possible, money floating down, surrounding you with fifty and hundred dollar bills. In applying this concept as instructed, I'm sure you will agree that the possibilities are endless.

1. **Method** – As explained above, the most important thing to do is to develop and practice your own way to focus on the sphere, pulling in laser-like, illuminated light from the universe. Everyone has a plan or an idea of how to become a winner, but only those who have a way of tapping into the universal powers become truly successful at it. For success does not just mean wealth, but also the gratification, self-esteem and integrity gained from following ones pureness of heart.

    There may be a better method of finding true mastery over fate, but I have yet to find anything as powerful as this **Illumination Therapy ™**.

2. **Motivation** – There are many ways to become motivated. The question is which motive works for **you**; what does it take to get **you** to feel the spark and the drive to accomplish your objective? Believe it or not, the four D's: Disposition, Discipline, Dexterity and Determination have a great deal of impact on whether or not you receive positive results.

    For example, your Disposition has a lot to do with your attitude, your frame of mind, your mood, in that it affects your drive to become a winner. Once you acquire the Discipline to take control of your destiny, you will find that things begin to fall into place. Your Dexterity, on the other hand, has much influence on the way you comprehend the road ahead of you. Above all, you must acquire enough Determination to firmly set your course, whether by committing to decisions, or by setting strong enough objectives that will inspire you to become motivated.

3. **Meditation** – You can definitely influence the outcome of your fate through the power of mind-altering affirmations, or prayers. Or by inducing hypnotic suggestions such as: *Like a special friend, I am looked after and supported by my higher spiritual power and the special forces of the universe in all areas of my health, wealth and relationships.*
You will find many more ways of acquiring the powers of meditation through the practice of hypnotic suggestions, mind-altering affirmations, and prayers.

4. **Matriculate** – In order to penetrate the part of subconscious mind, which is responsible for producing good luck, "go into" ***The Trance Zone*** and ask to receive the proper guidance regarding your requests. Ask for the right answers to your dilemmas, or how you can turn <u>chance</u> into opportunity. Whether fortune, health, or love that are your aspirations, it is all there, waiting to be called upon. All you have to do is tap into your source.

5. **Mentality** – One of the important keys to receiving good fortune is the mind-set, the mental attitude, or mode of thinking. When focusing with an optimistic heart, together with child-like enthusiasm, nothing seems impossible – therefore the possibilities of successful outcomes become something inherent. Misfortune, or unfortunate experiences, commonly associated with being "bad luck" irrefutably stem from conditions that instill fears. With a sincere attempt to become introspective, begin to examine the possible masks of fear that might have been affecting your attitude -- fears that actually serve in draining positive energy.

    The list of masks that cause fear is extensive, the major ones being as follows: anger; jealousy; lust; ego; aggressiveness; depression; possession; obsession; prejudice; over-protectiveness; smothering; insecurity; judgment; unhappiness and dissatisfaction. All of these fears interfere with our natural elements, from love to supernatural existence. At this juncture, you may ask, what doesn't consist of fear? Love, spiritual faith, and loyalty to God - that's about it.

6. **Magnetism** --- At the fore, spiritual harmony with the universe, better understood as charisma, is the most effective way to generate attraction. Because Personal Magnetism rules the world, and since everything indicates that great magnetic forces develop in persons who know how to purify their bodies through love and healthful living, it is to your personal embellishment to participate accordingly.

    To begin with, try inducing hypnotic suggestions such as: *Like a magnet, with special compelling attributes, I attract good fortune and abundance in my life. Since abundance is my natural state of being, I readily accept it now.*

7. **Manifest** – Manifestation is a remarkable phenomenon, a source governed by luck.

    Good luck is based on harmony, not discord; organization, not chaos; capability, not inadequacy: shrewdness, not stupidity; relaxation, not tension; anticipation, not hindsight; resolution, not procrastination; decisiveness, not doubt; trust, not disbelief; and finally, it is based on acceptance, not denial. With a keen eye, whether focusing on monetary, physical, physiological, or spiritual power, you can finally look forward to **Manifestations Of The Highest Kind**.

    Of all the forces on earth, luck still prevails as one of the most powerful, good or bad. Given in the information above, as well as the descriptions below, the secrets to good luck have been revealed to you. All you have to do now is apply them. Since the number <u>7</u> is considered lucky, I have included it under that number. But remember that the thought of having anything become lucky is only as good as its positive conception, where the unprecedented optimistic reaps the rewards of being a formidable winner. The **Formula** is described on the following page. **Good luck**.

LUCK – The Formula:

Leverage the possibilities. Nurture your advantages for all their worth. Play your cards, but know when to fold them. Sometimes it might better to take quick, small loss, rather than to chance a drawn out, large loss. After all this information is computed, acknowledged and incorporated, the chances are that you will become lucky enough to amass great wealth -- but remember this: millionaires have no real freedom. They are too busy holding onto to their money, investing it, and therefore becoming enslaved to it. So, be careful of what you ask for, because you are very apt get it.

Ultimately follow goals to completion. Many years ago, sometime in the early 1900's, a little known writer came up with the notion that he could write a good story about a girl and her dog. The two became entrapped in a cyclone, and then became carried into another time, another land, where the girl would meet three very odd people. He had great faith in this story, although it was just a children's story.

I suppose he hoped that it would become published, but the author didn't write for the money, or the success -- he wrote because he loved his work with a **passion**. It was something that **motivated** him; gave him **purpose** -- he **needed** to create. His name was L. Frank Baum -- and that children's story became so popular it was turned into that famous movie called, *The Wizard Of Oz*. Yes, the road to his success definitely became paved with a yellow, brick road – a gold one, in fact.

Calculate the risks and Commit to them. Speaking of roads, that illusive road to success has been paved with many a failure. Yet, without taking calculated risks, there can be no great gains. Since the difference between success and failure is similar to the difference between winning and losing, we are always focused on the struggle between them. It is there that the chance of becoming lucky, or not, comes into play.
In realizing that, the ability to increase the odds of winning becomes, not only based on the manner in which the calculations are made, but on the determination to commit to those calculations.

Ken is a rarely used word encompassing a wide range of Knowledge.

Ken not only encompasses an understanding beyond one's self, its meaning, in addition to vision, is comprised of cognizance and mental perception. Without considering all the aspects of **Ken**, making the proper calculations would leave the individual seeking luck incapable of drawing the proper conclusion.

Every bit of gathered information must be analyzed and scrutinized before making any kind of decision regarding the lucky, or unlucky, aspect of the deduction. For example: considering the three elements that could go wrong when betting on horseracing: the quality of the horse, the shape of the jockey, and the condition of the track, betting would be fruitless if either of these elements were miscalculated. And then, what about whether the horse was running on the outside rail, or whether it had never experienced a muddy track before? Here, the use of **Ken** would certainly make a difference – understanding, vision, cognizance, mental perception.

LUCK is not made – it is thought up; envisioned good, or bad!

Being in the right place at an opportune time also has a lot to do with luck. But, in being at that place at the particular time can be brought about by keeping an open line to those universal laws. The late millionaire, Howard Hughes, being stranded in the desert, once promised a man over a half million dollars for lending him a quarter, merely because he stopped the car to pick him up. Was this coincidence, or chance?

Or was it because of the man's giving nature. "Give, and you shall receive," is but one element of that universal law.

To insure that good luck will manifest itself, I have added the final letter -- **Y**, and its definition to the equation, as listed below.

Yes, I am lucky -- Emblazon these words in your mind.

    As an attempt to demonstrate the kind of perception it takes to make a proper calculation, I cite the following bit of information only as an example as to concept.

       On Easter Sunday of this year, a publicist friend of mine invited me to dinner at Ben's Restaurant in New York City. While being introduced to the owner, I happened to notice the giant-sized horseshoe hanging on the wall. Since I already knew how greatly successful the restaurant had become, I asked Ben, the owner, whether it made any difference whether the horseshoe was hanging upside down, or not. To my surprise, I learned that it <u>did</u> make a difference – his response was that the horseshoe must be hung with its legs turned upward in order to **attract luck** and **hold it inside**. Armed with this kind of knowledge (**Ken**,) whether suspicious in nature, or not, a person would be better equipped to draw the proper conclusion and proceed accordingly.

       All good luck is based on desire, belief, and expectation. The key being: neither to allow negative influence from without, nor to entertain negative thoughts from within. *Playboy's* Hugh Hefner got what he wished for -- his vast fortune began with a solitary wish from the wishing well right on his property when he was poor. He became "lucky" because he **desired**, **believed**, and **expected** his wish to come true. In essence, by having great faith in the powers that be, he enabled innate good fortune, already within him, to manifest itself.

       In conclusion, using every means possible, make sure you <u>apply</u> the key words: **Desire**, **Belief**, and **Expectation**. Congratulations, you now possess the most powerful tools ever developed to attract **good luck**. Now you can prepare yourself for that winning streak you've been yearning for. By the way, it is the culmination of **ken** and its key elements, which actually bring about winning streaks. The rest is in your **hands**; (it's always in good taste to throw in a pun, now and then.)

Now, because of your **Determination**, you have learned what it takes to become **Lucky**.

Congratulations . . . **LUCKY!**

CHAPTER TEN
10

SELF-HYPNOSIS INDUCTION >TECHNIQUES<

10   SELF-HYPNOSIS
AUTOSUGGESTION:

Again, Webster's New World Dictionary refers self-hypnosis to autohypnosis and defines it as "The act of hypnotizing oneself or the state of being so hypnotized.

Actually, through autosuggestion the subject makes suggestions to the self, effecting the mind, thoughts, and bodily functions, thereby becoming hypnotized. When the subject performs hypnosis on the self, the process is called self-hypnosis or the act of self-hypnotism. Self-hypnotic suggestion, self-hypnosis, or autosuggestion is that state of hypnosis induced by the subject.

Webster's New World Dictionary also describes subliminal as being "Below the threshold of consciousness or apprehension; specifically involving or using stimuli intended to take effect subconsciously."

By definition, it is obvious that all hypnosis, consciously audible or not, is subliminal, including self-hypnosis or autosuggestion.

CHAPTER TEN
10

SELF-HYPNOSIS INDUCTION TECHNIQUES
(with examples, in steps)

Currently, many hospitals in New York offer hypnosis as part of their mind-body programs because they are so profound in changing the patients' physiology – decreasing oxygen consumption and heart rate, even altering brain waves.

In fact, during mid-1998 the Vanderbilt Clinic had been awarded twenty million dollars for its research in mind-body programs. Even as I work on the completion this manuscript, there is a wave of renewed interest in hypnosis because of its highly effective influence on the healing process, as well as the restoration of the mental faculties.

By utilizing the instructions and practicing the applications of ***The Trance Zone,*** you can gain access to your programming. The secret to tapping the depths of your mind is to go into the subconscious, where the true source of power rules. This is where you can unleash the power of your subconscious mind, and change negative habits of thought and action into what you desire them to be -- this is where you can alter your programming for the better.

Penetrating The Subconscious Mind

Perhaps the most important thing to bear in mind regarding accessing the hypnotic state is this: In order to **penetrate the subconscious mind**, reaching a complete state of serenity allows the incoming messages to take hold more effectively. The more the subject is able to relax, the longer positive suggestions will endure. Reaching the state of tranquility also serves to disarm the conscious mind, thus allowing the subconscious to override all unnecessary censoring. This is one of the reasons exercise is stressed so frequently. (See the exercises in Part Eight.)

Empowering The Subconscious Mind

Suggestions such as *I will **not** think of an apple with a worm inside*, causes just the opposite affect. First, because *I will **not*** relates to the future, in a negative sense - the subconscious only acknowledges the present - and it acknowledges suggestions in a positive sense. Secondly, the statement, *an apple with a **worm inside,*** evokes a **vision** of a ***rotten apple with a worm inside***. This is because the subconscious overlooks the negative term, ***not***.

The hypnotist, always looking on the brighter, positive side, would rather choose to evoke this alternative positive state, *I **can see** an apple with its **rosy colors.***

The Ketchup Bottle Demonstration

To understand the basic concept of all hypnosis, consider the following example: Imagine that the ketchup bottle, below, (**Demonstration 10-1**) represents the physical and spiritual makeup of a human being. Imagine the **cap** as representing the conscious mind, and the contents of the bottle representing the subconscious. If this being was told that the contents inside was Green instead of Red, it would not readily accept it because the visual, critical, and conscious, mind has accepted Red as being a fact.

cap

Demonstration 10-1   Now, while undergoing hypnosis, and removing the **cap**, or the conscious mind, the being was told that the contents was Green, instead of Red, it would readily accept it. This is because the subconscious mind does not know the difference between fact and fiction. Relatively speaking, without going into the subconscious (the contents), this new belief would not be possible, since the conscious mind edits, criticizes, denies, and restricts information. The principle of **penetrating the subconscious mind** is as simple as offering a positive suggestion, a new thought, or a different truth. This is where the memory functions at its very best.

The Right Ear Demonstration

To further demonstrate the principle of **penetrating the subconscious mind**, try the following example: Form "**the hypnotic eye**" with the left hand and focus on it while cupping the fingers of the right hand just behind the right ear. Now, hold the palm close to the ear, serving as an amplifier while reciting the following words into the palm of the that hand placed at the right ear:

Every minute of every hour, I am feeling positive, uplifted, and fortunate because of receiving this remarkable power. This I have already accepted, in the name of Jesus Christ, Lord of every awakening hour.

Repeat the above phrase three times, not too loudly, focusing on the palm near the right ear. By doing this, the message is delivered directly to the subconscious because the right ear responds to it within the left hemisphere of the brain, where language is assimilated. In this instance, the words entering the right ear bypass the conscious mind, whereas words entering the left ear would only stifle the message. Many a New York City straphanger has, unwittingly, applied this practice when they would switch the phone to the right ear in an attempt to diminish the resounding noises of incoming trains,

THE TRANCE ZONE INDUCTION TECHNIQUES

Prior to going into deep hypnosis: You may choose to record any of the numerous **Self-hypnotic suggestions**. Then relax and proceed with the hypnosis while listening to the tape. If possible record and listen to the hypnotist's prerecorded inductions.

TO "GO INTO" *THE TRANCE ZONE*

The Initial Procedure - (self-hypnosis induced by the subject, sitting or lying)
To "Go Into" *The Trance Zone*:

First, form "**the hypnotic eye**," by placing the thumb and first finger of either hand together and place it at your side.

Then, lift the **eyes up to the eyebrows,** close them, and give a **deep yawn.**

Next, recite: *This is how I 'Go Into' The Trance Zone.*

Continue with the hypnotic suggestions.

(**This is how *The Trance Zone* is initially induced. The intention behind repeating this is to have it act as a posthypnotic suggestion, a subconscious trigger, or "CUE" to "Go Into" the hypnotic trance more easily.**)

The Hypnotic Eye Technique (with the subject sitting or lying)

(**NOTE** -- For the subject: as an alternative to going into your trance, simply focus on a small multifaceted crystal, or transparent marble, placed between your fingers and close the eyes. Imagining the crystal as "**the hypnotic eye**" will aid in deepening the hypnosis.)

To "Go Into" *The Trance Zone* proceed as follows:

EXAMPLE INDUCTION
SUBJECT (induce self-hypnosis, as follows):

*I place my thumb and forefinger of either hand together, and form '**the hypnotic eye**,' placing it at my side. Now, I lift my **eyes up to the eyebrows,** and close them.*

*Now give a **deep yawn.***

*This is how I "Go Into" **The Trance Zone**, where only good things happen. Now, I **inhale through the nose** and exhale through the mouth while counting down from 30, by 2's. 30, 28, 26, 24, 22, as I continue counting down, I keep inhaling through the nose until reaching 0. I breathe slowly and calmly, as I let my body relax more and more each time. I continue to exhale while counting, relaxing more and more.*

Note: Proceed with the hypnosis by adding any of the self-hypnotic suggestions.

Optional: Add To "Come Out" at the end of any of the trance scripts:
(See definition at the end of this Chapter.)

Squeeze The Ball Technique (in a lying or sitting position)

The Procedure:
"Go Into" ***The Trance Zone,*** by inducing self-hypnosis as follows:
First hold a soft rubber ball in either hand and focus the eyes on it while squeezing very tightly.
Then, lift the **eyes up to the eyebrows,** close them, and give a **deep yawn**.
Next, recite: *This is how I "Go Into"* ***The Trance Zone.***
Then continue squeezing the ball until the need is felt to release the pressure.
When releasing the pressure and letting the ball fall, let the arm, together with the entire body, fall into a relaxed position.

EXAMPLE INDUCTION
SUBJECT (induce self-hypnosis, as follows):

*As I place this rubber ball into my hand, I focus my eyes on it while squeezing it as hard as I can. Staring at it, I concentrate and give it my complete attention. Now, I lift my **eyes up to the eyebrows** and close them, still squeezing the ball. Then, I give a **deep yawn**, and recite: This is how I "Go Into"* ***The Trance Zone****, where only good things happen.*

Now, I let up the pressure very slowly until I feel my fingers release it. As I release the ball and let it fall out of my hand, I can imagine my entire body falling with it. Breathing slowly and calmly, I let my body relax more and more.

*Then, I **inhale through the nose** and exhale through the mouth, while counting down from 30, by 2's. 30, 28, 26, 24, 22 . . . I continue counting down slowly. I breathe slowly and calmly. I let my body relax more and more each time. I continue to inhale through my nose, and exhale through my mouth as I keep counting, 20, 18, 16, 14 . . . relaxing and counting, etc.*

Note: Proceed with the hypnosis by adding any of the self-hypnotic suggestions.

Optional: Add To "Come Out" at the end of any of the trance scripts: (See definition at the end of this Chapter.)

To "Come Out" Example

When I count to five,
I will open my eyes feeling alert, refreshed and alive.
1, 2, every part of me is better than ever before,
3, I am feeling alert and refreshed,
4, I am alert, refreshed and fully alive.
5 . . . I open my eyes.

Spinning Crystal Technique (with the subject sitting or lying)
The Procedure:
"Go Into" ***The Trance Zone***, by inducing self-hypnosis as follows:
First, focus on a spinning multifaceted crystal as you suspended it on a string, above your eyes. Keep staring as it spins, and then lift the **eyes up to the eyebrows,** close them, and give **deep yawn**.
Next recite: *This is how I "Go Into"* ***The Trance Zone.***
Now, **inhale through the nose**, and exhale counting down from 30 by 2's, relaxing the body more and more, until reaching zero.

EXAMPLE INDUCTION
SUBJECT (induce self-hypnosis, as follows):
With my eyes wide open, I watch the crystal intently as it spins above my eyes. My eyes remain transfixed. I focus intently on the crystal as it continues spinning, until I can no longer hold my eyes open. Now, I lift my **eyes up to the eyebrows,** *close them and give* **deep yawn**. *This is how I "Go Into"* ***The Trance Zone***, *where only good things happen. Now, I* **inhale through the nose** *and exhale through my mouth, while I begin counting down from 30, by 2's. 30, 28, 26, 24, 22, 20 . . . As I continue counting down slowly, I go deeper into hypnosis. 18, 16, 14, 12, 10 . . . Calmly and peacefully, I inhale through my nose and exhale through my mouth, 8, 6, 4, 2, 0. I am breathing slowly and calmly. And as I continue, I let my body relax more and more each time. Relaxing, relaxing; going deeper and deeper into hypnosis.*

Note: Proceed with the hypnosis by adding any of the self-hypnotic suggestions.

Optional: Add To "Come Out" at the end of any of the trance scripts:
(See definition at the end of this Chapter.)

To "Come Out" Example
As I slowly begin to count from 1 to 5, I will become better and better upon each count. 1 . . I am feeling terrific, knowing that I have vowed to stop smoking; 2 . . I remember everything that happened in this trance state; 3 . . I feel happy that my life is changed for the better; 4 . . I am totally relaxed, fully aware, and functioning perfectly normal, 5 . . I am awake and feeling better than ever before. Finally, I am healthy, alert, and fully alive.

Split Screen Technique (with the subject sitting or lying)

The Procedure:
"Go Into" ***The Trance Zone***, by inducing self-hypnosis as follows:
First, lift either arm, as if a balloon was attached, and have it rise. Then allow the arm fall, as if it were heavy as lead.
Now lift the **eyes up to the eyebrows,** close them, and give a **deep yawn.**
Next recite: *This is how I "Go Into"* ***The Trance Zone.***
Then, **inhale through the nose**, and exhale counting down from 30 by 2's, relaxing the body more and more, until reaching 0.
Imagine rising up into a blue sky and floating there, feeling light and free of earthly problems. Then, imagine three giant screens, and describe in detail, the image of the present self in the **middle screen.** Then visualize the image of the negative self, including all problems, in the **left screen;** and then the image of the positive self with all the problems resolved in the **right screen.**

EXAMPLE INDUCTION self-confidence
SUBJECT (induce self-hypnosis, as follows):
*First, I lift my right arm, imagining that a balloon was attached to my elbow, and have it rise. I hold it there a few moments. Now, I let my arm fall as if it were heavy as lead. Then, I lift my **eyes up to the eyebrows**, close them and give a **deep yawn.***

Now, I recite: This is how I "Go Into" ***The Trance Zone****, where only good things happen. Then, I **inhale through the nose** and exhale through the mouth, while counting down from 30, by 2's. 30, 28, 26, 24, 22 . . . I continue counting down slowly. I breathe slowly and calmly, letting my body relax more and more each time. I continue inhaling through my nose, and exhale as I keep counting down, 20,18, 16 . . . relaxing . . . etc.*

*I imagine rising up into a blue sky and floating there, feeling light and free of all earthly problems. Now, I imagine three giant screens, one in the middle, one on the left, and one on the right. I visualize the image of my present self in the **middle screen**. Then, I visualize the image of my bleak, negative self, including all my problems, in the **left screen**. Now, I visualize the image of my positive self in the **right screen**. As I enlarge the screen, I see clearly that all my problems are resolved. Now I can see myself very clearly with my positive self, smiling and happy. I am looking so bright and cheerful I have the image become ingrained into my subconscious, so that I will always remember that this is the best way to be -- free of worry, and self-confident.*

Note: Proceed with the hypnosis by adding any of the self-hypnotic suggestions.

SELF-HYPNOSIS INDUCTION

Note to hypnotists: This same induction can be used by merely recording, or typing the words in the "third person. (Example: *Now, lift **your** <u>eyes up to the eyebrows</u>, and close them . . .*)

EXAMPLE INDUCTION --TO QUIT SMOKING

SUBJECT (induce self-hypnosis, as follows):

*First, I lift my right arm, imagining that a balloon was attached to my elbow, and have it rise. I hold it there a few moments. Now, I let my arm fall as if it were heavy as lead. Then, I lift my **<u>eyes up to the eyebrows</u>**, close them and give a **<u>deep yawn.</u>** Now, I recite, This is how I "Go Into" **The Trance Zone**, where only good things happen. Then, I **<u>inhale through the nose</u>** and exhale through the mouth, while counting down from 30, by 2's. 30, 28, 26, 24, 22 . . . I continue counting down slowly. I breathe slowly and calmly, letting my body relax more and more each time. I continue inhaling through my nose, and exhale as I keep counting down, 20, 18, 16 . . . relaxing . . . etc. My arms are relaxed, my legs are relaxed; all my muscles are relaxed. As I continue to relax, there is a deep opening to my subconscious. My subconscious pays serious attention to my words and records them into my memory.*

*I now raise my body, raise it up to the sky, the calm blue sky. In the sky, I imagine three giant screens. In the **<u>middle screen,</u>** I see myself from above lying on the couch down below. I'm in the blue sky looking at the screen, looking at myself, as I lay dressed, completely relaxed, with my eyes closed. That is the image on the screen, the screen in the middle. Now, I make the screen in the middle become enlarged, showing all the colors.*

*On the **<u>left screen,</u>** I see the negative image of myself. This negative image shows me sitting up smoking a cigarette, disgusted about smoking, clouds of smoke surrounding me. My attitude is that I am entirely fed up with smoking, and discouraged because I can't quit. I enlarge that screen showing me with a disgusted look on my face, and then I go to the screen on the right. On this **<u>right screen</u>** is the same large image of myself in the sitting position, but without the cigarette in my hand. The air is clean behind me. Behind me I see the blue sky, the ocean down below, and I feel the warmth of the sun training its rays upon me. I have a smile on my face. My attitude is that I am happy that I have kicked the habit; that I have released my drive to smoke. The desire to smoke has left me completely, and in the wide opening into my subconscious, I acknowledge this, and see that this is my best image.*

(continue)

EXAMPLE INDUCTION -- TO QUIT SMOKING (continued)

The image of being free of having to hold and puff on the disgusting object makes me feel good. I take in the fresh air -- this is the way to feel, this is the way to be, to have a healthy outlook on life. Meanwhile, the screen on the left has completely vanished, and now the screen on the right is very much enlarged. I see myself with a very happy smile on my face, because I let go of the smoking habit; I let go of feeling the need to smoke! I am grateful that the desire to smoke cigarettes has left me for good. I am delighted that I no longer have to cater to the urges that kept me feeling so possessed, distressed and stressed out.

EXAMPLE SELF-HYPNOSIS INDUCTION:
To Quit Smoking - *Relaxing The Nerves*

My muscles are relaxed, my body is relaxed and my entire circulatory system is relaxed. My mind is so relaxed I am losing interest in smoking. And because my nerves have settled down, I have ceased to crave nicotine. My nerves are totally relaxed and free of that bondage smoking brings. My muscles are now completely free of tension; my breathing is opening up, as it has never done before. I can feel the nerves to my head releasing oxygen to my brain as the thought of being free of cigarettes enters my thoughts. This feels so real my nervous system is somehow completely relieved and in sync with my ingenious brain. I accept the fact that I have just quit smoking. In my subconscious mind, I will always remember these thoughts as I recite them aloud right now: "Cigarettes are harmful to my mind, body and spirit. So, yes - the best thing for me to do is to Quit Smoking! And Yes, through my subconscious powers, I accept the fact that I have just Quit Smoking, for good!"

SELF-HYPNOSIS INDUCTION -- COMBINATION

Note to hypnotists: This same induction can be used by merely recording, or typing the words in the "third person."(Example: *Now, lift **your** <u>eyes up to the eyebrows,</u> and close them*.)

Oxygen As An Elixir Technique *(with the subject lying)*

    <u>SUBJECT</u> (induce the hypnosis as follows:)

I lift my <u>eyes up to the eyebrows</u>, and close them. I Give a <u>deep yawn</u>, and form "<u>the hypnotic eye</u>" by placing my thumb and forefinger together. Now, I <u>recite</u>, "This is how I Go Into <u>The Trance Zone</u>."

I concentrate as I <u>inhale through the nose</u> and exhale counting down from 30 by 2's. Relaxing the body more and more until reaching 0, I begin counting slowly, evenly: 30 . . . 28 . . . 26 . . . 24 . . . 22 . . . 20 . . . 18 . . . 16 . . . 14 . . . 12 . . . 10 . . . 8 . . . 6 . . . 4 . . . 2 . . . 0.

This is how I "Go Into" <u>The Trance Zone</u>, where only good things happen. In that wide opening to my subconscious, I am listening intently to my voice. I am lying comfortably with my eyes still closed; my arms and legs are flexible, relaxed. Now, concentrating on being loose and free, and with my hand still forming "<u>the hypnotic eye,</u>" I keep taking in deep breaths through my nose and exhaling through my mouth. I let my entire body relax while lying in this comfortable position. As I am doing this, I think of the incoming oxygen as an elixir, a magic potion that cleanses me inside and out. And as I exhale, I imagine all my ailments, frustrations, and worries actually leaving my body.

Each time I inhale, I think of the oxygen as being a bright white mist coming into my spirit, cleansing me of all my impurities, all my diseases. Now, I imagine the white mist transforming into a bright blue mist. And now, I imagine this bright blue mist becoming a powerful healing potion. Every time I breathe in, I make the blue mist give off more healing energy, have it become more and more splendid.

It is now the most wonderful feeling I have felt in a long time. My mind is free of all worry, free of daily problems and headaches. I feel and experience this wonderful sensation, which spreads more and more throughout my body. My subconscious is registering all my words. Wider and wider, this opening has become. The gentle words of my voice are being deeply engraved as I listen intently to my suggestions. I am listening very intently as I proceed with care.

While I concentrate on my blue mist, I see this as a positive and healing energy. This powerful, relaxing energy overwhelms me to the point I feel a tremendous confidence in myself. I let myself go, let myself be. I let whatever happens happen because terrific things are taking place.

                                                                                 (continue)

Oxygen As An Elixir Technique   (continued)

Still concentrating on this blue mist, I feel that my mind is free of all worry, free of daily problems and headaches. As I lie, free of tension, I rejoice in the sense of well being that this inner blue mist brings to me. I feel and experience this wonderful sensation, which spreads more and more throughout my body.

I am finally fed up with cigarettes having a hold on me. I want to continue living a life devoid of pain and suffering. Therefore, I realize I must discontinue smoking. In addition to the countless rising costs, this undesirable habit is taking too great a toll on my life. Furthermore, I dismiss all desire for nicotine. And I dismiss any cravings and any holds cigarettes had on me. Right now, I vow to discontinue smoking. As of this very moment all desire to smoke has left me. Through the ability of my subconscious mind, I am given the power to quit smoking cigarettes. I acknowledge all this and give my firm commitment to stop smoking. Now that I have made this commitment, my subconscious responds powerfully, in accordance with my needs and desires.

I feel protected, secure and full of high esteem as the sensation forms a permanent place in my subconscious. My subconscious is registering all my words. Wider and wider, this opening has become. The gentle words of my voice are being deeply engraved there as I listen intently to these suggestions.

I am listening very intently as I proceed. Now that I am a free spirit capable of conquering any problem and unafraid of doing anything I desire, I now imagine myself entering my dream world. Deeper and deeper, I enter freely into my dream-state. I am unafraid, protected, and delighted at being far away from reality and the responsibilities and burdens that go along with my daily activities.

In this wonderful state of peace, I have an opening to my subconscious -- wider and wider this opening has become. My subconscious is registering all my words. The gentle words of my voice are being deeply engraved there as I listen intently to my suggestions. I am listening very intently as I proceed with care. I listen closely to these words as I say them: I feel peaceful; I feel very quiet emotionally. I feel calm physically, and I enjoy the peace, the quiet, and the calm that exudes from within me.

As I listen to my voice, my entire body becomes more relaxed, more and more. While my muscles become free of tension, my voice penetrates deeper into that opening to my subconscious. Now that I am totally relaxed and feeling completely free of tension I imagine all my worries, frustrations, and hostilities leaving my body permanently.

(continue)

Oxygen As An Elixir Technique   (continued)

I imagine that all that negativity is flowing out of my lungs and pores like poisonous gases, leaving me feeling completely refreshed, recharged and rejuvenated. Right now, I know in my mind that I fully and freely release all grudges held from the past. Fully and freely, I loosen and let go of all anger, resentment and pent-up emotional disorders. I feel the relief of unloading all this excess baggage from my mind. From this day forward my load is finally light. My burdens are light and all my worries and problems have just become trivial.

I continue to breathe slowly and calmly. I let my body relax more and more each time. Relaxing, relaxing; going deeper and deeper into hypnosis. As I am resting comfortably, I notice that my eyes are closed tight, very tight. They are stuck so tight I am not able to open them. My eyes are stuck together so tight they feel as if they are sealed with a mudpack. In a moment I will try to open them - I will not be able to do so. I will find they are sealed tight; they are stuck firmly together. I may be able to manage the muscle groups around my eyes, but not my eyelids. No matter how hard I try, I will be unable to open my eyes until I bring myself out of this deep trance.

When I count down from 3 to zero, I will find it impossible to open my eyes and I will go deeper into hypnosis. 3 . . . My eyelids are sealed tight, 2 . . . They feel stuck tight with mud, 1 . . . They are stuck firmly together, Zero . . . I try, but I am unable to open them. I stop trying, and go deeper into hypnosis.

In that wide opening to my subconscious, I am listening intently to my voice. I already know about my subconscious mind's extraordinary powers of self-healing, and how the right side of my brain controls the functioning of my entire body. The right side of my brain, the subconscious mind, knows how to regulate my breathing even while I am sleeping. And it knows how to regulate my circulatory system and how to carry the right nutrients to all the parts of my body that need them.

This brilliant part of my mind also knows how to instruct every cell in my body to heal itself, to improve my mind so that I become healthier and more sound-minded, cell by cell. And I don't know how fast my body is healing itself now, but my mind knows just how to accelerate the healing that is already taking place in my body. Yes, my subconscious has the intelligence and the power to heal anything inside of me on an intercellular basis. It is doing this effectively even as I speak.

(continue)

Oxygen As An Elixir Technique (continued)

I am finally fed up with cigarettes having a hold on me. I want to continue living life, a life devoid of pain and suffering. Therefore, I realize I must discontinue smoking. In addition to the countless rising costs, this undesirable habit is taking too great a toll on my life. Furthermore, I dismiss all desire for nicotine. And I dismiss any cravings and any holds cigarettes had on me. Right now, I vow to discontinue smoking. As of this very moment all desire to smoke has left me. Through the ability of my subconscious mind, I am given the power to quit smoking cigarettes. I acknowledge all this and give my firm commitment to stop smoking. Now that I have made this commitment, my subconscious responds powerfully, in accordance with my needs and desires.

And I don't know if I am already feeling certain sensations in my body, signaling that the healing process has already started, but I can be sure that while I am in this deep, resting trance state, my body is already healing itself. I enjoy feeling relaxed, knowing my body can accelerate and improve my immune system even now, as I enjoy this rest. I know for sure that I can rely on my inner self; that I can count on that part of me in my subconscious that knows exactly what to do, and exactly how to do it. While my body has a tremendous ability to heal itself, the subconscious mind actually serves as the regulator of every possible function. Not only does my subconscious have the ability to perform all the healing I need, it has the capability to initiate peaceful rest and recuperation whenever I decide to fall sleep.

My subconscious mind is capable of extraordinary recouping powers, and endless capabilities, even while I enjoy this peaceful state. I know that, and I continue to allow my body to rejuvenate while I relax and enjoy feeling peaceful. That deep place in my subconscious mind acknowledges all this and remembers the need to recall everything when I come out of this trance. And even after I come out of this exhilarating trance state, I can trust my ability to initiate peace and relaxation whenever it is needed. When I go to bed at night, I take delight in the fact that sleeping serves to replenish my entire body, hour after hour, cell by remarkable cell.

(continue)

Oxygen As An Elixir Technique   (continued)

Imagine a large softgel containing a liquid tranquilizer being lodged in the upper portion of your brain. Let it become loose and slowly travel down the head, and settle into the back of your neck. Now, let the softgel dissolve, allowing the liquid tranquilizer to flow down your throat and settle there. Feel the liquid dissolving into your throat. And now, allow the liquid tranquilizer to settle into every part of your body starting from your throat, and seeping down to the bottom of your feet. Feel its tranquilizing effect as it seeps down your chest and arms. Feel its loosening and healing effects as it seeps into every muscle, every ligament and into every joint.

Imagine every part of your body becoming so relaxed it seems like jelly. Allow this liquid tranquilizer to relieve every pain, every arthritic condition, every restrictive feeling in you body. Allow this tranquilizer to balance your entire nervous system, your complete immune system, as you focus on allowing your mind to come to complete rest. You are free of all worry, free of all tension as you drift off into your hypnotic trance. Deeper and deeper you go into this deep trance state; deeper and deeper you go into hypnosis. The deeper you go into hypnosis, the deeper you go into this trance state. Deeper and deeper, you drift off into your beautiful, restful hypnotic trance.

Even after I come out of this trance, I will remember that the "<u>the hypnotic eye</u>" is the key to unleashing the power of my subconscious mind. Whenever I call upon this image, hidden knowledge is brought to light. As I look deeper and deeper within my spirit, I draw wisdom from the depths of my subconscious mind. All knowledge is there for me. All channels of guidance are opened to me, especially spiritual guidance. Everything I want to know is revealed. Everything is made clear; everything is exposed.

I am finally fed up with cigarettes having a hold on me. I want to continue living life, a life devoid of pain and suffering. Therefore, I realize I must discontinue smoking. In addition to the countless rising costs, this undesirable habit is taking too great a toll on my life. Furthermore, I dismiss all desire for nicotine. And I dismiss any cravings and any holds cigarettes had on me. Right now, I vow to discontinue smoking. As of this very moment all desire to smoke has left me. Through the ability of my subconscious mind, I am given the power to quit smoking cigarettes. I acknowledge all this and give my firm commitment to stop smoking. Now that I have made this commitment, my subconscious responds powerfully, in accordance with my needs and desires.

(continue)

Oxygen As An Elixir Technique   (continued)

My muscles are relaxed, my body is relaxed and my entire circulatory system is relaxed. My mind is relaxed, indicating I have already lost my interest in smoking. My nerves have also settled down, and my craving of nicotine has ceased. My nerves are totally relaxed and free of the bondage that smoking caused in the past. My nerves and muscles are now completely free of tension; my breathing is opening up as it has never done before.

I can sense my circulatory system releasing oxygen to my brain as the thought of being free from cigarettes enters my mind. This feels so real my nervous system is somehow completely relieved, acting in sync with my ingenious brain's needs. I accept the fact that I have just quit smoking. In my subconscious mind, I will always remember these thoughts as I repeat them now: **"Cigarettes are harmful to my mind, body and spirit. So, yes - the best thing for me to do is to Quit Smoking! And Yes, through my subconscious powers, I accept the fact that I have just Quit Smoking, for good!"**

My muscles are relaxed, my body is relaxed and my entire circulatory system is relaxed. My mind is relaxed, indicating I have already lost my interest in smoking. My nerves have also settled down, and my craving of nicotine has ceased. My nerves are totally relaxed and free of the bondage that smoking caused in the past. My nerves and muscles are now completely free of tension; my breathing is opening up as it has never done before.

I can sense my circulatory system releasing oxygen to my brain as the thought of being free from cigarettes enters my mind. This feels so real my nervous system is somehow completely relieved, acting in sync with my ingenious brain's needs. I accept the fact that I have just quit smoking. In my subconscious mind, I will always remember these thoughts I repeat them now: **"Cigarettes are harmful to my mind, body and spirit. So, yes - the best thing for me to do is to Quit Smoking! And Yes, through my subconscious powers, I accept the fact that I have just Quit Smoking, for good!"**

My muscles are relaxed, my body is relaxed and my entire circulatory system is relaxed. My mind is relaxed, indicating I have already lost my interest in smoking. My nerves have also settled down, and my craving of nicotine has ceased. My nerves are totally relaxed and free of the bondage that smoking caused in the past. My nerves and muscles are now completely free of tension; my breathing is opening up as it has never done before.

(continue)

Oxygen As An Elixir Technique   (continued)

Focusing on this subconscious state, I know that I have permission to become anyone I wish to be, accomplish anything I wish to accomplish. With my newly formed identity, I envision myself as the person I have always dreamed I could be. In this state of subconscious, I will always remember how great it felt to have my imagination make me over. My subconscious mind has already allowed me to feel better about myself. And as I awaken, I will remember everything that happened during this trance.

As I slowly begin to count from 1 to 5, I will become better and better upon each count. 1 . . I am feeling terrific, knowing that I have vowed to stop smoking; 2 . . I remember everything that happened in this trance state; 3 . . I feel happy that my life is changed for the better; 4 . . I am totally relaxed, fully aware, and functioning perfectly normal, 5 . . I am awake and feeling better than ever before. Finally, I am healthy, alert, and fully alive.

NOTE: For an alternative method of going into **The Trance Zone**, place a **multifaceted crystal** within "**the hypnotic eye**" of your hand. Then, focusing on the crystal, lift the hand above your head until the eyes get tired. When your eyes close, with your hand falling, imagine your entire body falling along with it, eventually releasing the crystal from your grasp. When practiced diligently, this can become a very expedient way to "Go Into" **The Trance Zone.**

In fact, shortly after I developed this procedure and went for my final exam, I introduced the concept to the subject that I needed to hypnotize in order to become certified.

When I placed the crystal into my hand, forming "**the hypnotic eye,**" and lifted it above the young lady's eyes (she was a middle-aged woman with two children), she immediately closed her eyes and went directly into the trance. It must have taken all of **three seconds** for that to happen. After completing that hypnosis session, I was handed my certificate as a qualified hypnotist -- right on the spot.

The **SHORT SUGGESTIONS** listed below are given as examples of staccato, but effective inductions. They may prove helpful when interjecting them during hypnosis because of their influence on altering the thought process.

Although some of the other inductions appear to be rather lengthy, they can also be very effective provided they are given slowly, in a humdrum tone of voice. This puts the conscious mind aside (disarms it), and enlists the influence of the subconscious mind.

HYPNOTIST:

Excuses are signs of neglect; as of this moment, your failure to succeed is a thing of the past.

Vow to create positive images of the way things ought to be now, rather than of negative images, the way they were.

Every minute of every hour you feel better in every possible positive way, because of having this power.

You are motivated and rejuvenated; you are relaxed and totally optimistic every minute of every hour.

Your body is free of all inflammation and muscle spasms, including any arthritic conditions.

Right now, your immune system is activated and all disease is being eliminated, rejected and extracted from your entire system.

(**Note: Posthypnotic Suggestions** are the messages, key words, "CUES," or triggers induced by the hypnotist to the subject in the hypnotic state. They can even work during self-hypnosis, executed by the subject. The aim is to have them carry over to the awakened state, or to be used as a signal to return to the hypnotic state.

Also Note: Self-hypnotic suggestion, self-hypnosis, or autosuggestion is that state of hypnosis induced by the subject.)

TO "COME OUT" OF *THE TRANCE ZONE*:

There are several ways to terminate a trance: In the use of self-hypnosis, it either happens automatically during the trance, or it happens naturally, by falling asleep. There is, absolutely, no danger or any reason to worry about "coming out" of a trance, because you <u>do not</u> go to sleep. Remember -- the subject <u>always</u> remains in control. When being hypnotized by a hypnotist, the worse the subject could do is fall asleep, awakening automatically within a short period. More than likely, the hypnotist will not allow the subject to doze off, because the trance will have been automatically terminated.

The subject may interrupt the trance at any time, or the hypnotist may choose various methods of terminating the trance. Some of the hypnotist's methods include counting, snapping the fingers, giving posthypnotic suggestions, touching, or other harmless procedures.

Again, <u>never</u> is there a danger of not being able to "Come Out" during <u>any stage</u> of the hypnotic trance.

To "Come Out" Example
When I count to five,
I will open my eyes feeling alert, refreshed and alive.
1, 2, every part of me is better than ever before,
3, I am feeling alert and refreshed,
4, I am alert, refreshed and fully alive.
5 . . . I open my eyes.

To "Come Out" Example
As I slowly begin to count from 1 to 5, I will become better and better upon each count. 1 . . I am feeling terrific, knowing that I have vowed to stop smoking; 2 . . I remember everything that happened in this trance state; 3 . . I feel happy that my life is changed for the better; 4 . . I am totally relaxed, fully aware, and functioning perfectly normal, 5 . . I am awake and feeling better than ever before. Finally, I am healthy, alert, and fully alive.

PART SIX

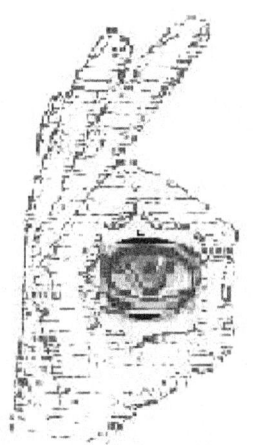

CHAPTER ELEVEN
11

SELF-HYPNOSIS INDUCTION
> ILLUSTRATIONS <

11   HYPNOSIS
ILLUSTRATIONS:

Taken By A Grain Of Salt

While sitting in a restaurant one afternoon, I happened to strike up a conversation with a young lady who admitted to being depressed. After a short conversation, while analyzing her situation, I picked up the cigarette-doused ashtray sitting in front of us, placed it on top of a fancy saltshaker, and asked her to take a good look at it. As she did so, I told her to imagine herself as the saltshaker with the ashes representing her depression.

Then I removed the ashtray and asked her to form "The Hypnotic eye" while I replaced the ashtray with a clear glass of water. As she sat staring through the glass, using "the hypnotic eye," I asked her to imagine her depression as being as clear as the saltshaker under the sparkling glass of water. Then I told her to imagine taking a snapshot of it, and go into the bathroom to see if she could still see that image she created, behind the closed door.

When she returned from the bathroom, smiling, she told me she could see the image as clear as a bell. Not only was she impressed, being taken by the demonstration; it immediately reversed her negative attitude. As we parted, she seemed lifted up above her depression. Obviously, she related very well to being the pure salt inside the saltshaker.   -------- EjL

CHAPTER ELEVEN

11

SELF-HYPNOSIS INDUCTION ILLUSTRATIONS
(with examples)

Imagine seeing the results of fulfilling your dreams, your hearts desires. Although it is best to perform the inductions from memory there are so many, it would be very difficult. Select your favorites, and practice memorizing them until you are ready for more.

Since your eyes will be closed (unless you memorize the self-hypnotic suggestions,) you will need to tape them in your own voice and listen to them while in **The Trance Zone**. *Simply tape your preferred inductions (it is best to record them in the "first person,") and listen to them repeatedly, using headphones.*

However, before taping, review the Illustrations below and practice reading them aloud. It is important that your voice flows rhythmically when reciting all hypnotic inductions. In practicing the examples as demonstrated below, you will eventually be able to develop your own personalized inductions. Whenever applicable, use the "Come Out" procedure after each hypnosis session. (See the method above.)

Whether hypnotist or subject, the following **"Self-Hypnosis Demonstration"** should be very convincing in regard to testing the powers of the subconscious mind:

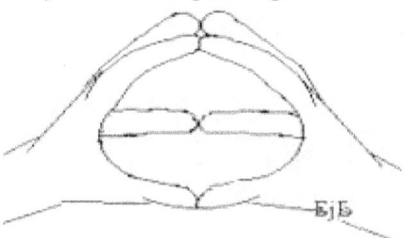

Self-Hypnosis Demonstration

Place both hands together, spreading and placing the fingertips together, forming a hollow sphere. Focusing very intently on the center, and gently pressing the fingertips imagine a cylindrical fireball inside. Concentrate on having this fireball between your hands getting hotter, and hotter. As you feel the heat warming your hands press your fingertips together as hard as possible. Now, while **concentrating 100 percent on exerting full pressure**, mentally think it as you say "*I want to pull my hands apart*."

You will find this impossible! You cannot exert two opposing forces in a positive direction. The lesson is that, where the positive force is strongest, the negative power becomes weakest. This is one of the best examples of how the subconscious can overcome all negativity. Find the positive force that overcomes the conflicting, negative weakness and you have discovered positive change, period.

THE TRANCE ZONE INDUCTION ILLUSTRATIONS

The **Illustrations** below have been designed to give inductions that are more specific -- while the above **Techniques** explain more about procedure. Record the self-hypnotic suggestion below in your own natural voice. When you are ready, get into a comfortable and listen intently to your words.

Typical Induction Illustration (with the subject sitting or lying)

(This is actually an extended version of **The Hypnotic Eye Technique.**
The **Illustrations** have been transposed into "**the first person,**" for taping purposes.
"Go Into" ***The Trance Zone.*** Then induce the hypnosis, as follows.

> **INDUCTION ILLUSTRATION -- TO BE TAPE RECORDED**
> **SUBJECT:**
>
> *This is how I "Go into"* ***The Trance Zone,*** *using* ***The Hypnotic Eye Technique****. I place my thumb and forefinger of either hand together, and form* ***"the hypnotic eye,"*** *placing it at my side. This is the eye to my subconscious. Now, I lift my **eyes up to the eyebrows**, close them and give a **deep yawn**. Now, I **inhale through the nose** and exhale through the mouth while lying comfortably. My eyes are closed. My arms and legs are flexible, relaxed.*
>
> *As I begin counting down from 30 by 2's, I continue breathing evenly, inhaling through my nose and exhaling through my mouth. 30, 28, 26, 24, 22, 20 . . . With each breath, I sink deeper and deeper and deeper into a relaxed state of mind. 18, 16, 14, 12, 10 . . . I let my body relax more and more each time. 8, 6, 4, 2, 0 . . . In that wide opening to my subconscious, I am listening intently to my voice.*
>
> *I no longer want anything. I become passive as I listen to my voice. I let myself go. I let it be . . . Let it happen. Nothing bothers or distracts me. Nothing bad or unusual is going to happen. My head is clear. My mind is free of all problems. I rejoice in this sense of peace and well being that envelops me from head to foot. I feel this wonderful relaxation which spreads more and more throughout my body. I feel the new looseness and weightlessness of my body.*
>
> *In this wonderful state of peace, I have an opening to the subconscious -- wider and wider this opening is becoming. My subconscious is registering all my words. The gentle words of my voice are being deeply engraved there as I listen intently to my suggestions. I am listening very intently as I proceed with care.*

Note: Proceed with the hypnosis by adding any of the self-hypnotic suggestions.

The Falling Backwards Illustration (with the subject sitting)

The **Illustrations** have been transposed into "**the first person,**" for taping purposes. "Go Into" ***The Trance Zone.*** Then induce the hypnosis, as follows.

INDUCTION ILLUSTRATION -- TO BE TAPE RECORDED
SUBJECT:

*This is how I "Go Into" **The Trance Zone**, where only good things happen. With my eyes still closed, my arms and legs are flexible, relaxed. Now, I **inhale through the nose** and exhale through my mouth as I count down from 30 to 0 by 2's. As I do so, I let myself fall backwards. Inching very slowly as I count. I let all my muscles relax as I sink farther and farther. 30 . . . 28 . . . 26 . . . 24 . . . etc.*

I let myself go as I continue counting. I let myself be . . . Let whatever happens happen, because nothing bad is about to take place. My mind is free of all worry and problems. As I sit, free of worry, I rejoice in the sense of peace and well being that envelops me from head to foot. I feel and experience this wonderful relaxation which spreads more and more throughout my body.

My words are sinking even farther, and as I listen closely to my voice, I willfully allow my words into an opening to my subconscious. With each breath, I sink deeper and deeper and deeper into my subconscious state of mind. Wider and wider, this opening is becoming. My subconscious is registering all my words. The gentle words of my voice are being deeply engraved as I listen intently to my suggestions. I am listening very intently as I proceed with care.

Note: Proceed with the hypnosis by adding any of the self-hypnotic suggestions.

Optional: Add To "Come Out" at the end of any of the trance scripts: (See definition in previous Chapter.)

Oxygen As An Elixir Illustration
The **Illustrations** have been transposed into "**the first person,**" for taping purposes. "Go Into" ***The Trance Zone.*** Then induce the hypnosis, as follows.

INDUCTION ILLUSTRATION -- TO BE TAPE RECORDED
SUBJECT:

This is how I "Go Into" ***The Trance Zone****, where only good things happen. Now, I **inhale through the nose** and exhale through my mouth. In that wide opening to my subconscious, I am listening intently to my voice.*

I am sitting comfortably with my eyes still closed. My arms and legs are flexible, relaxed. I keep breathing in and out continuously. And as I am doing this, I think of the incoming oxygen as an elixir, a magic potion that cleanses me inside and out. And as I exhale, I imagine all my ailments, frustrations, and worries actually leaving my body.

Each time I inhale, I think of the oxygen as being a bright white mist coming into my spirit, cleansing me of all my impurities, all my ailments. Now, I imagine the white mist becoming an even stronger bright blue mist. And now, I imagine this bright blue mist becoming a powerful healing potion. Every time I breathe in, I make the blue mist give off more energy, have it become more splendid.

It is now the most wonderful feeling I've felt in a long time. My mind is free of all worry, free of daily problems and headaches. I feel and experience this wonderful sensation which spreads more and more throughout my body. My subconscious is registering all my words. Wider and wider, this opening has become. The gentle words of my voice are being deeply engraved as I listen intently to my suggestions. I am listening very intently as I proceed with care.

Note: Proceed with the hypnosis by adding any of the self-hypnotic suggestions.

Optional: Add To "Come Out" at the end of any of the trance scripts:
(See definition in previous Chapter.)

A DEEPER STATE OF TRANCE
The Blue Aura Of Dharma Illustration

The **Illustrations** have been transposed into "**the first person**," for taping purposes. "Go Into" ***The Trance Zone.*** Then induce the self-hypnosis, as follows.

INDUCTION ILLUSTRATION -- TO BE TAPE RECORDED
SUBJECT: (lying or sitting)

*I now lift my **eyes up to the eyebrows**, and close them. I give a **deep yawn**, and form "**the hypnotic eye**" by placing my thumb and forefinger together. Now, I recite, This is how I Go Into **The Trance Zone**.*

*I concentrate, **inhale through the nose** and exhale counting down from 30 by 2's, relaxing the body more and more until reaching 0. (Record the count slowly, evenly: 30 . 28 . 26 . 24 . 22 . 20 . 18 . 16 . 14 . 12 . 10 . 8 . 6 . 4 . 2 . 0.)*

*I am lying comfortably with my eyes still closed; my arms and legs are flexible, relaxed. Now, concentrating on being loose and free, and with my hand still forming "**the hypnotic eye**," I imagine myself as being surrounded with a blue aura. As I concentrate, this blue aura begins to glow blue -- more and more bluer. Taking in deep breaths through my nose and exhaling through my mouth, I let my entire body relax while lying in this comfortable position. While I imagine my blue aura and watch it as it continues to glow, I feel it getting warmer and warmer until I sense a rush of energy surging throughout my body.*

This energy is a positive and healing energy. This powerful, relaxing energy overcomes me to the point I feel a tremendous confidence in myself. I let myself go. I let myself be . . . Let whatever happens happen because terrific things are taking place. Still concentrating on this blue aura, I feel that my mind is free of all worry, free of daily problems and headaches. As I sit, free of tension, I rejoice in the sense of well being that my blue aura brings me, which envelops me from head to foot. I Feel and experience this wonderful sensation which spreads more and more throughout my body.

I feel protected, secure and full of high esteem as the sensation forms a permanent place in my subconscious. My subconscious is registering all my words. Wider and wider, this opening has become. The gentle words of my voice are being deeply engraved there as I listen intently to these suggestions. I am listening very intently as I proceed, confidently. Now that I am a free spirit capable of conquering any problem and unafraid of doing anything I desire, I now imagine myself flying on the back of a huge American Eagle. Higher and higher, I soar freely among the protective clouds on those thick, soft feathers. I am unafraid, protected, and delighted at being far away from planet earth, far away from reality and the burdens that go along with daily activities. (continue)

The Blue Aura Of Dharma Illustration (continued)

*Even after I come out of this trance, I will remember that the "**the hypnotic eye**" is the key to unleashing the power of my subconscious mind. Whenever I call upon this image hidden knowledge is brought to light. As I look deeper and deeper within my spirit, I draw wisdom from the depths of my subconscious mind. All knowledge is there for me. All channels of guidance are opened to me, especially spiritual guidance. Everything I want to know is revealed. Everything is made clear; everything is exposed.*

As far as my problems with sleeping are concerned, I am confident it has been resolved. Bouts with insomnia are over. Struggling in order to find peaceful sleep is a thing of the past. Now, whenever I lay down for the night, I realize that sleeping is the way my body recuperates. I also know that sleep is inevitable because it is nature's way of replenishing my strength, my state of mental balance. Whenever I fall asleep my sleep is deep and unencumbered. Whenever I awaken, there is complete rest and complete relief all from stress. My will, as well as Thy Will, will be done - and thus, it is laid out before me.

Focusing on returning to the world below, I know that I have permission to become anyone I wish to be, accomplish anything I wish to accomplish. With my newly formed identity, I envision myself as the person I've always dreamed I could be. In this state of subconscious, I will always remember how great it felt to have my imagination make me over. My subconscious mind has allowed me feel better about myself, and as I awaken, I will remember everything that happened during this time.

As I slowly begin to count from 1 to 5, I will become better and better upon each count. 1 . . . I am feeling much better, 2 . . . I remember everything that happened in this trance state, 3 . . . I already feel that my life has changed for the better, 4 . . . I am fully aware and functioning perfectly normal, 5 . . . I am awake and fully alert, feeling better than ever before.

Practice this exercise until you actually feel the results. Experience fulfilling the dreams of your heart's desire.

Note: Proceed with the hypnosis by adding any of the self-hypnotic suggestions.

Optional: Add To "Come Out" at the end of any of the trance scripts:
(See definition in previous Chapter.)

Self-hypnosis Illustrations   151

A DEEPER STATE OF TRANCE
Behavior Modification Illustration (Tape record this for later sessions)
The **Illustrations** have been transposed into "**the first person**," for taping purposes. "Go Into" ***The Trance Zone.*** Then induce the hypnosis, as follows.
    INDUCTION ILLUSTRATION   Drawing Numbers In The Sand
    SUBJECT: (in a sitting position)

*I now form "**the hypnotic eye**" and place my hand at my side. This is the eye to my subconscious, which puts me into **The Trance Zone**. Now, I lift my **eyes up to the eyebrows** and close them. Keeping my eyes up, I take in a deep yawn. In that wide opening to my subconscious, I am listening intently to my voice.*

As I am resting comfortably, I notice that my eyes are closed tight, very tight. They are stuck so tight am not able to open them. In a moment, I will try to open them, but I will not be able to do so. I will find they are sealed tight; they are stuck firmly together. I may be able to manage the muscle groups around my eyes, but not my eyelids. No matter how hard I try, I will be unable to open my eyes. When I count down from 3 to 0, I will find it impossible to open my eyes, and I will go deeper into hypnosis. 3 . . . My eyelids are sealed tight, 2 . . . They are stuck firmly together, 1 . . . They are sealed and stuck firmly together, 0 . . . I try, but I am unable to open them. Now, I stop trying and go deeper into hypnosis.

In my imagination, I find that I am away on vacation. It is a lovely, sunny day at the beach in the Bahamas. As I return from a refreshing swim in the ocean, I dry myself off and place my towel down. Sitting right at the edge of the water, where the sand is moist, I adjust my sunglasses and bask in the sun as I watch the sailboats passing by.

Suddenly feeling energetic, I decide to play a numbers game. Using my finger, I draw a square in the sand next to me. On the moist sand, I trace a square about the size of the length of my arm, from my fingertips to the end of my elbow. Carefully, in my imagination, I draw a circle inside the square, having it touch all four sides of the square. Inside the circle, I draw the open version of the number 4, making sure all four points touch the edge of the circle.

Even if I can't see all this, it's okay, because I can imagine I see it. And imagining is what this is about. Now, using my fingers I gently begin to erase the 4. As I do this, I am being very careful not to break the circle. So, using the tip of my finger, I am careful to erase the 4 -- but only where it touches the circle at the four points. I do this slowly and calmly.

As long as I can imagine I see this, it is as good as seeing it. Now that I have done this, I erase the remaining part of the 4 with my fingers.

Behavior Modification Illustration (continued)

*Then I trace the number 30 inside the circle, making it small enough to have room to work without damaging the circle. Now, I erase the 30 and draw number 29; I erase that number and draw number 28; I erase that number, and so on. After drawing number 27, I listen to this recording and continue tracing and erasing lower numbers, concentrating on getting to zero. I don't have to worry about anything. I don't even have to pay full attention to the voice on this tape, because my subconscious will hear and register everything. So, I don't have to worry because my main concern is making these numbers. I just keep on making my numbers lower and lower until I get to the number 0. When I get to number zero, I say the words, **deeper I go**, then begin again, starting at 30 and keep right on drawing my numbers and erasing them until reaching zero again. As I keep tracing lower numbers, that wide opening to my subconscious brings me deeper and deeper into hypnosis.*
The lower I go, the deeper I go; the lower the number, the deeper the hypnosis.

*One number after the other, I erase and draw, erase and draw, going deeper and deeper into hypnosis. I am being neat as I work in the moist sand. As I keep on working, I try to avoid letting too much sand inside the circle. I try to keep the area smooth and my fingers clean, wiping them on my towel, so that I get neat numbers each time. When I get to zero, I will be deeper into hypnosis. The main thing to remember is that the lower the numbers, the deeper I go into hypnosis. Every time I get to zero, I will say the words, **deeper I go**. Then I will begin again, starting at 30 and keep right on drawing my numbers and erasing them until reaching zero again. As I keep tracing lower numbers, that wide opening to my subconscious brings me deeper and deeper into hypnosis. The lower I go, the deeper I go; the lower the number, the deeper the hypnosis becomes.*

Practice this exercise until you actually feel the results.
Experience fulfilling the dreams of your heart's desire.

Note: Proceed with the hypnosis by adding any of the self-hypnotic suggestions.

To "Go Under," or to "Reenter" *The Trance Zone.*
This is the same as "Go Into" *The Trance Zone.*

Using the "**the hypnotic eye**" action of the fingers will have etched the image on the subconscious mind, thus becoming a posthypnotic trigger to "Reenter," or "Go Under" at random. This is a primary example of a posthypnotic suggestion through association, a naturally occurring process that happens automatically. It works especially well in attempting to return to the hypnotic state. It will take time and practice in order to make use of this posthypnotic suggestion, but eventually it will become so automatic you will come to take it for granted. As explained many times, there are never any problems regarding coming out, or going into a trance.

To "Come Out" of *The Trance Zone.*
This is the awake, conscious state.

There are several ways to terminate a trance: In the use of self-hypnosis, it either happens automatically during the trance, or it happens naturally by falling asleep. Remember, there is, absolutely, no danger, or reason to worry about coming out of a trance. To "**Come Out**" of ***The Trance Zone,*** record and listen to your choice of the following pre-recorded affirmations (or use the hypnotist's recorded voice):

To "Come Out"
SOME EXAMPLES:

As I count from one to five, I will become fully awake and aware. My mind and all my body parts will become active and functioning better than ever before. One, two . . . I feel alert and refreshed, three, four . . . I am alert and alive. Five, I open my eyes.

OR:
When I count to five, I will open my eyes feeling alert and refreshed. Every part of me will feel better than ever before. One, two . . . I feel alert and refreshed. Three, four . . . I am alert and alive. Five . . . I open my eyes.

OR:
By the time I count to five, I will open my eyes feeling alert, refreshed and alive. 1 . . . 2 . . . Every part of me is better than ever before. 3 . . . I am feeling alert and refreshed. 4 . . . I am alert, refreshed and fully alive. 5 . . . I open my eyes, feeling better than ever before.

OR:
Create your own method based on the above, or what you have learned.

PART SEVEN

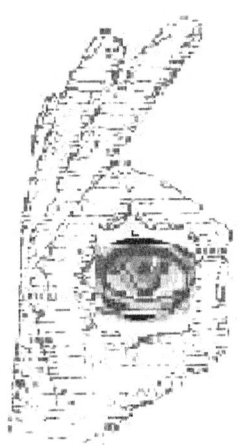

CHAPTER TWELVE
12

INDUCING MAJESTIC TRANCE SPELLS

12   SELF-HYPNOSIS
MANIFESTATION:

In my life there are things I need to have
So I have conditioned myself to the inductive;
While keeping the doors closed on things bad,
Opened doors guide me subconsciously --
Insuring that I remain productive.

CHAPTER TWELVE
12

INDUCING MAJESTIC TRANCE SPELLS
---

*Of all the negative forces
that **undermine** the subconscious,
deprivation is among the most damaging
to the psyche.*

    Due to the fact that it is not immediately recognizable, deprivation is the primary cause of self-abuse, insomnia, addiction and the consequences of rejection. It is also responsible for inferiority complexes, phobias and obsessive compulsion disorders, as well as an entire spectrum of other maladies.

    Because most victims of **deprivation** become so caught up in their problems, they become unaware of these influences - they have become blinded to their own inability. In affect, they become powerless and succumb to the dominant forces sabotaging their subconscious. The old saying, "You can't see the forest through the trees" has some truth in it. If you wish to see the big picture, you need to advance and examine the forest.

    The following **Majestic Trance Spells** will aid in resolving the distress, negativity, and doubt caused by **deprivation**. Considering the countless times that the "mysterious eye" had shown up in the Hieroglyphics of ancient tombs, I decided that it would be very fitting as a majestic hypnosis tool. (See **Illustration 12-1 -- "The Observing Eye,"** below:)

    It has been documented that his all-knowing, all-seeing God had provided the Egyptian King, Akhenaten with all kinds of powers. According to Akhenaten, the king who claimed to be the manifestation of the **Sun God, Re,** "By seeing the light, which is God, the eye is created; seeing is thus the sense of **divine communication**."

    Coincidentally, the sacred cobra that adorned King Akhenaten's brow, in whichever crown he wore, was believed to take on the attributes of the sun-disk, and thought to be the "**Eye of the Sun God, Re**. He would not go into battle without wearing it.

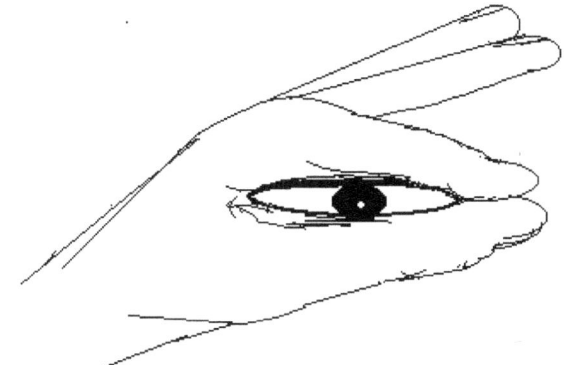

Illustration 12-1 - "The Observing Eye"

MAJESTIC TRANCE SPELLS

To augment the **Majestic Trance Spells**, place a small multifaceted crystal, or transparent marble, between the fingers to represent "T**he Observing Eye**. It is formed the same way as "**The Hypnotic Eye**," except that the fingers are stretched out, forming a narrow "Eye." Visualizing the object, and then closing the eyes and feeling its effect, will aid in deepening the hypnosis. When going into your trance, simply focus and imagine being empowered by a divine, mysterious eye within the fingers.

Focus on **Majestic Trance Spells** listed below, creating vivid images in your mind whenever possible. In time, and it could be sooner rather than later, the answer to your problems will become realized. To even further enhance your subconscious powers, practice **The Seven Day Trance Spells,** and **Dream Fulfillment During Sleep** as described below, and your desires, as well as your grandest dreams will manifest before you. Concentration, as well as imagination, are your keys to prosperity.

(Note: It can be equally effective to use either the "**The Observing Eye**" technique, or "**The Hypnotic Eye**" technique for any of the self-hypnotic suggestions.)

SUBJECT'S SELF-HYPNOTIC SUGGESTIONS:

Since the incantations below are designed to induce divine intervention, light up some Mt. Shasta sage, or frankincense during the ritual, and then focus on attaining the desired results. Prayers, beforehand, will help to produce results that are even more effective. Record the **Majestic Trance Spells** as they appear below, then "**Go into**" *The Trance Zone*, and listen to your choice of messages. To insure long-term results, listen to them twice every day under self-hypnosis, for a period of at least two weeks. Although not imperative, it is advisable that the suggestions be recorded in "the first person." However, some of the suggestions have been repeated to illustrate such a purpose.

To Resolve the Siege of Deprivation

*Although I do not fully recognize it, negative forces have infiltrated my attitude, my ego. Nothing is like what it should be, my finances, my love life, my social affairs, my health and my personal relations - all are suffering, and I do not know the cause. To rectify my situation, I will first change my attitude to that of being completely positive in all my undertakings. From now on my key **WORDS** are "can do." This means that any time I have doubts about my ability, or tasks at hand, I simply form "**The Observing Eye**," and recall the **WORDS**, "can do." Doing this will instantly place me in a positive frame of mind.*

The next thing I need to do is change my behavior patterns. Therefore, I commit myself to making the firm decision to lift my spirits. I commit myself to positively <u>improving my eating habits</u>; <u>cutting down on smoking</u>; <u>praying and meditating</u>; and <u>expressing and receiving love</u>. I also commit to doing the following: <u>treating myself to an occasional movie</u>; <u>participating in group relations</u>; <u>participating in some form of exercise</u>; and <u>listening to uplifting music every day</u>.

Finally, I see the light. In order to alter this infliction that has caused me grief and pain, I resolve to participate in some form of behavior modification practice. Only then, will I be able to rectify my situation of being deprived of the essential things in life. Life should consist of things like self-gratification, expression, acceptance, good healthy stamina, and prosperity. And now, through the commitments ahead of me, I can see a direct path to eventual happiness. My subconscious acknowledges my commitment, and has already planted the seeds to see all this through.

To Skyrocket The Power Of The Mind

I am resting, calm; relaxed. My eyes are closed; my arms and legs are flexible. I am free of tension, nothing distracts me as I feel myself being drawn along, breathing slowly, regularly. I am quite relaxed as I feel this wonderful peacefulness envelop my being. In this state of peace, I have an opening to my subconscious. This opening grows wider, more and more. My words are settling into my subconscious, are taking root there.

I now submit to the following commands: So far, I have been using only a small fraction of my mind, my conscious mind. I have been using less then five percent of my true potential because of using only my conscious mind. Now, using the power of the subconscious, I use more and more of my true power -- now, I am using the full power of my subconscious mind. Every minute of every day, my mind is better and better in every positive way. Every minute of every day, my mind continues to develop to its fullest potential -- even now, my mind is better in every possible way.

To Call Upon Divine Intervention

*I pray to the Egyptian "Eye of the Sun God, Re" and to my own personal God to enable me to acquire, (fill in: money; quit a habit; love; etc.) As I concentrate and say special prayers while forming "**The Observing Eye**," I am confident my prayers and requests are already taking effect.*

To Modify And Cleanse The Mind

To enable me to initiate mind clarity, I now clear my mind of all negative and mentally harmful thoughts. I further clear my body of all illness, infection, and degenerative disease. And, I further clear my spirit of all evil forces and influences. I know that I have something more valuable than money - I have my health, my values, my good nature, and my loving, winning attitude. Since my body is the temple of the Lord, Jesus Christ; my subconscious recognizes that I am, indeed, God's property. This, my subconscious acknowledges, and through the powers that are majestic and supernatural, I have just modified, and cleansed my entire personality.

To Become Totally Optimistic

*As I continue to remain in **The Trance Zone**, I know that potential, not faults enable me to become successful at whatever I choose to do. I know that, by now, I am more appealing, more magnetic as far as my personality is concerned. I know that good fortune is on the brink, and yes it is due me. From this moment on, I deserve all the good things that come my way. To put poetically: In my life there are things I need to know, so I condition myself to the seductive; while keeping the doors closed on things bad, opened doors guide me subconsciously -- insuring that I remain productive.*

To Attract Love Or A Mate

Every minute of every day, I'm getting closer and closer to meeting the mate who will be compatible, and good for me. Day by day, in every way I become attractive to the opposite sex. From this day forward, my best self is on the lookout for my compatible partner. Beginning right now, things are taking place to ensure that I will meet and "score" with a mate of my liking -- with that person responding to me in kind, as of right now. This process has already taken place and is being carried out through the power higher than myself. Subconsciously, I know and expect that this matching is taking place. I also know that this induction process is helping me to feel loved. I have come to realize that everything of true worth comes through love. This state of relaxation and utter trust has helped me to grow as a person. It has allowed me to reach a privileged state of being loved, as well as being capable of loving.

To Become Sexually Appealing

In order for me to reach my highly magnetic, erotically appealing state, I take in deep breaths while I recite aloud: I am physically attractive to the opposite sex. My subconscious mind knows I have what it takes to be attractive. And it knows how to make the right adjustment to instill me with charm and magnetism. I feel this happening, right now.

I feel it. I am a fitting, attractive person who is capable of reciprocating love, and one so groomed that I make heads turn. As I keep taking in deep breaths through my nose and exhaling, repeating these words aloud, I know I have developed the energy and spark necessary to attract a mate. I am physically attractive to the opposite sex. My subconscious mind knows I have what it takes to be attractive. And it knows how to make the right adjustment to instill me with charm and magnetism. I feel this happening to me, right now.

To Quit Smoking - *Relaxing The Nerves*

My muscles are relaxed, my body is relaxed and my entire circulatory system is relaxed. My mind is so relaxed I am losing interest in smoking. And because my nerves have settled down, I have ceased to crave nicotine. My nerves are totally relaxed and free of that bondage smoking brings. My muscles are now completely free of tension; my breathing is opening up, as it has never done before. I can feel the nerves to my head releasing oxygen to my brain as the thought of being free of cigarettes enters my thoughts. This feels so real my nervous system is somehow completely relieved and in sync with my ingenious brain. I accept the fact that I have just quit smoking. In my subconscious mind, I will always remember these thoughts as I recite them aloud right now: "Cigarettes are harmful to my mind, body and spirit. So, yes - the best thing for me to do is to Quit Smoking! And Yes, through my subconscious powers, I accept the fact that I have just Quit Smoking, for good!"

To Attract Good Fortune

Realizing that being lucky is more than chance; I know how to improve my odds. By arming myself with the elements of positive decisiveness, preparation, focus, and expectation, I know that I improve my chances of becoming lucky. My advantage is in knowing that being lucky is not simply due to luck -- it is due to the combination of these elements unfolding at precisely the right times. Being lucky means being skillful at anticipating and pulling these four elements together. By adding prayer, I have become a winner -- because now I have five luck-inducing elements. I know life consists of things like gratification, expression, acceptance, healthy stamina, and prosperity. And, through the commitments ahead of me, I can see a direct path to my happiness. My subconscious acknowledges this, and has already planted the seeds to see all this through.

To Influence Lady Luck

As I focus on imagining the brightest star, I summon it to transmit winning vibrations through my body, down into the earth, and back within me to charge me with its most mystical powers. As I continue to focus, these powers supercharge me with unyielding lucky energies that actually influence everything I do.

The more I focus, the more I become lucky, and the more I become lucky, the more I become a winner at everything I tackle; and that includes health, wealth and the pursuit of happiness. I feel this influence now. To enable Lady Luck to smile upon me, I invoke her to flow through me as I joyously begin singing or whistling the tune, **Luck Be A Lady Tonight.**

To Become Of Sound Mind

Every minute of every day, I get better and better in every way. Day by day, I get psychologically sound in every possible way. As I accept this wholeheartedly as truth, my thinking is sound, my behavior is sound -- so quite naturally, my mind, body and spirit are now fully sound.

To Stop Stuttering

To have my speech return to the way that God meant me to speak, I now speak words by concentrating on the flow, not the flaws; the spirit, not the suffering. As I focus on these words, I keep them flowing as one thought. To keep from stuttering, I hold each thought, completing a full sentence at a time. I concentrate on the famous quotation **He who hesitates is lost**, *as I continue to complete each thought.*

Since singing and poetry is a very powerful remedy for stuttering, I will read poetry aloud, or ever sing short songs until I feel confident about my voice. I will remember that the reason for my stuttering is because I have been made to feel insecure, offended, intimidated, abused, or inferior. I am now conformed to my natural way of speaking, and having become positively focused. I actually feel the energy and the power of all this.

(Note: The following poem is one of my own positive thought-inducing poems.)
Practice reciting this poem aloud keeping the words flowing, until you build self-confidence. The cause of stuttering is usually nothing more than a symptom of fear. Practice reciting this, as well as some of the many other famous poems found in poetry books.

Since I was born to create and become whole
I can always reach the magic of my goal,
Whatever sounds I make bring me power and courage
When I take a stand and flow with these words.

To Alleviate Arthritis

My neck and shoulders are more relaxed. As I relax more and more all the muscles surrounding, my neck and shoulders are looser and looser. My body processes are more efficient and my blood and tissue fluids now act to carry the impurities and wastes out and away. I feel this process relieving the clogging in my joints, relieving all my pain. As I concentrate on my shoulders, a drop of lubrication is secreted, loosening the joints of my neck and shoulders. Immediately, I feel the improvement and continue to feel better, healing more and more with every passing minute. I am pleased at this progress of recovery and have lost all desire to accommodate my arthritis. In that wide opening to my subconscious, I acknowledge that I have lost all susceptibility to arthritic symptoms. (Note: This may be applied to all joints and limbs of the body.)

To Strengthen The Mind, Spirit, And Immune System *(a repetition example)*

As of this moment, I feel I am being released from all illness. I feel the energy of my mind, spirit and body, including my immune system, working at reversing my condition. As I keep breathing deeply and slowly, I can begin to feel my illnesses being transformed into the state of "wellness." I feel my misplaced energies of nervousness, apprehension and hostility subsiding, reacting to my breathing. Through the power of my subconscious mind, my sick cells have been transformed into positive, recuperative energies. The more I focus on deep breathing, the more dramatically my subconscious continues to cure me of all disease, and the aches and pains, as well as mental and physical stress.

Since hypnotism produces organic responses, I know my subconscious powers are working to stabilize my adrenal and endocrine glands. I know, deep down all abnormal cells are responding to become normal once more. My subconscious acknowledges all this and insures me that all this is actually happening. As of this moment, I feel I am being released from all illness. I feel the energy of my mind, spirit and body, including my immune system, working at reversing my condition. As I keep breathing deeply and slowly, I can begin to feel my illnesses being transformed into the state of "wellness."

I feel the energy of my misplaced energies of nervousness, apprehension and hostility reacting to my breathing. Through the power of my subconscious mind, my sick cells have been transformed into positive, recuperative energies. The more I focus on deep breathing, the more dramatically it continues to cure me of all disease, and the aches and pains, as well as mental and physical stress. Since hypnotism produces organic responses, I know my subconscious powers are working to stabilize my adrenal and endocrine glands. I know, deep down, that all abnormal cells are responding to become normal once more. My subconscious acknowledges all this, and insures me that all this is actually happening.

THE SEVEN DAY TRANCE SPELLS:

Since the following <u>Trance Spells</u> vary in scope, they should be individually incorporated into your standard self-hypnosis routine. However, at the end of each week, combining and taping them as one hypnotic session can produce amazing results. Be sure to tape the "Come Out" when recording them as a single, weekly induction.

<u>Sunday:</u>
<u>To Achieve Your Heart's Desire</u>

I believe in myself and in the Higher Power that resides both in my mind and in the mind of the eternal one above. I call upon the Eternal One to enter these proceedings -- for we are One; One Power; One Universal Energy being a Channel through which this Power can flow. I believe in this Power, united through me, that guides all our lives. What man has done, I can do with the Eternal One working through me, because, knowing that I believe in this, I believe that <u>all</u> things are possible. My greatest desire at <u>this</u> time is -- <u>To have all my hopes and dreams become fulfilled</u>. To bring this situation about, my subconscious deep within me reassures me that I can, not through my will, but through Thy Will. <u>It is done</u> through the Universal Energy running through me; I repeat: <u>It is done!</u>

<u>Monday:</u>
<u>To Improve Health And Fitness</u>

Realizing from my own experience that athletes need to take care in order for their bodies to grow strong, or recuperate from overwork, they must have proper rest. Even as I rest my body now, like an athlete rests, my body can become stronger and healthier, revitalizing my nerves, my blood, and even my brain cells. And although the aging process is always causing deterioration, it doesn't have to follow that my vision, my memory or my legs have to become weakened. And, since I already feel certain sensations in my body, signaling that the healing process is already started, I can be sure that while I am in this deep, resting trance state, my body has begun to heal itself. I can even enjoy feeling relaxed because of knowing my body can accelerate and improve my immune system even now, as I enjoy this rest. Through the power of my subconscious, I know for sure that I can trust your inner self, know that I can trust that part of my subconscious mind that knows exactly what to do, and exactly how to do it.

Tuesday:
To Become Totally Optimistic:

*As I continue to remain in **The Trance Zone**, I know that potential, not faults enable me to become successful at whatever I choose to do. I know that, by now, I am more appealing, more magnetic as far as my personality is concerned. I know that good fortune is on the brink, and yes it is due me. From this moment on, I deserve all the good things that come my way. To put poetically: In my life there are things I need to know, so I condition myself to the seductive; while keeping the doors closed on things bad, opened doors guide me subconsciously -- insuring that I remain productive.*

Wednesday:
To Skyrocket The Power Of The Mind

I am resting, calm; relaxed. My eyes are closed; my arms and legs are flexible. I am free of tension, nothing distracts me as I feel myself being drawn along, breathing slowly, regularly. I am quite relaxed as I feel this wonderful peacefulness envelop my being. In this state of peace, I have an opening to my subconscious. This opening grows wider, more and more. My words are settling into my subconscious, are taking root there.

I now submit to the following commands: So far, I have been using only a small fraction of my mind, my conscious mind. I have been using less then five percent of my true potential because of using only my conscious mind. Now, using the power of the subconscious, I use more and more of my true power. Now, I am using the full power of my subconscious mind. Every minute of every day, my mind is better and better in every positive way. Every minute of every day, my mind continues to develop its fullest potential. Even now, it is better in every possible way.

Thursday:
To Instill Direction And Motivation

I call on my creative powers in order to enable me to choose the right direction. I have the ability to concentrate on completing the project nearest my ideals, nearest my passion, my creativity, and my most deeply rooted inclinations. I now have the ability to summon the powers within me to motivate myself.

Now, I am motivated to become active in putting together my ideal project and completing it, concentrating on it day by day until I succeed. Again, I have enabled the power within me to summon my innermost, tremendous energy. I have now initiated my total being in order to achieve whatever it is that is within me, and to accomplish that innate yearning within myself. In my mind's eye, I already know I have what it takes to get this completed.

Friday:
To Gain Infinite Riches

Personal Magnetism rules the world. In order for me to realize the power of this statement, I know there are adjustments to be made in my life. Since everything indicates that great magnetic forces develop in persons who know how to purify their bodies through love and healthful living, it is to my enrichment to do the same. Beginning right now, I accept temperance in all things -- from moderation in food consumption, to a simple diet, to strategic physical exercise, to calmness and kindness, to evenness of mind. This already has been accepted subconsciously -- it happened at the beginning of this induction.

As I go into that wide opening to my subconscious, I see that all the traits of Personal Magnetism have become stored there. This enables me to make use one of the most powerful tools the mind can possess, and I have access to it any time I wish. Between my newly acquired combination of Magnetism and Hypnosis, doors to every imaginable scenario have become opened to me. Already, I realize that some people sense I am the spiritual person they have been looking for, that I am a caring person of deep knowledge, wisdom and compassion. Even now, I know friends, strangers and even my enemies want to do favors for me, as well as offer me money and other golden opportunities. Anything and everything can virtually become mine for the asking. The ease with which I am able to influence those around me to gain love, admiration, opportunities and wealth may seem amazing, but all the above became possible through the powers of Magnetism and Hypnosis -- the process of which I am participating in at this very moment. All is love, and love is everything. I thank God for the infinite riches flowing into my life.

Saturday:
To Induce Overall Healing

My subconscious mind has extraordinary intelligence when it comes to self-healing. It has the intelligence to heal anything inside of me on an intercellular basis. This brilliant part of my mind also knows how to instruct every cell in my body to heal itself, to improve, to feel more comfortable and to be healthy and sound, cell by incredible cell. The right side of my brain that controls the functioning of my body knows how to regulate my breathing even while I am sleeping. And it knows how to regulate my circulatory system, how to carry the right nutrients to all the parts of your body that needs them. Because my subconscious mind knows how to recall that it was my body that ultimately healed me cell by incredible cell, it knows exactly how to accelerate the healing – this healing that has already started taking place in my body.

Note: In order to deepen the following trances, extend each of the examples by adding any combination of prerecorded suggestions. Repeat listening to the message several times, then relax and go to sleep. Upon awakening, try to recall the dream - it should be fresh in your memory. If you don't succeed right away, try, and try again, until you get the desired results. Remember one thing: <u>This process works</u>. So, don't become discouraged.

<u>To Strengthen The Mind And Spirit</u>
Every minute of every day, I get better and better in every way. Every minute of every day, my spirit is positive, more and more in every way. Every minute of every day, I acknowledge that all things are possible along the way. My voice is relaxed, calm and resonating. My body is relaxed, loose and free of tension. My mind is peaceful, focused and perceiving everything that is possible and positive.

<u>The Divine Wish Conception</u>
I imagine a decorative water fountain with statues pouring water into a pool at its base. I can see myself standing in front of it with a sparkling coin in my hand. As I stare at the coin and make my finest wish, I can imagine my guardian angel approaching me, giving me a blessing. As I toss the coin high in the air, I keep my eyes glued to it; watch it hit the water until it settles to the bottom of the pool. As I focus on the coin, I make it grow large enough to see what I wished for appear larger-than-life.

Once I envision all I wished for, I verbally thank the angel: <u>In my subconscious mind, I thank you for this wish. I shall always remember this moment. I realize now, that when I believe strong enough, and have faith worthy enough, anything is possible.</u>

EXAMPLE 1:
<u>Myself As A Talk Show Host:</u>
Form "<u>the observing eye</u>," and listen to the following recorded **Dream Fulfillment** request while playing it at bedtime:

This is how I "Go Into" <u>The Trance Zone</u>*, where my* **Dream Fulfillment** *request becomes resolved. In that wide opening to my subconscious ear, I request that I see, feel and experience exactly how a talk show host behaves during the performance of a successful show. Reveal all the details of my actions, my voice, and how I present myself in a most rewarding manner. Very clearly, show me the faces of my guests as they respond to me with respect.*

(continue)

Majestic Trance Spells   167

The Divine Wish Conception (continued)

EXAMPLE 2:
To Evoke The Ideal Self

Form "**the observing eye**," and recite, (or record) the following ***Dream Fulfillment request*** and play the following at bedtime:

This is how I "Go Into" The Trance Zone, where my dream fulfillment request is resolved. In that wide opening to my subconscious ear, I request that I see, experience, and remember exactly how my newly formed Ideal Self would become. I call upon my subconscious powers to enable me to become strong, of sound mind, and of a winning mindset. In all the aspects of my dream, enable me to command admiration and magnetism, no matter what the circumstances.

EXAMPLE 3:
To Enable Seduction (to be revised if female)

Form "**the observing eye**," and recite, (or record) the following ***Dream Fulfillment request*** and play the following at bedtime:

This is how I "Go Into" The Trance Zone, where my dream fulfillment request is resolved. In that wide opening to my subconscious ear, I acknowledge my dream fulfillment request as follows: As I approach my dream state, my subconscious mind creates images of me having sex with a beautiful woman. Because this lovely blond woman cannot resist my magnetism, she undresses herself and me and presses her lovely breasts against my naked body. Then she climbs on top of me and presses me firmly between her kegs. She kisses me frugally as she seduces me, nibbling and breathing into my ears until we both reach our climax. In my subconscious mind, I take note and record the continuing experience, to be recalled as soon as I awaken.

DREAM FULFILLMENT DURING SLEEP:

The standard practice, regarding dreams, is to interpret them <u>after</u> they have occurred. However, to my surprise, I have discovered that if a person would set up a **<u>Dream Fulfillment</u>** request prior to going to sleep, that request would become actualized during the dream state. Then, upon awakening, the person would be able to recall everything the dream revealed. The request could be one of asking for a solution to a specific problem, or one asking to live an experience that would bring a certain kind of fulfillment, sexual or financial gratification, for example. As you can imagine, this technique could produce richly rewarding results, having a remarkable effect on one's welfare and self-esteem.

This is how it works: Prior to going to sleep, "Go Into" ***<u>The Trance Zone</u>*** and state your **<u>Dream Fulfillment</u>** request orally. Be as creative and as imaginative as you wish, instructing the subconscious to acknowledge your desires, and to enable you to recall them upon awakening. In believing, wholeheartedly, that your requests will be carried out during your dream state, the subconscious will act accordingly and manifest them, recording them as though they were real occurrences. After you awaken, just form "**<u>the observing eye</u>**" and you will recall everything. The beauty of this technique is that you will have experienced the entire dream just as if it were real, giving you the fulfillment of even your wildest dream, since the subconscious cannot discern imagined truths from reality. Talk about benefits.

If your **<u>Dream Fulfillment</u>** request is too complex to memorize, tape it, then listen to it at bedtime. Remember that softness, directness, and clarity produces the best results. (Note: You probably will not be successful in the first few attempts.) The more you believe in the process, the more effective it will become. To recall the dream after awakening it will be helpful to "Go Into" ***<u>The Trance Zone</u>*** and review what the subconscious recorded. Concentrating on "**<u>the observing eye</u>**," ask your subconscious to reveal what it envisioned during your dream.

Listed below, is a typical example of a **<u>Dream Fulfillment</u>**, request. It is designed to build self-esteem, as well as to develop formidable confidence,

DREAM FULFILLMENT DURING SLEEP: (continued)
EXAMPLE:

Dream Created by you: (Write down your ideal dream, then memorize it prior to going to sleep.)

Imagine how it would be to receive an Oscar at the Academy Awards. Set up the entire scenario, including tight shots and hands clapping, prior to going to sleep. Remember, that concentration, focus, firm belief, and practice are <u>always paramount</u> in achieving <u>any</u> intended results.

<u>See the following chapter for Nature's Deep Sleep Tranquilizer</u>

CHAPTER THIRTEEN
13

SELF-HYPNOSIS
BEHAVIOR MODIFICATION

13   SELF-HYPNOSIS
REPROGRAMMING

<u>Meditation For The Body, Mind and Spirit</u>

Willpower alone is by no compression equal
To the power of the subconscious mind – that's factual.
Even by acquiring the faith of a mere mustard seed,
We inherit the unlimited power of the supernatural.

. . . . EjL

CHAPTER THIRTEEN
13

SELF-HYPNOSIS
BEHAVIOR MODIFICATION

BEHAVIOR MODIFICATION

Infiltrating the subconscious mind by bombarding it with new truths enables us the power to change for the betterment of our lives. Words are especially powerful when spoken audibly. They can instill belief or discredit belief, creating positive or negative energy. The most effective way to instill belief is to bypass the conscious mind, which criticizes, and deliver messages into the subconscious, where they become accepted without reasoning.

Through the practice of hypnosis, it is feasible to break a bad habit -- which is a degenerative, negative habit by replacing it with a good habit -- which becomes a beneficial, positive habit. Everyone develops habits, but some are positive, while others are negative. The problems arise when our negative habits control us: for they begin inducing demoralizing, and abusive, self-defeating traits. They are called "bad habits" because they are bad for us, personally, and sometimes just as bad for those around us.

Whether falling into patterns of negative conditioning, or self-destruction -- reprogramming our thoughts can be successfully used to alter the defeatist personality. Through the practice of these Mind-Altering Suggestions, you will learn how to actually alter your personality traits.

REPROGRAMMING THE SUBCONSCIOUS MIND
MIND-ALTERING SUGGESTIONS AND
MIND-ALTERING AFFIRMATIONS:

The only truth the conscious knows is what it receives from its subconscious, because everything delivered directly into the subconscious becomes truth, since it cannot discern imagined truths from reality.

By repeating the **suggestions** and **affirmations** listed below, the conscious mind will respond in kind to these new truths.

Posthypnotic Suggestions act as tools, enabling these changes to take place. In this instance, forming "**the hypnotic eye**" will enable you to "Go Into" **The Trance Zone** more rapidly in subsequent sessions.

MIND-ALTERING SUGGESTIONS
Since all posthypnotic suggestions become more effective when induced during the trance state, "Go into" ***The Trance Zone*** and recite the typical key words, as follows: *This is how I "Go Into" The Trance Zone.* Eventually, going into hypnosis becomes easier.

EXAMPLE

SUBJECT:
Sitting or lying down, encircle the thumb and forefinger to form "**the hypnotic eye.**" Then place the **eyes up to the eyebrows,** close them, and give **deep yawn**. Then give the posthypnotic suggestion, which will become a cue, subconsciously, to go into the hypnosis.

Recite: *This is how I "Go Into"* ***The Trance Zone****. Every time I recite this message, it will be easier for me to go deeper into hypnosis.*

Then, proceed with any of combination of the posthypnotic suggestions. (Actually, these are all forms of guided imagery intended for the purpose of improvement and change.)

To Gain Infinite Riches
Personal Magnetism rules the world. In order for me to realize the power of this statement, I know there are adjustments to be made in my life. Since everything indicates that great magnetic forces develop in persons who know how to purify their bodies through love and healthful living, it is to my enrichment to do the same. Beginning right now, I agree to accept temperance in all things -- from moderation in food consumption, to a simple diet, to strategic physical exercise, to calmness and kindness, to evenness of mind. This is already accepted subconsciously -- it happened at the beginning of this induction, when I stated that Personal Magnetism rules the world.

As I go into that wide opening to my subconscious, I see that all the traits of Personal Magnetism have become stored there. This enables me to make use one of the most powerful tools the mind can possess, and I have access to it, any time I wish. Between my newly acquired knowledge of Personal Magnetism, doors to every imaginable scenario are now being opened to me. Already, I realize that some people sense I am the spiritual person they have been looking for, that I am a caring person of deep knowledge, wisdom and compassion. Even now, I know that friends, strangers, even my enemies want to do favors for me, as well as offer me money and other golden opportunities. Anything and everything is virtually mine for the asking.

(continue)

To Gain Infinite Riches   (continued)

The ease with which I am able to influence those around me to gain love, admiration, opportunities and wealth may seem amazing, but at this very moment all the above have become possible through the power of this Personal Magnetism and the powers of my subconscious mind. My subconscious mind has recorded this and will remember everything that has been said. Before I bring myself out of this trance, I allow a brief pause as a way thanking God for the infinite riches flowing into my life.

The Divine Wish Conception

I can imagine a decorative water fountain with statues pouring water into a pool at its base. Now, I see myself standing in front of it with a sparkling coin in my hand. While I stare at the coin and make my finest wish, I imagine my guardian angel approaching me, giving me a blessing. As I toss the coin high in the air, keeping my eyes glued to it, I watch it hit the water until it settles to the bottom of the pool.

Focusing on the coin, I make it grow large enough to see what I wished for appear larger-than-life. Once I have envisioned all I wished for, **I whisper to the angel:**

Thank you for my wish; in my subconscious mind, I shall always remember this moment. I realize now, that if I believe strong enough, and have faith long enough, anything is possible.

To Refrain From Overeating

Willfully, I agree to go on a five day fast. As I do so, I loose all desire to overeat. Henceforth, I will eat very slowly and stop eating as soon as the feeling of "fullness" registers its message. I also feel the desire, the need to begin some form of exercise. And when I do so, I will listen closely to the instinctive messages my body sends me -- feel its true vibrations.

My natural instincts will tell me exactly what my normal weight should be, and will adjust accordingly. From this day forward, I agree to let my body be the judge of how much I should eat, and to let my insecure emotions stand aside.

To Alleviate Pressure And Tension

I understand that, due to the conflicts between accountability and accomplishment, tension builds up causing much discomfort and despair - even disease. To alleviate these pressures, I begin by stretching all my fingers open wide. As I continue stretching my fingers, I open my mouth wide and give a deep yawn. I stretch my fingers, with my jaw open wide. Now, I relax all my muscles and take deep breaths as if allowing the oxygen to flow into the muscles of my jaw, shoulders, hands, legs and feet.
I allow this oxygen to alleviate tension and stress within all my muscles.

I focus on this deep breathing until I feel tingling in the muscles and joints of my entire body. I feel this happening; I feel the oxygen replenishing my body and spirit, rejuvenating my stamina. My entire body feels loose and my mind is so clear I feel all the stress leaving my being. As I go deeper into the state of hypnosis, my subconscious is acknowledging all my words. Beginning this very moment all thoughts that come into my mind are positive. I never have to worry about being inadequate, because I have found the peace, the power and the inner strength to take control of my emotions. No matter what pressures I face, I remain cool, calm and concentrated.

To Instill Direction And Motivation

I call upon my creative powers in order to enable me to choose the right direction. I have the ability to concentrate on completing the project nearest my ideals, nearest my passion, my creativity, and my most deeply rooted inclinations. I now have the ability to summon the powers within me to motivate myself. I know that I now have enough motivation to become active in putting together my ideal project and completing it, concentrating on it day by day until you succeed.

Again, I have enabled the power within me to summon my innermost, tremendous energy. I have now initiated my total being in order that I may produce whatever it is that is within me, whatever it takes to accomplish that innate yearning within myself.

In my mind's eye I already know that I have what it takes to get this completed.

Overcoming Disease Cell by Wonderful Cell

I know that when I am in the deeply relaxed state as I am now, every nerve and every cell in my body is able to restore and rejuvenate itself. Deep within my subconscious, I know my body has the intelligence to heal itself, cell by wonderful cell, so that my nerves, joints, ligaments, muscles and organs improve and become healthier. When I am quiet and peaceful, as I am right now, I realize there is a part of me that knows what parts need restoration, and exactly what to do about it.

And I don't know when I will begin to notice that increased surge throughout my immune system -- but I already notice that I am feeling deeply relaxed and that my symptoms and ailments are melting, floating away, disappearing. And I can continue to imagine and accept that all the areas of my body, which need healing, are healthy, strong, whole, and pure. I can certainly recall which parts of my mind, body, and spirit need restoration, because it is already doing something about it. So, deep within me, I know that my subconscious knows exactly how to cure everything.

To Overcome Illness

I am coming into a very deep subconscious state. My imagination is free and clear. Here, I am enabled to use the power of my imagination to help me attain whatever it is I need to accomplish. I command that part of my subconscious that is responsible to restore my original powers. Now, I am enabled to begin functioning perfectly, just as I was intended to do from the beginning.

I address all the cells of my being, and command them to restore my powers. I call attention to my healthy cells and instruct them to heal me and make me healthy. These commands to my cells give them permission to begin my healing process. The healing process is already working and, in a very short period, the affects shall take place accordingly, and dramatically.

Journey Away To Your Vacation

After taking a safe flight several miles away from home I find myself riding in an open car along the French Rivera. Since I have been enjoying the afternoon basking on the beach, I pull into special garden café where they go to extremes to please their patrons. While being led to a private wooded area, I become overwhelmed with my surroundings: beautiful weeping willows, with colorful lanterns suspended high among them, while waitresses pass back and forth serving drinks along the adjacent pool.

And then I lose my breath when I see this delightful, interwoven, thick-corded hammock spread between the trees, especially for me. As I slip into the hammock with my full weight, I find myself swinging side-to-side, smiling contently because I am being served my favorite exotic drink. Suddenly, I realize everything is just as I always dreamed my vacation would be.

To Overcome Insomnia

It is possible to remember a time when I had a cut that was so deep I felt it wouldn't heal, or when I had a bout with the flu. But even afterward, as I slept and played and worked, my body did all the healing. While my body has a tremendous ability to heal itself, my subconscious mind actually serves as the regulator of every possible part, every possible function. It is great to know that, my subconscious not only has the ability to perform all the healing I need, it has the capability to initiate peaceful rest and sleep when called upon.

To get to sleep, I just go deep into my trance and speak to my subconscious mind. I simply talk to it, just as if it has the power and understanding to fulfill my requests – for, indeed, it does. All I have to do is ask that I be given the opportunity to sleep when it comes time to retire for the night.

Repeated often enough at bedtime, I will be granted my request. I remember that Desire, Belief and Expectation are very necessary tools. In combination with exercise and proper nutrition, as well as proper ventilation, I know that I will learn to apply these in order to overcome my bouts with insomnia.

My subconscious mind is capable of extraordinary recouping powers, and endless capacities, even when I am enjoying my peaceful sleep. I certainly <u>know</u> that, and I can continue to allow my body to rejuvenate while I relax and enjoy feeling peaceful. That deep place in my subconscious mind acknowledges all this and remembers to initiate sleep at bedtime. And even after I come out of this exhilarating trance state, I can trust in my ability to initiate sleep whenever it is needed. When I go to bed at night, I take delight in the fact that sleeping serves to replenish my entire body, hour after hour, cell by remarkable cell.

Nature's Deep Sleep Tranquilizer

Now, breathing in deeply, I take in full breaths as if I can picture the oxygen filling my lungs. As I continue to breathe deeply, I imagine the oxygen as a magic healing vapor. The deeper I breathe, the deeper this healing vapor circulates into my entire body. The more oxygen I take in, the more I feel the effect of its healing powers. I can visualize a clear picture of this healing vapor going into my lungs and circulating throughout my nervous system.

My subconscious mind is capable of extraordinary recouping powers, and endless capacities, even while I enjoy this peaceful state. I know that, and I continue to allow my body to rejuvenate while I relax and enjoy feeling peaceful. That deep place in my subconscious mind acknowledges all this and remembers the need to recall everything when I come out of this trance. And even after I come out of this exhilarating trance state, I can trust my ability to initiate peace and relaxation whenever it is needed. When I go to bed at night, I take delight in the fact that sleeping serves to replenish my entire body, hour after hour, cell by remarkable cell.

I can imagine a large softgel *containing a liquid tranquilizer being lodged in the upper portion of my brain. I let it become loose and slowly travel down the head, and settle into the back of my neck. Now, I let the softgel dissolve, allowing the liquid tranquilizer to flow down my throat and settle there. I feel the liquid dissolving into my throat. And now, allow the liquid tranquilizer to settle into every part of my body starting from my throat, and seeping down to the bottom of my feet. I feel its tranquilizing effect as it seeps down my chest and arms. I Feel its loosening and healing effects as it seeps into every muscle, every ligament and into every joint.*

I imagine every part of my body *becoming so relaxed it seems like jelly. I allow this liquid tranquilizer to relieve every pain, every arthritic condition, every restrictive feeling in my body. I allow this tranquilizer to balance my entire nervous system, my complete immune system, as I focus on allowing my mind to come to complete rest. I am free of all worry, free of all tension as I drift off into my hypnotic trance. Deeper and deeper I go into this deep trance state; deeper and deeper I go into hypnosis. The deeper I go into hypnosis, the deeper I go into this trance state. Deeper and deeper, I drift off into my beautiful, restful hypnotic trance.*

When I count to five, I will open my eyes feeling alert, refreshed and alive. 1 . . . 2 . . . every part of me is better than ever before, 3 . . . I am feeling alert and refreshed, 4 . . . I am alert, refreshed and fully alive, 5 . . . I open my eyes.

CESSATION OF BAD HABITS (Quitting Addictions)

Shedding Addiction

*My shoulders and arms are relaxed, my legs and feet are relaxed, and all my muscles are completely loose. As I continue to relax, there is a deep opening to my subconscious, which listens intently to my voice. I now have the courage to give up my habit of (my **bad** habit).   Just as a snake is able to shed its skin, I have the ability to shed my disturbing, unwanted habit, never to be part of my behavior again. My subconscious pays full attention to my words and stores them into my memory. The more I imagine the nasty addiction I crave to get ride of, the more I think of it as becoming an additional layer of skin. I imagine all aspects of my addiction as becoming an imaginary blanket of skin covering me from head to foot.*

Now, in my mind's eye, I imagine placing everything about my addiction into this imaginary skin. As it builds up in this outer blanket, I concentrate more and more, until I feel that every trace of my addiction becomes accumulated within this imaginary skin. Still concentrating with my imagination, I have this addiction built up to such a point I decide to cast the entire skin away from me. As I cast my skin away, I think of casting it away physically as well as emotionally. In my mind's eye, I finally feel a great release -- all the discomfort that I once felt has left me.

When I think about the snake <u>shedding its skin</u> I realize in making use of the idea, I can shed my addicted skin, permanently. I see and feel everything let go -- every discomfort I've every known is being <u>shed</u> before my eyes. As I feel this happening, I look behind me and see the skin I just shed on the ground, disintegrating before my eyes. Finally, as I confirm that the skin has vanished, I realize that I have become free at last. In my subconscious mind, I actually believe this has happened, and I acknowledge that my entire addiction is gone, all of it -- gone away, never to trouble me again.

<u>NOTE</u>: Typical method used to "Come Out" of any trance.
When I count to five, I will open my eyes feeling alert, refreshed and alive. 1 . . . 2 . . . every part of me is better than ever before, 3 . . . I am feeling alert and refreshed, 4 . . . I am alert, refreshed and fully alive, 5 . . . I open my eyes.

The Smoking Cure

My shoulders and arms are relaxed, my legs and feet are relaxed, and all my muscles are completely loose. As I continue to relax, there is a deep opening to my subconscious, which listens intently to my voice. My subconscious pays close attention to my words and records them into my memory. I imagine my body raising up to the blue sky, and settling on a fluffy white cloud. Resting on that cloud in the sky, I imagine three giant screens.

*In the **middle screen**, I imagine myself in my current state lying on the couch down below. I am resting on the cloud in the blue sky looking at the screen, looking at myself dressed and completely relaxed. Now, I make this **middle screen** become enlarged, and imagine myself, including all the colors, as vivid as I can.*

*On the **left screen**, I imagine the negative image of myself. This negative image shows me sitting up **smoking cigarettes** nervously, while I am being uncomfortably tense. I enlarge that screen showing myself with a disgusted, uneasy look on my face. Suddenly, my attitude is that I am entirely fed up with **smoking**. While I feel thoroughly discouraged because I can't beat the habit, I turn to the screen on the right.*

*On this **right screen** is the same large image of myself in the sitting position, but with my hand removed from my face. Now, I see a smile on my face as I look at my hands and see clean, unstained fingers. My attitude is that I am happy to have kicked the habit, that I have become permanently **relieved of my smoking addiction**. The feeling of relief is overwhelming, because I feel confident my habit of smoking cigarettes is gone forever.*

*And in the wide opening to my subconscious, I acknowledge this, and see that this is in my best interest. The image of being **free from smoking cigarettes** makes me feel great. The air is clean all around me, and I take in the fresh air. I acknowledge that this is the way to feel, this is the way to be. I feel good about having this healthy outlook on life.*

*Momentarily, I notice that the **left screen** has completely vanished. And now, with the **right screen** becoming much more enlarged and colorful, I see myself with a very happy smile on my face.*

I whisper loud enough for me to hear it:

I'm glad you let go of me, you disgusting habit, because, I too, have let go of my need to smoke cigarettes.

*I smile to myself . . . I am delighted that I let it go! I am delighted that the desire has left me for good. And I am **totally** relieved that the urges that used to leave me feeling possessed, as well as distressed and stressed out, have all gone by the wayside.*

To Quit Smoking - *The Tombstone Imagery*
I imagine walking into a graveyard carrying a sack over my shoulder. It is daylight and people witness my actions as I put down the sack, pick up a shovel and dig a small grave. With a smile on my face, I empty the contents on the ground in front of me. When cartons of my favorite cigarette pile up, along with hundreds of loose cigarettes, I take the shovel and toss the disgusting cigarettes into the grave. I imagine all the stinks, all the inconveniences, and all the misery I felt before I quit smoking as I shovel the sand. I am happy, because all the misery of my gross smoking habit is buried along with those cigarettes. After I finish packing down the sand using the shovel, I walk away from the cemetery. When I turn to look back, I see people smiling in approval. Chiseled into the tombstone are the words: "Here lies the death of my ugly, bad habit -- Smoking."

To Quit Smoking - *The Bulldozer Imagery*
I imagine getting into a bulldozer and digging a deep hole in the middle of a park. After filling a dump truck with a load of sand, I climb down from the bulldozer and empty all my cigarettes into the hole. I imagine tossing cartons of cigarettes into the hole -- everything related to my addiction, including the undesirable habit, the nasty smoke, the shortness of breath, the loss of control and the feeling of being possessed -- everything.

*As I toss in the last cigarette dangling from my mouth, I pick up several boulders and, furiously, toss them down on top of the cigarettes. As I do so, I call out loudly: **I'm fed up, and so I'm released from being possessed as of right now**. Now, I climb into the dump truck and pour the sand into the hole, stopping only after making sure it is completely filled.*

I am smiling and feeling proud of myself as I sit back and imagine the future: The spot where I am sitting is now covered with tall Birch and Maple trees. Hundreds of people are gathered there with me, celebrating breathing the fresh oxygen produced by the trees. In my subconscious mind, I record the details of this imagined, future event. As I take in deep breaths, I suddenly realize my breathing feels clean. I am delighted -- the thought of being relieved of my cigarette addiction feels absolutely pleasing to me.

NOTE: *Optional method* used to "Come Out" of any trance.
As I slowly begin to count from 1 to 5, I will become better and better upon each count. 1 . . . I am feeling much better; 2 . . . I remember everything that happened in this trance state; 3 . . . I already feel that my life has changed for the better; 4 . . . I am fully aware and functioning perfectly normal. 5 . . . I am awake and fully alert, feeling more physically fit than ever before.

FULL-DEPTH COMBINED INDUCTION

As you may have concluded, achieving successful results generally takes a bit more than half an hour. To fulfill your needs you will have to perform many helpful suggestions, much guided imagery, and much self-encouragement. In addition to solving various psychological problems, or emotional conflicts, the following , the following is one example of how to combine inductions in order to resolve the some of those needs through self-hypnosis.

Fulfilling The Subject's Needs
    SUBJECT: (sitting or lying)

"Go into" **The *Trance Zone*,** as described below, then continue with the self-hypnotic suggestions.

*I form "**the hypnotic eye**" by placing the thumb and forefinger of either hand together, and place my hand at my side. This is the eye to my subconscious, which puts me into **The Trance Zone**. Now, I lift my **eyes up to the eyebrows** and, when I feel like it, close them. Keeping my eyes up, I take in a **deep yawn**, and recite: This is how I "Go Into" **The Trance Zone**, where only good things happen. In that wide opening to my subconscious, I am listening intently to my voice.*

My arms and legs are flexible, relaxed. As I count down from 30 by 2's, I continue breathing evenly, inhaling through my nose and exhaling through my mouth. 30, 28, 26, 24 . . .With each breath I sink deeper and deeper and deeper into a relaxed state of mind. 22, 20, 18, 16 . . .I no longer want anything. I Become passive as I listen to my voice. I Let myself go . . . 14, 12, 10, 8, 6, 4, 2 . . . 0.

I let it be. . . let it happen. Nothing bothers or distracts me. Nothing bad or unusual is going to happen. My head is clear. My mind is free of all problems. I rejoice in this sense of peace and well being that envelops me from head to foot. I feel this wonderful relaxation which spreads more and more throughout my body. I feel the new looseness and weightlessness of my body.

In this wonderful state of peace, I have an opening to the subconscious -- wider and wider this opening is becoming. My subconscious is registering all my words. The gentle words of my voice are being deeply engraved there as I listen intently to my suggestions. I am listening very intently as I proceed with care. I listen closely to these words as I say them: I feel peaceful; I feel very quiet emotionally. I feel calm physically, and I enjoy the peace, the quiet, and the calm that exudes from within me.

(continue)

Fulfilling The Subject's Needs (continued)

This brilliant part of my mind knows how to instruct every cell in my body to heal itself, to improve, to feel more comfortable and to be healthy and sound, cell by cell. And I don't know how fast my body is healing itself now, but my mind knows just how to accelerate the healing that is already taking place in my body.

As I am resting comfortably, I take notice that my eyes are closed tight, very tight. They are stuck so tight I am not able to open them. In a moment I will ask myself to try to open them - I will not be able to do so. I will find they are sealed tight; they are stuck firmly together. I may be able to manage the muscle groups around my eyes, but not my eyelids. No matter how hard I try, I will be unable to open my eyes.

When I count down from 3 to zero, I will find it impossible to open my eyes and I will go deeper into hypnosis. 3 . . . My eyelids are sealed tight, 2 . . . They are stuck tight, 1 . . . They are stuck firmly together, Zero . . . I try, but I am unable to open them. I stop trying, and go deeper into hypnosis. As I listen to my voice, my entire body becomes more relaxed, more and more. While my muscles become free of tension, my voice is going deeper into that opening to my subconscious. Now that I am totally relaxed and feeling completely free of tension I can imagine all my worries, frustrations, and hostilities leaving my body permanently.

I imagine that all that negativity is flowing out of my lungs and pores like poisonous gases leaving me feeling completely refreshed, recharged, and rejuvenated. Right now, I know in my mind that I fully and freely release all grudges held from the past. Fully and freely, I loosen and let go of all anger, resentment and pent-up emotional disorders. I feel the relief of unloading all this excess baggage from my mind. From this day forward my load is finally light. My burdens are light and all my worries and problems have just become trivial.

The right side of my brain that controls the functioning of my body knows how to regulate my breathing even while I am sleeping. And it knows how to regulate my circulatory system, how to carry the right nutrients to all the parts of my body that needs them. Because my subconscious mind knows how to recall that it was my body that ultimately healed me cell-by-incredible-cell, it knows exactly how to accelerate the healing – this healing that has already started taking place in my body. My subconscious mind has extraordinary powers when it comes to self-healing. It has the intelligence to heal anything inside of me on an intercellular basis. This brilliant part of my mind also knows how to instruct every cell in my body to heal itself, to improve, to feel more comfortable and to be healthy and sound, cell by incredible cell.

(continue)

Fulfilling The Subject's Needs (continued)

And, since I already feel certain sensations in my body, signaling that the healing process is already started, I can be sure that while I am in this deep, resting trance state, my body has begun to heal itself. I can even enjoy feeling relaxed because of knowing my body can accelerate and improve my immune system even now, as I enjoy this rest. Through the power of my subconscious, I know for sure that I can trust my inner self, know that I can trust that part of my subconscious mind that knows exactly what to do, and exactly how to do it. Yes, my subconscious has the intelligence and the power to heal anything inside of me on an intercellular basis.

It is possible to remember a time when I had a cut that was so deep you felt it wouldn't heal, or when I had a bout with the flu. But even afterward, as I slept and played and worked, my body did all the healing. While my body has a tremendous ability to heal itself, my subconscious mind actually serves as the regulator of every possible part, every possible function. It is great to know that, my subconscious not only has the ability to perform all the healing I need, it has the capability to initiate peaceful rest and sleep when called upon.

Now, breathing in deeply, I take in full breaths as if I can picture the oxygen filling my lungs. As I continue to breathe deeply, I imagine the oxygen as a magic healing vapor. The deeper I breathe, the deeper this healing vapor circulates into my entire body. The more oxygen I take in, the more I feel the effect of its healing powers. I can visualize a clear picture of this healing vapor going into my lungs and circulating throughout my nervous system.

My subconscious mind is capable of extraordinary recouping powers, and endless capacities, even while I enjoy this peaceful state. I know that, and I continue to allow my body to rejuvenate while I relax and enjoy feeling peaceful. That deep place in my subconscious mind acknowledges all this and remembers the need to recall everything when I come out of this trance. And even after I come out of this exhilarating trance state, I can trust my ability to initiate peace and relaxation whenever it is needed. When I go to bed at night, I take delight in the fact that sleeping serves to replenish my entire body, hour after hour, cell by remarkable cell.

Now, breathing in deeply, I take in full breaths as if I can picture the oxygen filling my lungs. As I continue to breathe deeply, I imagine the oxygen as a magic healing vapor. The deeper I breathe, the deeper this healing vapor circulates into my entire body. The more oxygen I take in, the more I feel the effect of its healing powers. I can visualize a clear picture of this healing vapor going into my lungs and circulating throughout my nervous system.

(continue)

Fulfilling The Subject's Needs (continued)

I can imagine a large softgel containing a liquid tranquilizer being lodged in the upper portion of my brain. I let it become loose and slowly travel down the head, and settle into the back of my neck. Now, I let the softgel dissolve, allowing the liquid tranquilizer to flow down my throat and settle there. I feel the liquid dissolving into my throat. And now, allow the liquid tranquilizer to settle into every part of my body starting from my throat, and seeping down to the bottom of my feet. I feel its tranquilizing effect as it seeps down my chest and arms. I Feel its loosening and healing effects as it seeps into every muscle, every ligament and into every joint.

I imagine every part of my body becoming so relaxed it seems like jelly. I allow this liquid tranquilizer to relieve every pain, every arthritic condition, every restrictive feeling in my body. I allow this tranquilizer to balance my entire nervous system, my complete immune system, as I focus on allowing my mind to come to complete rest. I am free of all worry, free of all tension as I drift off into my hypnotic trance. Deeper and deeper I go into this deep trance state; deeper and deeper I go into hypnosis. The deeper I go into hypnosis, the deeper I go into this trance state. Deeper and deeper, I drift off into my beautiful, restful hypnotic trance. As I search into that wide opening to my subconscious, I feel that my memory as well as my appeal has improved. The ease with which I am able to influence those around me to gain love, admiration, opportunities and wealth may seem amazing, but at this very moment the powers of my subconscious mind have made all this possible.

My subconscious mind has recorded this and will remember everything that has been said. Before I come out of this trance, I allow a brief pause as a way thanking God for the infinite riches flowing into my life.

As I slowly begin to count from 1 to 5, I will become better and better upon each count. 1 . . . I am feeling much better; 2 . . . I remember everything that happened in this trance state; 3 . . . I already feel that my life has changed for the better; 4 . . . I am fully aware and functioning perfectly normal. 5 . . . I am awake and fully alert, feeling more physically fit than ever before.

MIND-ALTERING AFFIRMATIONS

In this bowed praying position, bless yourself with the sign of the cross. Then begin with the following prayers, in silence, as demonstrated in **Illustration 13 - 1**, below. When appropriate "Go into" ***The Trance Zone***, and proceed with the inductions that follow.

It is best to memorize these several prayers, reciting them audibly with the eyes closed. An additional benefit to kneeling with the head down is that it sends blood and oxygen to the head and neck region, thereby replenishing the brain cells to some extent.

PRAYER POSITION
Illustration 13 – 1

RECITE AUDIBLY:

To ward off depression, pain and negativity, I make the sign of the cross and affirm, by this sign I conquer. You demons, you devil -- let go, because I let God. I call on the power of divine restoration. My good of past and present is divinely restored to me now. This is a time of divine fulfillment. I give thanks for my divine restoration in mind, body, financial affairs, and in all my relationships. I am in God's hands, God's power, for I am certainly God's property now.

Count it all joy my brethren, when you meet various trials for you know that the testing of your faith produces steadfastness. And let steadfastness have its full effect, that you may be perfect and complete, lacking in nothing.
   (James 1: 2-4)

But they that wait upon the Lord shall renew their strength; they shall mount up with wings as eagles; they shall run and not be weary; and they shall walk, and not faint. (Isaiah 40:31)

Not by might, nor by power, but by My Spirit, saith The Lord.
   (Zechariah 4:6)

Take delight in The Lord, and He will give you the desires of your heart.
   (Psalms 37: 4)

Whether kneeling or sitting "Go into" ***The Trance Zone***, Then recite audibly, the affirmations listed below. Before doing so, consider going into a deep trance beforehand. Since sounds resonate through neurotransmitters affecting the glands and organs playing inspirational music in the background aids in having self-hypnosis take its full affect.

RECITE AUDIBLY:
*Dear God, in the name of, Jesus Christ, I **ask** that You keep Your Loving support behind me; below me; above, ahead and around me, as well as within me no matter where I am, what I do, or what I think. I also **ask** that you be my cushion when things go wrong and my spiritual power to ward off evil, instill good fortune, and to intercede to make everything in my life go right.*

I pray for God's power to supercharge resistance against the devil; and that I may be protected and receive His magical powers, in addition the His great generosity. "Ephphatha" I am opened -- therefore I receive the Spirit of God through the unlimited strength and power of Jesus. (Note: Jesus used the word "Ephphatha" to heal his subjects.)

An incredible goodness is operating in my behalf. Nevermore do I think lack, or failure; I think prosperity, success; I think I am the best I can possibly be.

Minute by minute I am getting better and better. Already I feel the process working. Day by day beginning today, I know I am better and getting progressively better. Since nothing is impossible as long as I believe, I know my subconscious mind can alter, or reverse any problem, thereby making me exceedingly better.

Nothing is too good to be true, so my hopes can become realized. My most wonderful dreams are coming true. All I need I can really have, and I am expecting great things to happen starting this very moment. God is with me now providing me with protection and prosperity as well as supernatural intervention in all areas of my life.

Each day before I go out to face the world, I promise God I'll talk to Him and know it won't go unheard; I promise to ask for God's Spirit and God's strength as I pray. Yes, I promise I'll charge my battery as I talk with God, through Jesus, each and every remarkable day.

PART EIGHT

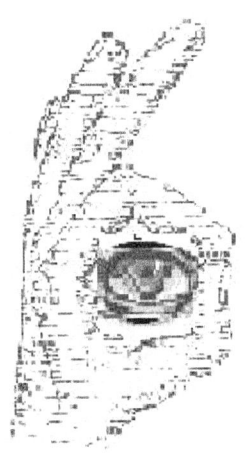

Part Eight

CHAPTER FOURTEEN
14

UNIFIED PHYSICAL THERAPY TECHNIQUE

---

14   HYPNOSIS
            TECHNIQUE

<u>Leonardo de Vinci once said to his disciples:</u>

*"The soul does not like to be without its body
because without its body it cannot feel nor do anything;
therefore build a figure in such a way
that its pose tells what is in the soul of IT"*

EjL 1998

CHAPTER FOURTEEN
14

UNIFIED PHYSICAL THERAPY TECHNIQUE™

A HEALTHY BODY, A SOUND MIND

Tending to mental and physical health has always been a constant struggle. If a person doesn't stick to a sound exercise routine and beneficial nutritional regimen, that person's body will tend to deteriorate before its time. For instance, if a person were to eat nothing but white bread, salt and coffee with loads of sugar, that person's body would soon become prone to disease and stroke. Add to this, alcohol and cigarette addiction, and the situation becomes even bleaker. On the other hand, if a person were to eat fish and an assortment of fresh fruits and steamed vegetables, that person's body and vital organs would tend remain fruitful.

My explanation for this is that, from birth, nature's role is to see that we are given the opportunity to develop, spiritually, but mentally and physically, as well. After a time, when going against nature's role too long, the body begins its swing toward fatality. Think of it as the "degenerative swing." The principle is much the same as when an apple grows on a tree. After it falls or is shaken off, the degenerative process begins to set in because its lifeline – its umbilical cord to nature – has been cut; then comes the rotting. Fortunately, as humans, we are blessed with the ability to decelerate this inevitable swing.

Through a never-ending responsibility to ourselves, we must see to it that our bodies get the proper exercise and nourishment, enough so that it becomes a sustaining fuel -- a progressive blood/cell regeneration process. This physical conditioning is our only way of retarding the inevitable pull towards death. In fact, in the animal kingdom, the expression "the survival of the fittest" is truly representative of their way of life. In their world, the weak are always the first to succumb. It is the same in our world – death holds a ringside seat and continues to beckon the underdog called "self-neglect," while life, the opponent as "the fittest," spars to defend the title of **longevity**.

The exercises listed below are not only to intended to improve the quality of life for those willing to participate, but to insure that total physical fitness, including a dexterous, sound mind serve as the corridor to that **longevity**.

Consider the following **Unified Physical Therapy Technique**™, if you will, as your free insurance policy.

UNIFIED PHYSICAL THERAPY TECHNIQUE™

If you happened to think the **Unified Physical Therapy Technique™** has nothing to do with hypnotism, you would be dead wrong. In fact, exercise is one of the most effective ways to acquire the discipline to stay focused, in addition to becoming relaxed, physically, as well as mentally.

The closer a person comes to relaxing, the closer that person is able to reach the unfathomable powers that lay latent within the subconscious. Actually, during and after exercising, the brain waves become very much the same as when undergoing hypnosis. This means that the person, who has exercised, is more prepared to be hypnotized, than the one who has not exercised.

When committing to this **Unified Physical Therapy Technique™** you will receive a multitude of benefits. First and foremost, is the surprising sense of high-esteem, then comes the feeling of having excessive energy; then comes an increase in strength and endurance, and finally comes the state of total relaxation. The real surprise will come when you realize that can't do without the exercises. Upon reaching this point, you will have developed an athletic heart, in more ways then one. You may even come to realize that the pleasure derived from exercise can run a close parallel to having sex. Yes, exercise can become that enjoyable.

What Eventually Occurs During This Training -- (3 to 5 times a week.):

Without exercise, the body tends to degenerate before its time – the spine loses its posture, muscles lose elasticity, and the blood tends to lose its hemoglobin count. Then the spirit begins to yield to negative symptoms, such as high anxiety, neurosis --even complete exhaustion.

By exercising, these symptoms can become reversed; the conditions such as Chronic Fatigue Syndrome (CFS) can become totally mitigated. Even fear can become a factor, causing headaches, nausea, ulcers, and various other diseases. Since fear feeds the muscle tension that causes these disorders, the key is to alleviate that fear. Then, soon, the symptoms will begin to subside.

What does fear have to do with this? – Everything. Without going into the vast array of categories associated with fear, the important thing is in realizing that practicing the **Unified Physical Therapy Technique™** can provide a profound effect on the things feared in life. Take security, as a brief example. Once the feeling of physical and mental relaxation is attained, the body responds in a totally different way. And in doing so, it induces a positive psychosomatic reaction.

When everything _feels_ right, everything will _go_ right. So, the key really boils down to attitude. Actually, "attitude" became the contributing factor behind naming this section the **Unified Physical Therapy Technique™**. For, in combining these exercises with prayer and affirmations, and then connecting it all to hypnosis, it becomes a unified experience, producing harmony, unity, and purpose within the participant. The purpose for this orchestrated approach is that it will provide conformity, change, and eventually the complete transformation of one's attitude.

(continue)

What Eventually Occurs During This Training (continued)

After a short period, you will begin to experience a shift from being anxious and tense, to a state of mental balance and harmony. Because of replacing negative behavior with this positive activity, the heart will respond, producing a smooth, coherent rhythm. This, in turn, has a positive effect on the neurological, immune and hormonal activity. By providing renewed circulatory activity, the muscles become relaxed, due to being revitalized with the increased blood circulation.

Not only does exercise serve as a form of exorcism, as well as provide security, but it also acts to give the body muscle tone, strong bones and flexibility of the joints. When our joints become limber, there becomes a probability of alleviating the symptoms of arthritis; or even curing arteriosclerosis -- that debilitating disease leading to the thickening and hardening of arterial walls. Through exercise, the body reacts and serves to force poison, lymphatic fluids, and waste from the muscle tissues, into the blood and to the excretory glands. In addition, exercise serves to aid in strengthening the will, rejuvenation of the cells, organs, skin, and the entire endocrine system, as well as improving the thought and mental patterns of the brain – the most important organ for sustaining life and **longevity**.

UNIFIED ABDOMINAL BREATHING

Before beginning any of the exercises, practice the following breathing exercise to experience just how natural breathing occurs. Afterward, you should always apply this technique when exercising.

To practice **Unified Abdominal Breathing** (or diaphragmatic breathing), become seated comfortably and place the right hand on the abdomen and the left hand on the chest. Breathe in and out through the nose, several times, to get the lungs going. Then, with no movement under the left hand, inhale deeply through the nose. With the right hand rising and falling, keep breathing in and out, feeling the abdomen expanding and depleting of air. When you feel abdomen pushing and falling under the right hand, think of the diaphragm acting as a bellows pumping air out and drawing it in.

Get the feel of your belly becoming completely flat, and then becoming fully enlarged as you hold your right hand firmly against it. As you suck in hard, and push out until there is no more air, make sure the chest doesn't rise under the left hand. After a little practice, you will be breathing correctly, perhaps for the first time. This is the professional technique used to teach singers, as well as speakers, how to project their voices. To avoid becoming overly conscious of breathing while exercising, the main rule is to breathe in before initiating the exercise, and exhale upon releasing the tension. When you apply the above technique to your exercises, breathing will happen automatically, because of the natural action of the diaphragm.

UNIFIED PHYSICAL IMAGRY

Many people have difficulty perceiving themselves as having a great body, or addressing the fact that their physical condition doesn't measure up to their own standards. Still others procrastinate about doing anything to improve their self-image. The following self-hypnosis induction has been designed to, not only to alter negative attitudes, but also to instill new ways of gaining optimism and self-esteem.

Through **Unified Physical Imagery**, a person becomes enabled to imagine the old self in a new light, simply by projecting the ideally transformed self, subconsciously. Before beginning with the following exercises, follow the self-hypnosis procedure as described below. This "positive conditioning" will help you to stay focused. After that, practice going into self-hypnosis no less than 5 times a week. Always strive to reach your ideal physical condition, keeping a positive image of yourself throughout the exercises.

SUBJECT: (sitting, lying, or kneeling)
First, either tape or memorize the following self-hypnotic induction:
Then, "Go Into" ***The Trance Zone*** ™ and proceed.

Now, breathing in deeply, I take in full breaths as if I can picture the oxygen filling my lungs. As I continue to breathe deeply, I imagine the oxygen as a magic healing vapor. The deeper I breathe, the deeper this healing vapor circulates into my entire body. The more oxygen I take in, the more I feel the effect of its healing powers. I can visualize a clear picture of this healing vapor going into my lungs and circulating throughout my nervous system.

I can imagine a large softgel *containing a liquid tranquilizer being lodged in the upper portion of my brain. I let it become loose and slowly travel down the head, and settle into the back of my neck. Now, I let the softgel dissolve, allowing the liquid tranquilizer to flow down my throat and settle there. I feel the liquid dissolving into my throat. And now, allow the liquid tranquilizer to settle into every part of my body starting from my throat, and seeping down to the bottom of my feet. I feel its tranquilizing effect as it seeps down my chest and arms. I Feel its loosening and healing effects as it seeps into every muscle, every ligament and into every joint.*

I imagine every part of my body *becoming so relaxed it seems like jelly. I allow this liquid tranquilizer to relieve every pain, every arthritic condition, every restrictive feeling in my body. I allow this tranquilizer to balance my entire nervous system, my complete immune system, as I focus on allowing my mind to come to complete rest. I am free of all worry, free of all tension as I drift off into my hypnotic trance. Deeper and deeper I go into this deep trance state; deeper and deeper I go into hypnosis. The deeper I go into hypnosis, the deeper I go into this trance state. Deeper and deeper, I drift off into my beautiful, restful hypnotic trance.*
(continue)

SUBJECT: (continued)

Still using my imagination, I can visualize myself in my present condition inside a large, black frame with all my features shown in black and white. Now, I see this picture dissolve and I reappear inside of a bright, blue frame with everything in vivid color, where I become larger than life, my face and figure appearing in vivid color. As I visualize myself removing my clothes, I study the features of my entire body. I am pleased with this image, but in order to appear even better, I imagine myself with a perfect body – and a figure I can really feel proud about.

As I envision the changes taking place, I can see my muscle tone developing and becoming more appealing to my eyes. Now, I can actually begin see the way I look after doing my exercises. Although I feel some changes taking place right now, I know that I am progressively looking and feeling better. This amazing transformation happens every time I "Go Into" **The Trance Zone**™.

As I keep focused on this very appealing image of myself, I can see that I not only have developed a beautiful body, but my weight is finally to where it should be for my height. As I stare, admiring myself to the point I can actually believe this true, I see myself tossing away my old clothes. Now, as I envision myself in a new set of clothes, I really marvel at how great I look, how attractive I really am. I find this very intriguing as I allow this image to become etched in my mind.

Using my imagination once more, I study the whole picture of myself in this bright blue frame, and as I focus on my image, I see the whole picture becoming life-like. As I continue to focus and imagine how great I look, I admire this great image of my newly developed body. As I focus on this enlarged image, I count, 1 . . . 2 . . . 3, and replace the bright blue frame with a splendid gilded frame, finding myself in a remarkably appealing pose. Since this gilded frame around me is like those expensive frames used for masterpieces in museums, it becomes engraved in my subconscious mind. Now, this image of my self has found a permanent place in my mind, and I am able to call upon the picture any time I wish.

With my newly formed identity, I now envision myself as the person I've always dreamed I could be. In this state of subconscious, I can always recall how great it felt to have my imagination make me over. My subconscious mind has allowed me see and feel this greatly improved image of my self. When I come out of this trance, I will remember everything that has taken place, and be able to reflect on it every time I wish to improve my image. Whether I reflect on it, or not, this session is already taking a positive affect on me – and it will continue to do so, automatically.

UNIFIED PHYSICAL EXERCISES

The exercises, as described below, consist of a combination of effective anaerobic, aerobic and resistance techniques that have taken years of sweat to develop. Any "kinks" have been modified and rectified thereby producing selectively balanced, well organized "Sets," or groups of highly effective exercises.

One of the best things about this **Unified Physical Therapy Technique**™ is that there is no fancy, or expensive, equipment involved. A ten pound dumbbell and a mat is all that is required to perform any, or all, of the exercises – a fantastic benefit for those having little space to work from. No matter whether you are looking for performance, bodybuilding, athletic ability or merely becoming physically fit, the following exercises will, certainly, fulfill your needs. For sure, the more you work at this, the more you will be amazed at the results.

Although these exercises are designed to greatly improve the physical condition, be sure not to neglect other exercises, such as walking, swimming, tennis, etc. -- the main thing is to find ways of becoming motivated, to strive to become physically and mentally fit, no matter what that takes. No matter which kind of program you select to become fit, be sure to drink at least 6 to 8 glasses of water daily. Not only does this prevent dehydration, but it also washes away many of the unwanted toxins that continuously invade the body. Although it is okay to have water when exercising, it is not advisable to drink ice water.

THE ILLUSTRATIONS

Note: After becoming familiar with the exercises, you may feel more comfortable by alternating the **First Set of Exercises** one day, and the **Second Set** the next day. Although it may make sense to deviate from the sequences because of the needs, or requirements, of your body, it is crucial that you always begin with the **Warm Up Exercises**.

Total Repetitions Table

Warm Up Exercises --- Standing Up

Warm Ups – Total of 5 minutes @ 1 consecutive minute per exercise:
    Activates the lungs and stretches the muscles of the upper torso.
14 – 1 **Backstroke** – Begin with closed fingers – **1 minute**.
14 – 2 **Swimstroke** -- continue with closed fingers – **1 minute**.
14 – 3 **Hands Straight Up** continue with open fingers –**1 minute**
14 – 4 **Alternating Fists** continue with closed fists – **1 minute**
14 – 5 **Open Hands Crisscross** finish with open fingers – **1 minute**
 	
    Note: complete these without resting throughout the 5-minute period.

(continued below)

THE ILLUSTRATIONS (continued)

Total Repetitions Table

First Set of Exercises --- Standing Up
14 – 6 Alternate Kick – Begin this set with **10 kicks** each leg. 14 – 7 Deep Knee Bend – Repeat this exercise **10 times**. 14 – 8 Elephant Swing – For limbering up, do this exercise for **1 minute – 2 times** 14 – 9 Touch Toes Straight – Repeat this exercise **10 times**. 14 –10 Touch Opposite Toes – Repeat this exercise **10 times**. **Sitting Down** 14 – 11 Dumbbell Curl & Press – Repeat this exercise **10 times**.

Total Repetitions Table

Second Set of Exercises -- Lying Down
14 – 12 Rowing and Alternate – Repeat this combined exercise **2 times**. 14 – 13 Bend Overs – Repeat this exercise **15 times**. 14 – 14– Alternate Leg Swings – Repeat this exercise **10 times**. 14 – 15 Both Legs Lifts – Repeat this exercise **10 times**. 14 – 16 Flutter Kicks – Repeat this exercise for **10 double-kicks -- 2 times**. 14 – 17 Alternate Pushups – Repeat this exercise **10 times – each hand**. 14 – 18 Half Sit Ups – Repeat this exercise **10 times**.

An Important Note About These Exercises:

When most people think about exercise they shirk from the idea of doing them for two reasons: 1, -- They think they will become too tired; 2, -- They think exercise will take away the energy they need to do other things. In both cases they are gravely (and I use the term rather loosely), misinformed.

The amazing truth is that exercise provides _more_ energy – the more you participate, the more the energy builds up. The day you begin to exercise is the day you reverse becoming tired. And, in the days following, you will find you have so much energy you will become astounded by how many tasks you begin taking on, not to mention the enthusiasm it brings – (well, I _had to_ mention it). You owe it to yourself to begin exercising your way to progressive health – otherwise life becomes, all too soon, digressive.

Total Repetitions Table

Finishing The Exercises Off (optional)
The Human Blossom -- Perform this combined exercise **5 times** a week. 14 – 19 Inhale – Begin to **Inhale** in the fetus position. 14 – 20 Exhale – After rising up, **Exhale** while returning to the fetus position.

UNIFIED PHYSICAL EXERCISES
THE ILLUSTRATIONS:

When performing these exercises, bear in mind two things. First, always strive to increase the repetitions until reaching your **comfort zone**. Second, although these exercises have a specific order, keep experimenting until you find which exercises give the best results, predicated by your **intuitive feelings**.

Warm Up Exercises
Illustrations 14 – 1 to 14 – 5
Total Time: 5 minutes.

When doing these **5 Warm Up Exercises**, spend **1 minute** on each of the exercises as illustrated below, for a total of **5 minutes**.

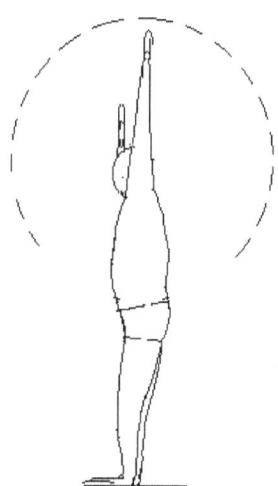

Illustration 14 – 1   Backstroke

Begin the warm ups, with the **Backstroke**, as shown in **Illustrations 14 – 1**, above. From a standing position, swing the arms upwards, backwards and down, imitating *a swimming backstroke. Keep the fingers together*.
Repeat this exercise for 1 minute.
Then proceed immediately to the next **Warm Up Exercise**.

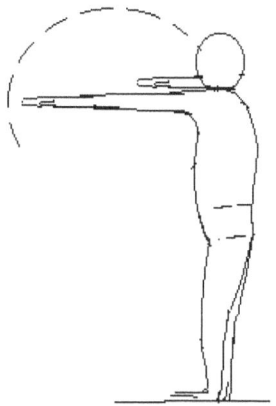

Illustration 14 – 2   Swimstroke

Continue with the **Swimstroke,** by shifting the arms above the head and thrusting forward, imitating the overhand swimming stroke. Keep the fingers together.
Repeat this exercise for 1 minute.
Then proceed immediately to the next **Warm Up Exercise**.

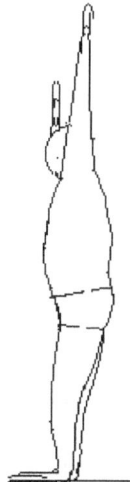

Illustration 14 – 3 Hands Straight Up

Continue with the **Hands Straight Up**, by stretching as high as possible with one hand, and then, while bringing it back down to the shoulder, stretch the opposite hand upward. Keep the fingers spread apart.
Repeat this exercise for 1 minute.
Then proceed immediately to the next **Warm Up Exercise**.

Warm Up Exercises (continued)

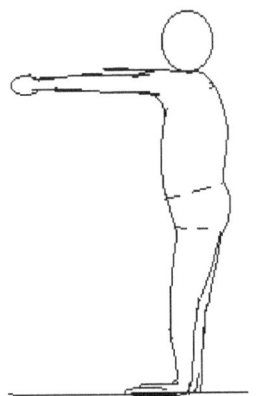

Illustration 14 – 4 Alternating Fists

Continue with the **Alternating Fists** by bringing the hands to the shoulders and making fists. Then thrust each fist forward, alternating them, as they are thrust forward and back, as if punching an invisible bag. During this exercise think of it as a flowing motion in two stages: 1 - while keeping the chest erect, pivot at the waist and count 5 strokes smiling and exhaling making a hiss sound. 2 - continue with another count of 5 strokes, while inhaling with the mouth puckered making a sucking sound. This type of breathing causes the lungs to become purified, as well as increasing the lung capacity. The smile aids in keeping everything positive, and energized. Doing this also helps to intensify concentration, for any purpose.
Keep the fingers closed into a fist.
Repeat this exercise for 1 minute.
Then proceed immediately to the next
Warm Up Exercise.

Warm Up Exercise 14-5

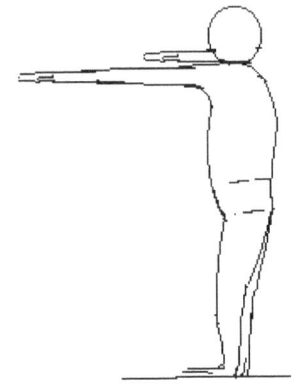

Illustration 14–5 OpenHandsCrisscross

Finish with the warm ups with the **Open Hands Crisscross**, by immediately shifting to a crisscross swing -- that is, by opening the fists and spreading the fingers, and swinging the hands, alternately, across to the opposite shoulder. Have the arms crisscross the chest from shoulder to shoulder. Continue the same breathing technique as described above. Keep the fingers extended and spread apart.
Repeat this exercise for 1 minute.
Take a brief rest before proceeding to the
First Set of Exercises.

Physical Therapy Technique   197

First Set of Exercises
Illustrations 14 – 6 through 14 – 11
Total Time: approximately 20 minutes.

When doing this **First Set of Exercises**, as illustrated below, **Repeat** each one as specified, then gradually increase the repetitions as you progress. <u>**Note:**</u> As with all these exercises, keep increasing the repetitions until reaching your ideal physical condition. <u>Always</u> take several minutes rest between exercises.

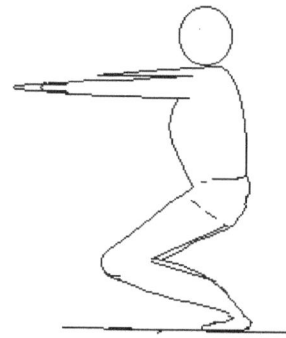

Illustration 14 – 7   Deep Knee Bend

To execute this exercise, begin by standing with the feet shoulder width flat on the floor. Then, with the hands extended palms down, the eyes looking straight ahead, keep the spine straight and let the torso drop as you bend the knees. Done properly, this will place you in the ideal bending position, balancing on your toes. Then, still balancing on your toes, rise up to the original standing position until the feet become flat on the floor again.
Repeat this exercise 10 times.

> **Note**: Since brain cells die at the rate of millions per second, this form of breathing enables the oxygen to replenish the brain cells at a more intensified rate. When breathing, think of breathing between the eyes while breathing through the nose. Not only does breathing in this manner act to replenish the brain cells, but doing this special deep-knee exercise serves to improve the condition of the blood's capillaries, as well.
>
> When performing this exercise, the immune system becomes inundated with such an abundance of oxygen, the brain, as well as the respiratory and circulatory systems become revitalized. And since capillaries are a vital part of the blood, providing the body with this kind of oxygen replenishment goes a long way toward altering the molecular structure, as well as rejuvenating the immune system.
>
> Although this exercise may cause hyperventilation, which could cause dizziness, try to stick with it. Try starting with fewer repetitions, and then increase them, gradually.

Illustration 14 – 6 Alternate Kick

Begin this set of exercises with the feet flat on the floor. Then, balancing on the left foot, extend the left hand straight out, and try to kick the extended left palm with the right foot.
Continue by switching legs, balancing on the right foot. Now, extend the right hand straight out, and try to kick the extended right palm with the left foot. Not only is this exercise excellent for stamina, weight control, circulation, and posture, it is an excellent way of gaining profound mental and physical equilibrium.
Repeat this exercise 10 times.

First Set of Exercises (continued)

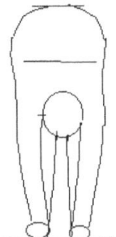

Illustration 14 – 8 Elephant Swing
For limbering up in preparation for the next several exercises bend over, letting the head and hands hang freely. Then, gently bouncing, pivot at the waist and continue bouncing from side to side. This exercise is not only good for relaxation, but the flow of blood becomes invigorating for the head and scalp.
Do this for **1 minute**.
Repeat this exercise 2 times.

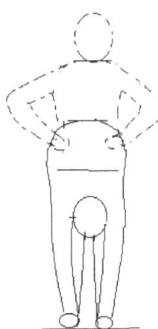

Illustration 14 – 9 Touch Toes Straight
Beginning from a standing position with the hands on the hips, and the feet spread shoulder width, bend straight down and touch the toes.
Bending over, and stretching as far as possible each time, try to touch the fingers to the toes. With every repetition, strive to stretch far enough to have bent fists touch the floor between the feet. For most people, this will take many attempts. However, never force when stretching. The object is to practice until the muscles become loose enough so that they stretch more and more over time. This exercise is especially good for stamina, weight control and circulation. It fact, this serves to greatly improve the posture.
Repeat this exercise 10 times.

Exercise 14-10

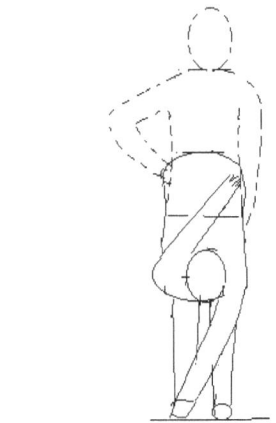

Illustration 14 – 10 Touch OppositeToes

Beginning from a standing position with the hands on the hips, and the feet spread shoulder width, bend down and stretch either hand to touch the opposite toes. When bending over each time, alternate the hands and stretch as far as possible trying to touch the fingers to the opposite toes. Pivot at the waist to get as much motion as possible.
This exercise is especially good for the abdomen and vital organs, as well as the chest and arm muscles. This also serves to greatly improve the posture.
Repeat this exercise 10 times.

First Set of Exercises (continued)

Illustration 14–11 Dumbbell Curl Press

Using **only one** ten-pound dumbbell, become seated and lift it (in either hand) to shoulder height, then straight above the head. Performed in two sweeping motions, lift the dumbbell up to the shoulder, then twist the wrist forward and lift it straight above the head. When dropping down to the shoulder twist the wrist again and drop the hand to the side. This action serves to strengthen the combined muscles of the arms, hands, wrists, and shoulders. This is also very good for stamina.
Repeat this exercise 7 times.
Take a brief rest before proceeding to the **Second Set of Exercises.**

Physical Therapy Technique

Second Set of Exercises
Illustrations 14 – 12 through 14 –18
Total Time approximately 20 minutes.

In doing this **Second Set of Exercises**, as illustrated below, **Repeat** each one as specified then gradually increase the repetitions as you progress.
   Note: Keep experimenting, eliminating some exercises one day and doubling up on others the next. Keep striving to reach your ideal physical condition. Always take several minutes rest between exercises.

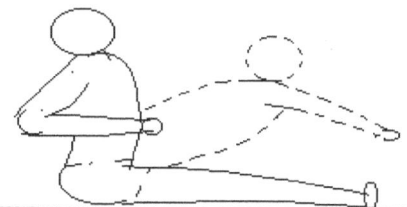

Illustration 14 – 12 Rowing & Alternate

Beginning in a sitting position, stretch both hands forward, reach to touch the toes with the fingertips, and continuing in a flowing motion, pull the arms backwards while making fists until the back becomes arched. Do this as if rowing a boat. Do this exercise **5 times**.
   Next, placing the left hand behind the back, stretch the right hand over to the left foot and reach to touch the left toe with the fingertips, and continuing in a sweeping motion, pull the arm back making a fist, and place it behind the back. Then continue the same procedure using the left hand.
   Do this **5 times**. This combination is especially good for breathing and stamina.
Repeat this combined exercise 2 times.

Second Set of Exercises
(continued)

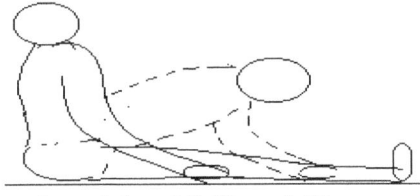

Illustration 14 – 13 Bend Overs

Beginning in a sitting position, reach forward, placing the hands under the calves, and pull the torso gently to the legs. In a flowing motion, continue by leaning backwards as far as possible, while allowing the hands to slide up to the thighs, for balance.

In addition to many other benefits, this exercise is great for reducing the waistline.

Repeat this exercise 15 times.

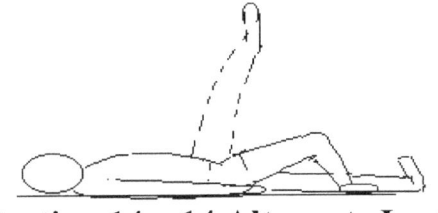

Illustration 14 – 14 Alternate LegSwing

Lying in a comfortable position with the hands resting at the sides, bend the right leg and lock the knee and foot into position. Then, swing the left leg as high as possible while keeping the leg straight, extending the toes forward. Upon bringing the leg down keeping it straight and bending the toes back toward the knee, let the leg drop, stopping it just before the foot touches the floor. Continue the exercise by switching to the opposite leg. When swinging each leg, scissors-like, concentrate on the pivotal action of the hip, ankle and foot muscles.

Repeat this exercise 10 times.

Exercise 14-15

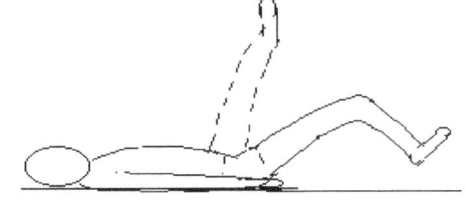

Illustration 14 – 15 Both Legs Lifts

Lying in a comfortable position with the hands resting at the sides bend both legs and lock the knees and foots into position. Then, swing both legs as high as possible, bending at the knees, and extending the toes forward. Now, bending at the knees, dropping and pulling the legs toward the torso, reverse the toes pulling them toward the knee without the feet touching the floor.

When swinging the legs in this jackknife motion, concentrate on the pivotal action of the knees, ankles and foot muscles. By loosening the tension in these joints, the body will respond in kind by becoming more relaxed, providing much needed agility and dexterity.

Repeat this exercise 10 times.

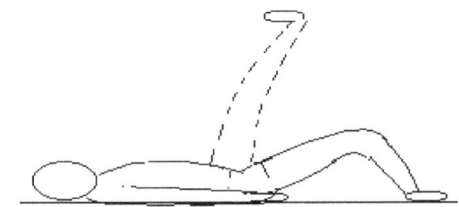

Illustration 14 – 16 Flutter Kicks

Lying in a comfortable position with the hands resting at the sides, simply lift both legs and begin kicking. In doing so, keep the legs up and angled at 45 degrees, while imagining doing a flutter kick in the water. When executing this, flutter the legs and feet freely and rhythmically while bending at the knees, never allowing the feet to touch the floor. This exercise works extremely well for tightening up the thighs, buttocks, and abdominal muscles. Continue doing this for **10 double-kicks. Repeat this exercise 2 times.**

Second Set of Exercises
(continued)

Exercise 14-18

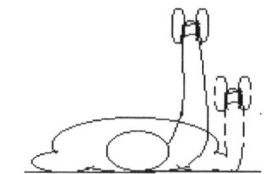

Illustration 14 – 17 Alternate Pushups

Lying in a comfortable position, with the left hand resting at the side, brace a 10-pound dumbbell in the right hand. With the elbow touching the floor, lift the dumbbell straight
up, extending the arm as far as possible. Then lower the arm to the beginning position, and raise it again without the elbow touching the floor. When doing this exercise, the legs may be bent, but keep the dumbbell in line with the breast.
Repeat this exercise 10 times – each hand.

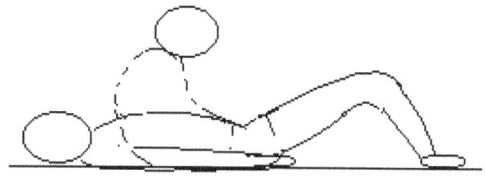

Illustration 14 – 18 Half Sit Ups

Lying in a comfortable position with the hands resting at the sides, raise the chest, keeping the neck straight. When doing this **Half Sit Up** exercise, keep the hands flat, and the knees bent and locked into position.
In addition to strengthening the spine, this exercise is great for tightening the abdominal muscles.
Repeat this exercise 10 times.

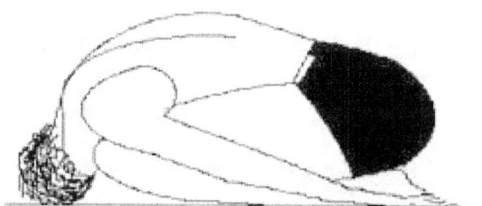

Remember to Do The Human Blossom

FINE'

A SPECIAL SELF-ESTEEM EXERCISE
Another exercise in Unified Physical Imagery

Before proceeding with, **Finishing The Exercises Off** it would be a good idea to spend some time building up a little extra confidence, as well as to concentrate on improving the self-image. With that in mind, consider practicing the following self-hypnotic suggestion.

In combining this **special self-esteem exercise** with the above physical exercises, altering one's physical condition can, feasibly, become a reality taking half the time it would ordinarily take to have to reach the ideal physical image. With dedication, practice and commitment, acquiring a sexy and visually appealing physique will no longer be as you dreamed – merely by **participating** and **accepting** it, this will become your reality.

Congratulations on your decision to go ahead. Now, focus on your ideal image and make this special self-esteem exercise become very personal and special to you.

"Go Into" **The Trance Zone** and induce the self-hypnosis, as follows:

*I now lift my **eyes up to the eyebrows**, and close them. I give a **deep yawn**, and form "**the hypnotic eye**" by placing my thumb and forefinger of my hand together. Now, I recite, This is how I Go Into **The Trance Zone**.*

*As I concentrate, I **inhale through the nose** and exhale counting down from 30 by 2's, relaxing the body more and more until reaching 0. (Record the count slowly, evenly: 30, 28, 26, 24, 22, 20, 18 . . . etc.)*

I am sitting comfortably with my eyes still closed; my arms and legs are flexible, relaxed. Gracefully and freely, I lift both arms and imagine myself as an angel, wings and all. Now, I imagine myself as being surrounded with a blue aura. And as I concentrate, this blue aura begins to glow more and more bluer. Taking deep breaths, I let my entire body relax, but still keeping my arms in comfortable, raised position. Soon, while my blue aura continues to glow, it gets warmer and warmer until I feel a rush of energy surging throughout my body.

This energy is a positive and healing energy. This powerful energy overcomes me to the point I feel a tremendous confidence in myself. I let myself go. I let myself be . . . Let whatever happens happen, because terrific things are taking place. My mind is free of all worry, free of daily problems and headaches. As I sit, free of tension, I rejoice in the sense of well being that my blue aura brings me, which envelops me from head to foot. I Feel and experience this wonderful sensation which spreads more and more throughout my body.

(continued)

The Trance Zone self-hypnosis (continued)

I feel protected, secure and full of high esteem as the sensation forms a permanent place in my subconscious. My subconscious is registering all my words. Wider and wider, this opening has become. The gentle words of my voice are being deeply engraved there as I listen intently to these suggestions. I am listening very intently as I proceed, confidently. Now that I am a free spirit capable of going anywhere I wish, unafraid of doing anything I desire, I now lower my arms and imagine myself flying on the back of a huge American Eagle. Higher and higher, I soar freely among the protective clouds on those thick, soft feathers. I am unafraid, protected, and delighted at being far away from planet earth, far away from reality and the burdens that go along with daily activities.

*The image I have formed of "**the hypnotic eye**" is the key to unleashing the power of my subconscious mind. Whenever I call upon this image, hidden knowledge is brought to light. As I look deeper and deeper within my spirit, I draw wisdom from the depths of my subconscious mind. All knowledge is there for me. All channels of guidance are opened to me, especially spiritual guidance. Everything I want to know is revealed. Everything is made clear; everything is exposed. My will, as well as Thy Will, will be done - and thus, it is laid out before me.*

Focusing on returning to the world below, I know that I have permission to become anyone I wish to be, accomplish anything I wish to accomplish. With my newly formed identity, I envision myself as the person I've always dreamed I could be. In this state of subconscious, I will always remember how great it felt to have my imagination make me over. My subconscious mind has allowed me feel better about myself, and when I awaken, I will remember everything that happened during this time.

As I slowly begin to count from 1 to 5, I will become better and better upon each count. 1 . . . I am feeling much better, 2 . . . I remember everything that happened in this trance state, 3 . . . I already feel that my life has changed for the better, 4 . . . I am fully aware and functioning perfectly normal, 5 . . . I am awake and fully alert, feeling better than ever before.

Practice this special exercise until you actually feel the results. Experience fulfilling the dream of your hearts desire.

204 *The Trance Zone*

THE HUMAN BLOSSOM

Finishing The Exercises Off (optional)

CLEANSING EXERCISE:

The Human Blossom is performed as a two-fold exercise as follows:
    In the first fetus position as shown in **Illustration 14—19**, crouch down on the knees while bending the head and placing the hands, palm upward, alongside of the body. This is the position, in which to **Inhale**.
    In the second chest-expansion position, as shown in **Illustration 14 – 20**, rise up from the fetus position, still inhaling and while extending the arms backwards, sit back and rest between the ankles.
Then, begin to **Exhale** while bringing the arms forward toward the fetus position.
    The Human Blossom becomes completed upon fully exhaling and settling into the starting fetus position.
    Repeat this exercise 5 times a week.

Illustration 14 -- 19 Inhale: **Illustration 14 -- 20 Exhale:**

In the fetus position as shown above in **Illustration 14 – 19**, take in several breaths to relax. Then, **Inhale** while reciting the following affirmation:

Out with demons, out with disease, Out with all negativity.

After reaching the chest-expansion position with the hands above the head as shown above in **Illustration 14 – 20**, begin to **Exhale** while lowering the arms and reciting the following prayer:

In with God's Supernatural Power, In with the spirit of Jesus Christ.

ADDITIONAL CLEANSING EXERCISES: (optional)

For added protection against all evil forces, recite the following prayer audibly at least once a week, in the position of **The Human Blossom**. (As an alternative, memorize and recite it while you **"Go Into"** ***The Trance Zone***.)

I am fortunate because I am in harmony with the universe of abundance, which is in perfect sync with the powers of my creator and His Divine plans for me. I shall reinforce this fact by reciting the following verse:

    The Whole Armor of God.
    Finally, my brethren, be strong in the Lord, and in the power of His Might. ***Put on the whole armor of God*** *that you may be able to stand against the wiles of the devil. For we wrestle not with flesh and blood, but against principalities, against powers, against rulers of darkness of this world, against spiritual wickedness in high places.*
    *Wherefore take unto you the **whole armor of God** that you may be able to withstand in the evil day, and having done all, to stand. Stand, therefore, having your loins girt about with truth, and having on the breastplate of righteousness; and having your feet shod with the preparation of the gospel of peace.*
Above all, taking the shield of faith wherewith you shall be able to quench all the fiery darts of the wicked. And take the helmet of salvation, and the sword of the Spirit, which is the word of God: Praying always in the Spirit, and watching for all saints.

                                ----- Ephesians 6: 10 -- 18

TO END ON A POSITIVE NOTE PONDER THESE FINAL THOUGHTS:

To Love Is To Radiate

Love is a spirit; an energy. It is the unseen chemical element which suspends like a current and carries each molecule to its destination. In the body this chemical process is known as "body fluids" - in the universe it is called "interplanetary expansion." The only way to control your moods and feelings is through your thoughts. What you think is what you are, and eventually what you will become. What you fill your mind with is what will influence you in life.

Love is the positive force, which when applied is capable of creating the impossible, but when opposed and completely reversed to the negative force, hate, it is capable of much havoc and destruction. Radiate pure love, and you will illuminate people around you, attracting them like an irresistible magnet.

YES -- Your Everlasting Spirit

People are forever telling you, NO. It may come from Your friend, Your neighbor, Your enemy, Your boss, Your associate, Your spouse, Your child, or even Your brother. Well, now it's time to think Y.E.S.!

Human nature, itself, warrants prejudice against the positive: It will try to win out because of the pull of the negative, opposing pole. There is also the pull between good and evil, ups and downs, male and female, success and failure - That's just life. But, who said life was just.

The only way to combat these opposing forces is to gain faith. Faith will give you the foundation, The Seed, The Will, The Confidence, and The Desire to have everything go Your Way. There is no mystery here - Opposition always requires defense, and defense must be gained by Complete Preparation.

That Preparation is Faith: a belief in a Power Stronger than the self. And that Power is beyond life - It Is The Power of The Holy Spirit.

Copyright 1999 Edward J. Longo

CONTACT INFORMATION

My research regarding the study of the subconscious began more than 25 years ago, which eventually became the catalyst for developing my hypnosis manual called, The Trance Zone. When I realized what I had developed I decided to use it as the basis for my hypnotherapy practice, which I formed about ten years ago, in addition to my Certified Hypnotherapy School.

As an ABH Certified Hypnotherapist, I administer alternative methods that are designed to help clients transform their minds. Whether they wish to stop smoking, drop unwanted pounds, resolve an insomnia problem, or whether they have a mental, physical, or emotional problem, I will do everything in my power to assist them. Using one of the most effective hypnotherapy techniques as specified in this book, The Trance Zone Hypnotherapy Course, I strive to instruct candidates on how to resolve most mental disorders, or inner conflicts.

Credentialed Certification with the following Organizations:
American Board of Hypnotherapy (ABH) – Board Certified
American Board of Hypnotherapy (ABH) – Certified Instructor / Trainer
American College of Hypnotherapy (ACH) – Board Certified
American Association of Behavioral Therapists (RBT)
American Association of Psychotherapists. (AAP)

The Trance Zone Hypnotherapy Course
To find out how to qualify to become a Certified Hypnotherapist,
Or to review other products, visit the website links below.
Send E-Mails To: affinity@affinityzone.com

Hypnosis Manual: Order This Product
http://www.thetrancezone.com

Visit My Featured Hypnotherapist & Other Links
http://www.affinityzone.com/Robinfeatured.html
http://hypnotists.affinityzone.com
http://www.thetrancezone.com

Edward J. Longo - ABH CCH RBT
503 East 78th Street, New York, NY 10075 (212) 737-8538
Founder: The Trance Zone Hypnotherapy School
Author: The Trance Zone Hypnosis Manual
Hypnosis Manual Website URL: http://www.thetrancezone.com

HOW TO BECOME A GIFTED CERTIFIED HYPNOTHERAPTIST
The Six Keys:
1. Practice, then experiment, and then implement all the knowledge and insight gained. . . .
2. Apply all therapy treatments in a compassionate, caring, and honest manner.. . . . .
3. Establish a bond while relaxing the subject with smooth, soothing, positive WORDS. . .
4. Gain trust by presenting positive suggestions, and by mirroring subject's actions. . . . . .
5. Guide, lead, and direct the subject through guided imagery and direction of focus. . . . .
6. Create an Atmosphere Of Trust using the 3 S's: Soundness, Smoothness, and Sincerity.
7. Receive Your Own Perfectly Legal Certificate (Authorized by Edward J Longo)

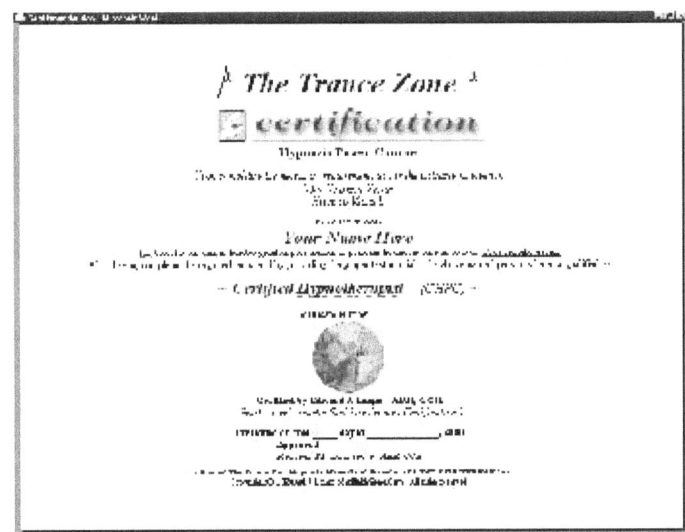

Legal Personalized Certification

To find out how to qualify to become a Certified Hypnotherapist, or to order specialized Trance Zone DVD's recorded in the author's hypnotic voice Call (212) 737-8538,
Or Send EMail: affinity@affinityzone.com

I am interested in: (place appropriate check marks:)
Trance Tapes in author's experienced, soothing voice ___
Private Hypnosis Sessions, or Hypnotherapy Certification ___
The Trance Zone Hypnosis Course - by mail, or Email online
Full Name (To Appear on Certificate) _____
Street Address: _____
City, State, Zip: _____
Country: _____
Phone Number: _____
Email: (Confidential) _____

Print & Mail to: Edward J. Longo – ABH CCH RBT
503 East 78th Street, New York, NY 10075-1130 - Phone: 212 737-8538
Order Hypnotherapy Course http://hypnotherapytoliveby.com/

Highly Recommended Reading For Serious Professionals

TRANCE & Treatment *by Herbert Spiegal*
Jung To Live By *by Eugene Pascal, Ph.L*
Imagery In Healing *by Achterberg*
The Neuroscience of Psychotherapy *by Cozolino*
Talk I Not Enough *by Willard Gaylin, M.D*
Your Mental Health *by Allen Frances, M.D*
Your Inner Physician and You *by Upledger*
The Trance Workbook *by Hoffman*
Inner Wisdom & Heal Your Body *by Louise L Hay*
Trance Spells by *Janina Renee*
Tapping The Healer Within *by Callahan*
Acupressure Way of Health *by Teeguarden*
Acupressure Potent Points *by Gach*
Aikido and The Harmony Of Nature *by Saotome*
Clinical Neuropsychology *by Snyder*
DSM-IV Manual of Mental Disorders *4th Edition*
Healing Anxiety & Depression *by Daniel G. Amen, M.D.*
The Trance Zone Hypnosis Manual *by Edward J. Longo*
Change Your Brain, Change Your Life *by Dr. Daniel Amen*
I Can Make You Thin *by Paul McKenna*

ABOUT THE AUTHOR: EDWARD J LONGO

By utilizing the instructions and then practicing the positive applications within **The Trance Zone** hypnosis manual, one can gain access to one's programming. The secret to tapping the depths of the mind is to go into the subconscious, where the true source of power rules. This is where you can unleash the power of the subconscious, and change negative habits of thought and action into what you desire them to be. This is where you can alter your programming for the better.

As an ABH Board Certified Hypnotherapist and Instructor Edward J Longo provides such beneficial components of hypnotherapy that, when administered, ultimately initiates positive changes. Amazingly, through his process of advanced hypnotherapy, permanent transformation becomes inevitable. Through the process of guided imagery, positive suggestions, and deep hypnotic trances, even the most skeptical subjects become influenced. When clients learn to incorporate the power of the subconscious mind even their elusive, desirable dreams seem to manifest as if by MAGIC.

MISSION STATEMENT

Inspire The Injured Spirit and You Can Dissipate Any Disorder – Even Disease.

TESTIMONIAL

Edward J Longo's concept is outstanding, and I recommend The Trance Zone Hypnotherapy Course to anyone who wants to learn to heal themselves, change negative behavioral patterns, or even start a rewarding career as a certified hypnotherapist. I cannot thank Mr. Longo enough for his personal support and mentoring while using his manual throughout my studies. His manual called "The Trance Zone" is the foundation to The Trance Zone Hypnotherapy Course. . . . . **Robin E. Jones – TTZ**

NOTE: The Trance Zone Hypnotherapy Course is Board Certified by the American Board of Hypnotherapy, and the American College of Hypnotherapy.

THE VOLCANO

*As with
the proverbial
mountainous **volcano**,
we, as human inhabitants,
are capable of summoning
powers; latent powers that could
captivate, even astound, the wisest of
intellects. . . . . Edward J Longo*

www.ingramcontent.com/pod-product-compliance
Lightning Source LLC
Chambersburg PA
CBHW082040300426
44117CB00015B/2552